RTI AND MATHEMATICS

Practical Tools for Teachers in K–8 Classrooms

Regina "Gina" Harwood Gresham
University of Central Florida

Mary Little
University of Central Florida

PEARSON

Boston   Columbus   Indianapolis   New York   San Francisco   Upper Saddle River
Amsterdam   Cape Town   Dubai   London   Madrid   Milan   Munich   Paris   Montreal   Toronto
Delhi   Mexico City   São Paulo   Sydney   Hong Kong   Seoul   Singapore   Taipei   Tokyo

Vice President and Editor-in-Chief: Aurora Martínez Ramos
Executive Editor: Linda Ashe Bishop
Editorial Assistant: Michelle Hochberg and Katie Wiley
Senior Marketing Manager: Christine Gatchell
Production Editor: Janet Domingo
Editorial Production Service: Electronic Publishing Services Inc.
Manufacturing Buyer: Megan Cochran
Electronic Composition: Jouve
Interior Design: Electronic Publishing Services Inc.
Photographer: Keith Ford, Rhino Graphics
Cover Designer: Diane Lorenzo and Jennifer Hart

10 9 8 7 6 5 4 3 2 1

ISBN-10: 0-13-300701-4
ISBN-13: 978-0-13-300701-5

How blessed I am! I have been touched by so many people throughout my teaching career: my parents, family, loved ones, friends, students, colleagues...what an endless list. Many very special people have entered into my life and I am forever grateful to have you there! Many of you know who you are, but I want to particularly thank my friend, my guide, my supporter, and my mentor, Dr. Douglas K. Brumbaugh, for getting me started along this journey. I am so thankful and forever grateful to you for your guidance in helping me see what I can do and be. I wish you were still here to see this in print. May you rest in peace and know the impact you had on me and others was priceless.

Most important, I dedicate my life's work to my precious daddy, Randal "Ronnie" Frank Harwood, Sr., for the tremendous unselfish and unconditional love you gave to me and to all you knew. Thank you, Daddy, for loving me, believing in me, guiding me, and supporting me in everything I did. It is through your strength that I continue to help others and seek out the best life has to offer. You are simply the best! Roll Tide Paw-Paw... Roll Tide!

Also, may the life of my mother, Glenda Kidd Harwood, be celebrated as the blessing she brought to this world as we all engrave a piece of her beauty within ourselves. It is my most sincere belief that she is home now with a pair of wings guarding and protecting each of us as she awaits the children she has raised and those who crossed her path. She was such a nurturing, caring soul who took great joy and pride in the caring of others. Thank you for holding me eternally in your arms.

I miss you both more than my words could ever describe and I love you both tremendously. Until we see each other again. I humbly dedicate this book in honor and loving memory of my beloved daddy and mother.

"If you believe in yourself and have dedication and pride; you'll be a winner.
The price of victory is high but so are the rewards" (Paul "Bear" Bryant).
To all teachers: We shall always be partners in education!
To students past, present, and future: "14437"

Dr. Regina "Gina" Harwood Gresham

Sincere thanks to our teachers and educators who inspire daily with their effective teaching, instructional decision making, continuous learning, collaboration, and reflection. Your knowledge, dedication, and commitment to improved learning for all students in mathematics make the difference!

Dr. Mary Little

About the Authors

Dr. Regina "Gina" Harwood Gresham, Ph.D., is an educational psychologist, behavioral specialist, and Associate Professor in Mathematics Education at the University of Central Florida in Orlando. She is also a national mathematics consultant and is actively involved in presenting professional development workshops to improve mathematics achievement and implementing RTI in mathematics classrooms across the United States. As a national trainer and speaker on RTI in mathematics, she is featured in a national video on RTI in mathematics with the Bureau of Education and Research. In addition, Dr. Gresham has published numerous international and national research articles and authored or coauthored five books including *Teaching Middle School Mathematics, TAG Middle Math Is It!, TAG for Grades 3–5,* and *Response to Intervention in Elementary School.* She is a former public school teacher and has taught learners in high-risk urban settings. Dr. Gresham's current research, writing, and professional development topics of interest include: response to intervention in the mathematics classrooms; the psychology of mathematics, particularly mathematics anxiety; teacher self-efficacy; and learning styles. She has received her university's Scholarship in Teaching and Learning Award, Excellence in Undergraduate Teaching Award, Teacher Recognition and Appreciation Award, and the Christa McAuliffe Teaching Award–Lockheed Martin/ UCF K–8 Program Award. She has an undergraduate degree in education from Jacksonville State University. She earned her master's in education, educational specialist, and Ph.D. with special emphasis in education, educational psychology, cognition and instruction, and neurophysiology/neuropsychology from the University of Alabama in Tuscaloosa. Dr. Gresham was also a Graduate Fellow at the University of Alabama.

Dr. Mary Little is an Associate Professor in Exceptional Student Education at the University of Central Florida in Orlando and also currently serves as the Coordinator of Graduate Programs. She received her graduate and undergraduate degrees in special education and curriculum and instruction from the State University College at Buffalo and her Ph.D. in special education from the University of Kansas. Her professional experiences in K–12 schools include roles as a secondary teacher, coteacher, program coordinator, and principal. Her interests include evidence-based instructional practices, interventions, teacher efficacy, and student learning related to teacher learning. She teaches courses at the graduate and undergraduate levels using traditional and online formats, specifically in mathematics, assessment, instruction, action research, and program evaluation. In addition, she has received over $15 million in external funding for research and development from federal, state, and private funding agencies including the Institute for Educational Sciences (IES) and the Office of Special Education Programs (OSEP). Currently, she serves as the principal investigator for Building Bridges in Teacher Education, a federally funded research and development project through OSEP. The purpose of this project is to research, develop, and enhance the existing graduate programs at the University of Central Florida to ensure highly qualified special education teachers in the content areas of mathematics and science to improve learning outcomes for secondary students, especially within diverse, urban schools.

Contents

Preface

We know that when you think about teaching mathematics, you can probably think of students who struggle with learning and mastering the curricular standards we are required to teach for mathematics. What can we offer to increase our students' active engagement and achievement with learning mathematics and help our struggling learners be mathematically successful? We know that students learn in different ways and have different strengths and needs. The challenge of meeting the needs of the diverse learners in our classrooms continues to grow. Instructional demands are becoming increasingly complex, including the alignment of federal and state policies and mandates that increase the accountability emphasis. New curriculum standards in mathematics and current implementation of Response to Intervention (RTI) places new awareness on instruction. Therefore, we have developed this book as a practical teaching guide to empower you to learn or continue to learn about and implement RTI in mathematics classrooms. Even with new changes and responsibilities, we know the focus remains the same: Teach so that students successfully learn the mathematical content while ensuring that high-quality instruction and interventions continue for each student each day in our classrooms.

Purposes of this Book

We believe that learning mathematics is now more multifaceted than ever and it requires critical resources for mathematics teachers as related to curricular revisions and recent legislative mandates. We designed *RTI and Mathematics: Practical Tools for Teachers in K–8 Classrooms* to provide an interactive, practical resource for mathematics educators to actively participate in the instructional processes within the RTI framework, with the goal of improving student conceptual learning in mathematics. This book offers a blueprint for a coordinated, comprehensive resource to plan, implement, and evaluate instruction, present interventions, and recommend assessments for working with diverse students. The purpose is to provide evidence-based instruction and intervention resources, including numerous examples, case studies, planning forms, and templates for classroom use when constructing lessons and implementing RTI in K–8 mathematics classrooms.

Why Is This Book Needed?

Although there is much literature on RTI, there is little that speaks to the educator in a practical, how-to format. Our goal with this text is to collaboratively build on and enrich your knowledge and expertise through professional learning about RTI in mathematics to address some of the continued challenges. We know teachers' days are already filled with many instructional activities: we are planning lessons, reviewing various types of assessments, and providing enrichment and reteaching students as indicated by assessment results. Teachers review resources that align with the grade-level standards and objectives for students, both in large and smaller groups, to ensure that *all* students are learning. When necessary, they solicit additional information and support from other teachers, support staff, parents, and other resources. Therefore, we wrote this book with you in mind! We know that you hold the key to our students' future mathematical successes. Together we can make a difference. Together we will make a difference. Together we *are* making a difference!

For Whom Is This Book Written?

The primary audience for this book includes those who are directly responsible for the mathematics curriculum within the RTI model. This includes mathematics teachers, special education classroom teachers, mathematics coaches, instructional/ mathematics specialists, school-based interventionists, administrators, professors, and professional development coordinators. In addition, various support personnel (school psychologists, counselors, assessment specialists, paraprofessionals) will find this book of value as they adjust their roles to best meet the mathematical needs of all students. Because RTI in mathematics is a relatively new concept in our schools, both novice and veteran educators will find our contents and resources helpful. Educators will be thinking about how to teach all students at various tiers of intervention within the mathematics classroom and can easily plan to use this book with their curriculum standards and resources.

Intended Outcomes

We have been inspired by the following quote by William Butler Yeats: "Education is not the filling of a pail, but the lighting of a fire." The goals of this book are to "fill your pail" with knowledge about Response to Instruction/Intervention (RTI) as related to mathematics, as well as to "light your fire" as you consider and act on *your* critical role within the RTI process in your school and classroom.

The chapters in this book are designed to produce the following outcomes:

- Briefly clarify and establish clear definitions of common language, core principles, implementation practices, and procedures as related to or involved with RTI.

- Describe the connections among teachers' knowledge and skills and their important use with RTI.

- Understand your role within the classroom and school to meet the instructional goals in mathematics for all students.

- Offer clear and evidence-based content, scenarios, examples, resources, and activities.

- Provide modeling, description, and reflection on the key learning outcomes of RTI.

- Provide a continuous case study of a mathematics teacher as she implements RTI in her classroom.

- Fill your professional toolbox with information and resources that can be immediately used within K–8 classrooms to successfully implement RTI in mathematics.

Once the definitions and principles are described, the multiple components of RTI are then illustrated and connected through the eyes of the mathematics teacher. Specifically, resources within this book address *how* mathematics teachers and other educators in a school provide services and collaborate to teach within the tiers of instruction and intervention to meet the diverse learning needs of students. Strategies and methods of curriculum, instruction, and environmental supports, as well as accommodations and resources that intensify instruction, are included within the lesson plan format. The emphasis is on *what to do* to plan, instruct, assess, and support students during instruction and intervention within the school-wide RTI system. Finally, instructional decision making and problem solving with members of the school's RTI team are addressed, again through the eyes of mathematics teachers. Curriculum-based assessments of student achievement are incorporated to ensure accountability for continuous progress monitoring.

Keep in mind that as you implement RTI in your mathematics classroom, you will not be learning and working in isolation. RTI requires teamwork and collaboration with your colleagues in your school. Therefore, the roles and services that can be provided by a mathematics interventionist, a mathematics coach, a school psychologist, a counselor, or other members of your school's instructional support personnel will be explored as part of the services for students who are in need of more intensive interventions. One goal of this book is to describe the processes and resources clearly and systematically so teachers and their school colleagues will implement RTI as a collaborative extension of their professional knowledge and skills, focusing on learning by *all* students in mathematics. But remember, the personnel and resources differ among schools. You may or may not, for example, have a specific mathematics interventionist, a mathematics coach, a school psychologist, or a counselor in your school. This may require you to have several roles within the RTI framework. You and your colleagues must make decisions regarding the personnel and resources that are currently present in your school and work with what is there. Therefore, as you read this book, consider how you will structure RTI in your school or how RTI may already be structured in your school, which colleagues are there to collaborate with, and what is available in your school to effectively implement RTI in mathematics.

Key Features of This Book

We are defining RTI within this book as Response to Instruction/Intervention because we feel that RTI is part of the educator's instructional decision-making processes to meet the learning needs in mathematics for *all* students. The book is designed to include the "need to know" evidence-based resources and materials just in time for instruction and intervention by teachers and other school professionals within an RTI framework. This book focuses on classroom instruction in mathematics through comprehensive planning. It includes reflective questions, resources, and samples of instructional interventions that teachers can use. Examples and practical suggestions are provided to illustrate and support implementation. The book is filled with ideas, resources, case studies, and current information about RTI, and is organized for busy mathematics teachers around their central professional activity—teaching! We have worked with many teachers and other educators through professional development, courses, workshops, presentations, and conferences. Therefore, we have placed emphasis on the "teacher's voice" and designed the text to be practical and teacher-friendly for any educators working within a school and district system that is implementing an RTI model. You will be able to see glimpses of your classroom in the examples and ideas. You will see how your efforts to meet the diverse needs of students are aligned to the larger framework of RTI and you will gain insights regarding your students and your teaching. Implementation of RTI should not be something to fear. RTI is composed of skills that teachers use daily, such as using classroom-based assessments, grouping and regrouping students for instruction, and reassessing and reteaching to ensure that students are learning the grade-level curriculum and achieving standards and goals. This book provides comprehensive resources for mathematics teachers to effectively plan for instruction within their K–8 mathematics classrooms to implement RTI. Evidence-based instruction, intervention, and progress-monitoring resources are provided for educators to consult and use during the planning process.

In Chapter 1, we start with the basics of RTI to provide an overview of the rationale, principles, and implications of implementing RTI in mathematics classrooms. Definitions, components, and legislation describe and develop common language and knowledge of RTI as related to content in mathematics (especially the Common Core State Standards) and instruction. It describes and connects your knowledge and skills with the principles of RTI to demystify the RTI process and connect it to your current knowledge and skills. Chapter 2 focuses on the data-based instructional decision-making process related to the multiple variables in teaching, such as grouping, resources, types of instruction, and so forth, as related to the RTI framework. This chapter focuses on instructional flexibility and thoughtful instruction. It is showcased to offer specific classroom-based tasks, activities, and resources that serve as instructional tools for RTI in mathematics. Critical instructional variables to consider for intensifying instruction and interventions are described, with specific classroom application examples for implementation. Chapter 3 is based on the use and interpretation of multiple assessments: universal screening, progress monitoring, diagnostic, and outcome. Evidence-based progress-monitoring assessments, including curriculum-based measurements, are provided for use with groups and individual students for formative and summative assessments within mathematics.

Chapters 4, 5, and 6 offer the essential components of assessing effective instruction, curriculum, and differentiated instructional practices throughout RTI Tiers 1, 2, and 3. Specifically, the concepts of differentiating instruction (including the levels of support offered to learners within the mathematics classrooms), multiple representations, curriculum enhancement, and intensifying and scaffolding lesson components are featured. Also included in these chapters are the continuous formative assessment, progress-monitoring, and curriculum-based measurements to inform instructional decision making. These measurements allow teachers to take the pulse of their own teaching to reflect on how much their students are learning in the mathematics classroom. Critical instructional variables with specific classroom application examples are presented for intensifying instruction and interventions in the tiers. Scenarios distinguish between interventions in Tiers 1, 2, and 3, as well as discussion of other services, if warranted. Considerations and discussions of curriculum focus and alignment, in conjunction with supports, accommodations, and resources to meet individual student needs in mathematics are also included. Diagnostic assessments and teaching for individual students are described, using case studies. Discussions related to intensifying instruction, classroom interventions, other educator supports and collaboration, and organizational procedures for the classroom illuminate the concepts.

Chapter 7 supports the building of professional and collegial conversations centered on enhancing lessons and serves as a cornerstone for continuous improvement. Specific strategies for school reform and renewal based on continuous learning serve as the catalyst for maximizing the potential for student improvement for RTI in the mathematics classroom. The focus of this chapter is professional colearning to improve teaching by all educators who serve students in the mathematics classroom. Rationale and opportunities for enhanced roles and increased collaboration for educators are discussed. Considerations for action research, professional learning communities, and lesson study within the RTI framework are also included.

Additional resources that you will find throughout this book include:

- **Initial advance organizers and questions** that focus the readers for learning within each chapter

- **Reflective questions** that provide readers with considerations, checklists, and explicit information when implementing RTI concepts and/or practices in their mathematics classroom
- **Student case studies** that engage the reader with instructional decision making related to conceptual learning and resources and include samples of student data, work, and characteristics
- **Vignettes and scenarios** with "how-to" examples for classroom application of organization, procedures, and so forth, to facilitate RTI implementation (e.g., classroom arrangement, schedules, learning centers)
- **Teacher's Corner** features at the end of each chapter that highlight main ideas, practical suggestions, and tips for getting you started with RTI implementation in the classroom
- **Summaries, figures, tables, and charts** that highlight and emphasize main points and resources
- **Websites** highlighting RTI, evidence-based instruction and interventions, and multiple assessments in mathematics

The following additional resources appear in the appendices for this book:

- Reproducible instructional tools for RTI
- Book study questions for each chapter that enhance knowledge of RTI and can be used for individual and/or group discussion
- Lesson study format questions and reflections for use within Professional Learning Communities (PLCs)
- A glossary of key terms highlighted throughout the text

Authors' Note

How special education fits into a tiered instructional model is a question that always arises when developing comprehensive school-wide RTI models. Different RTI models have placed special education in different ways within the process. We are using a three-tiered model of RTI as the framework for our book. RTI models may vary slightly across states and school districts with regard to the number of tiers (three or four) and the specific roles of educators, especially as related to determining special education eligibility in the states. We know there may be controversy regarding Tier 3, as some schools have students progress through each of the tiers (Tier 1, Tier 2, Tier 3), whereas other schools may have students jump from Tier 1 directly to Tier 3. Finally, other schools may have students go through Tiers 1 and 2, then refer students to Tier 3, in which they consider special education services or define as special education. This level of intensity is typically for students who have not been responsive to the Tier 2 level of instruction and intervention. Therefore, the students are considered in need of more individualized instructional delivery consistent with individualized education programs (IEPs). For this text, we are referring to Tier 3 as intensive supports provided by a mathematics coach, a mathematics specialist, an interventionist, designated educational personnel, and/or possibly the special education teacher. If Tier 3 services are not working, *then* the student may need referral to special education services. Also, throughout this book, we use the term *interventionist* to refer to those teaching the interventions. At a given school, the interventionist may be the classroom teacher, a special education instructor, other certified school personnel, or an instructional assistant, depending on the different personnel available to fill these roles. You are encouraged to investigate the specific RTI model and related regulations and procedures in your state and school district.

Regardless of the model your school chooses, it is of utmost importance that we have the flexibility to do what works for *our* students in *our* schools. This will be based on the personnel and resources that are available within a particular school. Remember that flexibility, team-based decisions, and accountability are what we are striving for in addressing our students' particular mathematical needs.

Acknowledgments

We wish to offer a very, very special thank you to our friend, graphic artist Keith Ford from Rhino Graphics in Edgewater, Florida, for his dedicated work and perfection in his photography, including the front cover page and author photos. Your knowledge and expertise, as well as time and attention to detail, certainly bring out the best in all of us. They are most appreciated!

Featured on the front cover is Ms. Holly, the "Teacher's Voice" used throughout this book. We sincerely thank you, Ms. Holly, for allowing us to see your teaching in action. We are truly blessed to have you as a colleague and we look forward to working with you as partners in education! Ms. Holly is an elementary education graduate from the University of Alabama in Tuscaloosa and is an elementary school teacher in Texas.

We also thank our loved ones, including family and close friends, for their love and support throughout this adventure. We could not have managed without your unconditional love and patience.

Finally, we would like to thank the following reviewers for their helpful comments on the manuscript: Ellen S. Baker, Countryside Elementary School; Susan M. Burris, Cambridge-Isanti School District #911; Russell Gersten, Instructional Research Group; Debra (Debbie) S. Hicks, Whitford Middle School; Lisa Hicks, Corkscrew Middle School; Sheryl Kirkey, Glenwood Elementary School; Kelly Krownapple, Phelps Luck Elementary School; Amanda McCray, Clymore Elementary School; Constance Sauer, Enemy Swim Day School; and Eunetra Simpson, Parker Intermediate.

Chapter 1

Response to Instruction and Intervention in Mathematics

*"At the end of each day, ask yourself whether
you have taught anyone anything or
whether you have learned anything yourself."*

—Dr. Henri Sue Bynum

What You Will Find in This Chapter

- Definitions and core components of RTI
- Challenges to teach all students to mastery in mathematics
- Connections: RTI with Common Core Standards and NCTM Focal Points in Mathematics
- Getting started with RTI in your classroom

Teacher's Voice

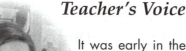

It was early in the school year in Ms. Holly's fourth-grade classroom. She had just posed to her students a mathematical word problem based on curriculum standards that incorporated several grade-level concepts and skills. Could the students draw from their previous knowledge of mathematical skills to determine the answer? What strategies or manipulatives could they use to solve it? Ms. Holly had organized the students into cooperative groups of four students of mixed abilities based on screening assessments from the beginning of the school year. As Ms. Holly walked around the classroom to observe her students, she quickly noticed that some students understood the word problem, explained and wrote the correct equation, and possessed skills for multiplying two-digit numbers rather quickly, while others struggled with the content presented. There appeared to be several students who had difficulty setting up the equation and some who could not multiply two-digit numbers. One student in particular, Heather, showed signs of frustration and confusion.

Ms. Holly asked her to explain what she knew about solving her multiplication problem of 78 × 43. Heather's explanation for multiplication did contain some correct information about the presented multiplication problem, but her answer to the problem was incorrect. Heather knew some but not all of the basic multiplication facts, and she struggled with addition and place value. Ms. Holly continued to observe Heather and other students and wrote notes related to their knowledge and use of the concepts and skills needed to solve the word problem. From her observations she knew that several more students needed additional instruction to demonstrate mastery of the mathematical content presented in the day's lesson.

One of the most difficult tasks that we face as classroom teachers is finding ways to reach *each* student's level of mathematical readiness. In our classrooms and schools, current federal and state requirements have increased the emphasis on accountability for improved achievement in mathematics for all students through effective teaching by both professional organizations and legislation. In 2007, the National Council of Teachers of Mathematics (NCTM) stated that all students' instructional needs can be met by knowledgeable teachers who use evidence-based instructional practices and strategies designed to increase student achievement. The Individuals with Disabilities Education Improvement Act (IDEA) of 2004, specifically, outlines Response to Intervention (RTI) as a process for continuously improving the achievement of students struggling to learn and to reduce the number of students who are being referred for special education services. The definitions, components, and goals of the recent legislative mandates of RTI and revised curriculum standards in mathematics focus on instruction, intervention, and assessments aligned with revised mathematics standards.

What Is Response to Instruction/Intervention (RTI)?

Response to Instruction/Intervention (RTI) is a systematic, data-based method for identifying, defining, and resolving students' academic difficulties using collaborative, school-wide, problem-solving approaches. The definition of RTI is the practice of (1) providing high-quality instruction/intervention matched to student needs and (2) using learning rate over time and level of performance to (3) make important educational decisions to guide instruction (National Association of State Directors of Special Education, 2005). As a proactive and prevention-focused approach, RTI relies on instructional problem solving within classrooms and schools. It encourages teams of educators to develop dynamic instructional plans to address academic or behavioral concerns of individual students within classrooms. RTI focuses on using evidence-based instructional approaches, interventions, resources, and strategies within the classroom, while continuously monitoring student learning through classroom-based assessments. Instructional problem solving, based on assessment data, is the continuous decision-making process used throughout RTI. Because the goal is to increase achievement for all students, classroom teachers must be the primary participants in the RTI process. RTI's comprehensive and continuous process, however, may include other educators (e.g., mathematics teacher, instructional coach, school psychologist, special education teacher) on the school-based team who can help identify and participate in possible solutions for instructional concerns of students. This may require us to learn new methods and use new resources to teach and differentiate instruction in math. Figure 1.1 lists the core components for the framework for RTI.

FIGURE 1.1 Core Components of RTI

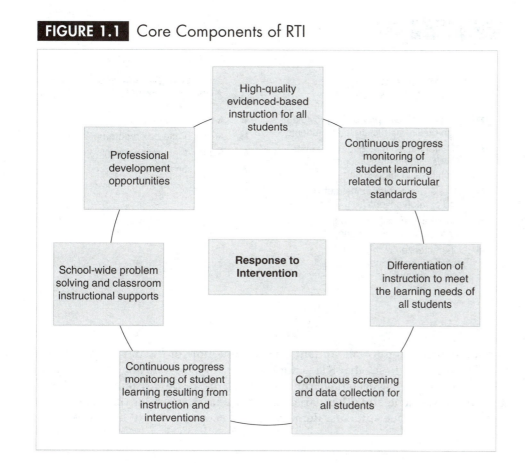

What RTI Is Not

As we consider the definitions and components of RTI, we also want to discuss and identify what RTI is *not* (see Figure 1.2). We want you to view RTI as a practice of what effective teachers are already doing. Effective teachers provide high-quality instruction within classrooms to meet students' needs so each student becomes academically successful in learning mathematics. RTI is not considered a special education eligibility tracking system to monitor students or to place them in a special needs program. Although some students may need special services, RTI is not a pre-referral model or a separate stand-alone initiative. We do not want to wait and see if students fail, but rather offer opportunities for them to *respond* to lessons that differentiate and scaffold to build on the skills necessary to develop the knowledge base, competencies, and skills in mathematics. RTI is about instruction, not just intervention. It is not a mathematics program. It is not a separate class for mathematics instruction or individual tutoring. Nor is it adding

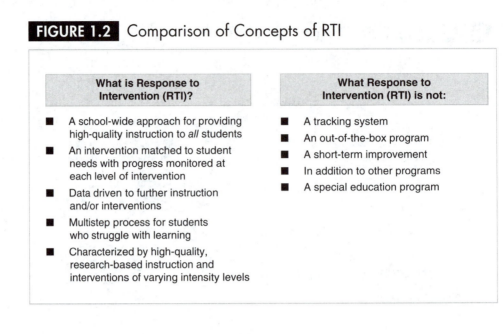

FIGURE 1.2 Comparison of Concepts of RTI

What is Response to Intervention (RTI)?	What Response to Intervention (RTI) is not:
■ A school-wide approach for providing high-quality instruction to *all* students	■ A tracking system
■ An intervention matched to student needs with progress monitored at each level of intervention	■ An out-of-the-box program
■ Data driven to further instruction and/or interventions	■ A short-term improvement
■ Multistep process for students who struggle with learning	■ In addition to other programs
■ Characterized by high-quality, research-based instruction and interventions of varying intensity levels	■ A special education program

the same instruction for all students at the same time of the day each and every day. We want you to see that RTI is not the same for everyone nor do we want it to be. Why? Because we each have different strengths, resources, students, administrative involvement, and other variables that we use to meet the different learning needs of each of our students. Remember, one size does not fit all and we never want it to!

Meeting the Instructional Needs of All Learners in Mathematics

Learning mathematics is often challenging for students both with and without differences and disabilities. We know that:

- Children who have had less experience with or exposure to mathematical concepts and numeracy are at high risk for mathematics failure (Griffin & Case, 1997).

- Most students fail to meet minimal mathematics proficiency standards by the end of their formal schooling (U.S. Department of Education, 2010).

- Relative to their peers, students identified as having specific learning disabilities perform at a lower level and grow at a slower pace in learning mathematics (Gresham, 2009; Little & Witzel, 2009).

- Existing instructional tools and textbooks often do a poor job of adhering to important instructional principles for learning in mathematics (National Mathematics Advisory Panel, 2008).

- Math is highly proceduralized and continually builds on previous knowledge for successful learning. Hence, early deficits have enduring and devastating effects on later learning, as indicated in *The Head Start Path to Positive Child Outcomes* (U.S. Department of Health and Human Services, 2001) and elsewhere (e.g., National Council of Teachers of Mathematics, 2000; National Mathematics Advisory Panel, 2008; U.S. Department of Education, 2010).

- Early mathematics intervention can repair deficits and prevent future deficits (Clements & Sarama, 2007; Fuchs & Fuchs, 2005; Gresham, 2009; Griffin & Case, 1997).

Our classroom experiences mirror this research and drive the renewed emphasis on improving achievement in mathematics for all students. It is important for us to build on this knowledge and magnify, enhance, and increase our learning to address these challenges for the reasons that we entered education: to make positive differences in student learning. Through our commitment to our students and the knowledge about these current educational changes we are called to action to lead and inform conversations and decisions impacting the teaching and learning processes. Our knowledge is critical to the solutions enacted to address the educational changes and reforms. Ultimately, to improve educational results in mathematics for all children, including students with disabilities, we must focus on the strengths and needs of the learner through the use of differentiated, evidence-based instructional practices in the implementation of RTI. Teaching, therefore, calls for the knowledge and use of various instructional practices, as well as multiple strategies and techniques to scaffold instruction to ensure that students reach increasing levels of mathematical understanding (Berch & Mazzocco, 2007; Gresham, 2009; Little, 2009a; NCTM, 2008).

> 1. Teachers need to be committed to ensure that all students will learn mathematics.
> 2. Teachers have background knowledge as to why struggling learners have difficulties with learning mathematics.
> 3. Teachers have deep pedagogical content knowledge and knowledge of cognitive strategies to meet the learning needs of students, thereby allowing students to understand mathematics (Allsopp, Kyger, & Lovin, 2008).

Effective teaching within RTI classrooms is adaptive teaching. It is changing and adapting standard lessons and standard units in ways that make them fit our students. No two lessons or units will be the same because teachers use their knowledge and skills to adapt and enhance lessons based on what *their* students do and say. We use instructional planning and decision-making process (i.e., instructional problem solving) to make important instructional decisions to meet the needs of our students. This instructional planning and decision-making process is used by teachers and other professionals within classrooms daily. The instructional decisions and the results of student learning collected by progress-monitoring assessments and probes are the critical first phases in the RTI process.

As we consider the instructional planning and decision-making planning process, we must also stop and critically analyze our own teaching practices. Taking a long hard look in the mirror allows us to reflect on our own content knowledge and pedagogy. This is important if we are to increase our students' mathematical performance. Our mathematical strengths become our students' mathematical strengths. In turn, our mathematical weaknesses become our students' mathematical weaknesses. Pedagogical content knowledge and a deep understanding of mathematics are needed to enhance and diversify instructional approaches, explanations, and supports to meet students' needs. We want to also think about and analyze our students' knowledge, interests, and needs, and make decisions about the multiple variables of teaching and learning so that each student learns the curriculum. During the instructional process of planning, teaching, and assessing student learning, strategic use of evidence-based instructional practices, interventions, and various cognitive and metacognitive strategies are important to meet the needs of a wide range of students, particularly those who struggle with learning mathematics. Additionally, strategic use of instructional materials, such as manipulatives, graphic organizers specific to mathematics, visuals, and models (representations) are necessary for supporting conceptual understanding of mathematics and providing students with a solid foundation for the continuous learning and mastery of mathematics. As we continue to learn about the new standards, teaching methods, and resources, we enhance our professional skills and experiences and are able to answer more of our students' questions and meet their learning needs.

Connections: RTI with Common Core Standards and NCTM Focal Points in Mathematics

Many states are working together to increase students' mathematical performance by developing and adopting new standards in mathematics or upgrading their existing standards through the Common Core State Standards. The Common Core Standards were developed in collaboration with teachers, school administrators, and experts to provide a clear and consistent framework to prepare children for the future (National Governors Association, 2009). These standards are designed to ensure that students graduating from high school are prepared to go to college or enter the workforce, and that parents, teachers, and students have a clear understanding of what is expected of them. The Common Core Standards are benchmarked to international standards to guarantee that our students are competitive in the emerging global marketplace (National Governors Association, 2009). The goal of the Common Core Standards is to enhance collaboration among participating states in order to:

- Make expectations for students clear to parents, teachers, and the general public;

- Encourage the development of textbooks, digital media, and other teaching materials aligned to the standards;

- Develop and implement comprehensive assessment systems to measure student performance against the Common Core State Standards that will replace the existing testing systems that too often are inconsistent, burdensome, and confusing; and,

- Evaluate policy changes needed to help students and educators meet the standards (National Governors Association, 2009).

Most importantly, the idea of the Common Core State Standards is to provide more clarity and consistency in what is expected of student learning across the country. Until now, every state has had its own set of academic standards. Therefore, students at the same grade level in different states could be required to meet different curricular standards. Common Core Standards adopted by states will provide consistency among curriculums so that all students will have equal opportunities for an education that will prepare them to go to college or enter the workforce, regardless of where they live. (To view states that have adopted the Common Core Standards visit the website listed in the sidebar). Common standards will not prevent different levels of achievement among students. Rather, they will ensure more consistent student outcomes through similar curriculum, instruction, and teacher preparation (National Governors Association, 2009).

In addition to the Common Core Standards, the National Council of Teachers of Mathematics (NCTM) initiated reform efforts in mathematics education (NCTM, 2000). As a response to the overwhelming number of grade-level mathematics standards required in some states, NCTM presented the Curriculum Focal Points. The purpose of the focal points is to narrow the emphasis to essential learning at each grade level. The focal points address a shift in curriculum rather than instructional pedagogy. The focus of the revised standards is on high-level conceptual

READ MORE ABOUT IT!

Visit the following websites for additional information:

Common Core State Standards: www.corestandards.org

National Center on Response to Intervention: www.RTI4success.org

National Council of Teachers of Mathematics (NCTM): www.nctm.org

understanding and problem solving rather than procedural knowledge and rule-driven computation (Maccini & Gagnon, 2002). To meet these revised standards, teachers will need to differentiate and scaffold instruction of abstract concepts so that students master mathematical problems (National Research Council, 2001). We must review our primary responsibilities as mathematics educators within the context of the definitions, components, and goals of the recent legislative mandates and revised curriculum standards in mathematics. Based on student assessment results from state, school, and classroom data, we must make instructional decisions and problem solve additional solutions to ensure that the instructional goals and standards in mathematics are achieved by each student. The goal is to ensure that all students learn mathematics through high-quality instruction using evidence-based instructional and intervention methods, products, and practices. There appear to be multiple similarities among these revised mandates that directly impact the teaching–learning–assessing process within the mathematics classrooms and schools (see Table 1.1).

The revised standards encourage an increased process approach for a deeper understanding of a decreased number of standards, providing additional instructional opportunities for teachers and instructional coaches in mathematics to differentiate instruction and implement additional resources. As a teacher or educator in mathematics, the focus will continue to be the teaching, learning, and assessing process within the mathematics classroom. Our increased learning about our role in RTI in mathematics will make all the difference.

A TIME TO REFLECT

What do I know about legislation that affects my classroom teaching in mathematics? What adjustments are needed to enhance the mathematical learning process to address components of RTI and the Common Core Standards?

TABLE 1.1 Comparison of Revised Mandates

Attribute	Response to Intervention	Common Core State Standards and NCTM Curriculum Focal Points
Goal	To increase achievement for all students	To improve student achievement in mathematics
Components	Multiple tiers of evidence-based instruction service delivery A problem-solving method designed to inform the development of interventions An integrated data collection and assessment system that informs decisions at each tier of service delivery	Use of evidence-based instruction and interventions that support learning and high achievement for all through a continuous process of instructional decision making using assessment data

We know that mathematics educators have incredible knowledge and expertise in the teaching–learning–assessing process; that is the core of RTI within our schools and classrooms. With new standards in mathematics and RTI, there is a unique and immediate call to action for us to learn and engage in implementation of RTI in mathematics in our classrooms. The next chapter will discuss enhanced opportunities to deepen your professional knowledge, expertise, and skills and focus on setting the stage for RTI in your mathematics classroom through instructional decision making.

As we help you connect the dots with RTI and implementation, we also want to provide you with professional learning opportunities that will support you and your colleagues in your classrooms and schools. Whether you are just beginning or are an experienced teacher, there is always something new to learn and add to your professional toolbox.

TEACHERS' CORNER

Keys to Getting You Started with RTI

- Complete the Personal Action Plan in RTI. This framework will not only help guide your goals for learning about RTI in mathematics, but will also encourage you to open the doors for collaboration with colleagues as you identify and discuss your current teaching practices and the various resources within your school. (Reproducible #1)
- Complete the Professional Learning Community Chapter 1 activities.
- Complete the Book Study questions for Chapter 1.
- Review the following websites for additional information about RTI in schools:

RTI Action Network / www.RTInetwork.org

RTI, properly understood and used, is focused on improving student learning. The RTI Action Network provides information on how to use RTI to improve instruction.

Center on Instruction / www.centeroninstruction.org/resources

The Center on Instruction is a collection of scientifically based research and information on K–12 instruction in reading, math, science, special education, and English language learning. The Center on Instruction offers materials and resources to build educators' knowledge of instruction for students. There are over thirty resources for grades K–12.

Chapter 2

Setting the Stage for RTI in the Classroom by Understanding the Fundamentals

"The question for the educator/leader is not whether all humans can learn, but what conditions we can create so they will learn. For only when the school house becomes a context for adult development will it become hospitable to student development."

—*Roland Barth*

What You Will Find in This Chapter

- The tiers and how they work
- RTI vocabulary
- Data-based instructional decision-making processes
- Instructional variables for RTI considerations

Teacher's Voice

I finished a whole-group instruction lesson with my fourth graders and they were now working independently for more practice on multiplying two-digit numbers. Some of my students worked diligently, while others seemed uninterested or disengaged. A few weren't "getting it" as quickly as I had hoped. Seeing them appear confused and unmotivated about the math lesson made me think about the RTI workshop I attended yesterday. There was a lot of information presented in the after-school workshop. The presenter talked about evidence-based core instruction, differentiated instructional practices, tiers, interventions, and progress monitoring, and about what we were doing in our classrooms to meet our students' needs. Although I brought back a lot of good information on RTI to share with my colleagues, I wish I had asked more questions during the workshop for clarification. I know I must find a way to work with my students, particularly those who struggle with the content and specific skills in mathematics, but I am a little overwhelmed at the prospect of trying to implement RTI in my classroom. I already feel that there is so much to do with testing my students and the pressures of paperwork, curriculum mandates by my district, and so forth. Perhaps I am fearful and afraid of the RTI unknowns. What is it and how does it work? Where and how do I begin the RTI process? How will it work for me and my students? But most of all, what is my role in this process? I want all my students to have mathematical success. I know I want to change what I am doing to help my students, but how?

Ms. Holly, fourth-grade teacher

The ultimate goal for our students is increased academic achievement and improved results in mathematics. We make decisions every day about *what* to teach and *how* to teach. On an ongoing basis we reflect on questions such as: "What are my students learning?" "How do I improve and adjust the rate and level of learning for all of my students?" and "How effective are the instructional practices I use to teach my students mathematics?" We want to ensure that students' difficulties in mathematics are not due to lack of effective instruction. We want students to be engaged in high-quality instructional practices that promote interest and active engagement in learning mathematics every day. Based on our answers to the questions above, we may need to adjust, enhance, and differentiate our instructional practices in mathematics. As Ms. Holly's story indicated, we may sometimes feel uncertain as to what instructional practices and decisions need to be made and how those practices and decisions should be used in our classrooms. As we learn more about implementing RTI, we may have more questions than answers. How will the decision-making process help my struggling students effectively learn mathematics? How does RTI work for those struggling learners who do not understand the content as I teach it? How do I begin implementing RTI in my classroom? The goal of this chapter is help you set the stage for RTI in your classroom and school or to review and evaluate your current RTI framework if you already have it in place. We want to provide information that will help you know the fundamentals of RTI in mathematics and encourage you to reflect on the current RTI knowledge you may have.

RTI and How It Works

The goal of RTI is to meet the learning needs of the students by considering, analyzing, and differentiating the learning environment, the mathematics curriculum and skills being taught, and the delivery of that instruction within a comprehensive system of school improvement. To accomplish this goal, teachers, math coaches, interventionists, and special education teachers who provide instruction and intervention are responsible for:

- Planning, implementing, and adjusting evidence-based core instruction to meet curriculum standards and interventions based on individual student needs to ensure student success

- Providing appropriate instruction and interventions with fidelity, or as designed

- Continuously making instructional and intervention decisions by collecting and examining student progress-monitoring assessment data (Hoover & Love, 2011).

The key responsibilities within RTI are focused on instruction, interventions, and assessment practices within a continuous process of improvement. In addition, teachers and other school professionals provide more assistance if students are not mastering the content, or if the student needs more challenging expectations.

Authors' Note: As with any new process, there are many new definitions and terms to learn and to relate to our current knowledge and practices. As we review the concepts and components of RTI in this chapter and others, all of the words in bold are defined in the Glossary at the end of this book. This will help you understand the fundamentals of RTI, or it may serve as a refresher of your RTI knowledge.

The Goal of RTI Is a Continuous Process of . . .

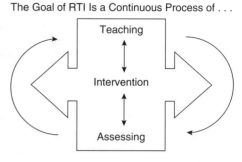

Tiered Instruction: Why and How It Works

Various RTI models will describe either three or four **tiers** of services and interventions to meet students' instructional needs with increasing levels of **intensity**, depending on student assessment data (Jankowski, 2003; Jimerson, Burns, & VanDerheyden, 2007). For the purposes of this book, a three-tiered model will be used (see Figure 2.1). Assessment data from multiple sources provides the necessary information for making instructional decisions within the tiers of RTI. **Universal screening** is the assessment we use for initial determination of students' current performance, identifying students in need of additional interventions. The universal screening of assessment data in mathematics is used to determine

FIGURE 2.1 Three-Tiered Model of RTI with the Instructional Data-Based Decision-Making Process

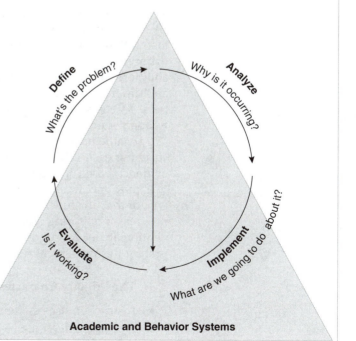

ACADEMIC AND BEHAVIOR SYSTEMS

Tier 3: Intensive, Individualized Interventions and Supports

The most intense (increased time, narrowed focus, reduced group size) instruction and intervention based on individual student needs provided in addition to and aligned with Tier 1 and 2 academic and behavior instruction and supports.
(1–5% of population)

Tier 2: Targeted, Supplemental Interventions and Supports

More targeted instruction/intervention and supplemental support that is aligned with the core academic and behavior curriculum.
(10–15% of population)

Tier 1: Core, Universal Instruction and Supports

General instruction and support provided to all students in all settings.
(80–90% of population)

individual students' instructional needs. One common source of these assessment data is mandated state or district assessments that are used to plan for instruction and student services.

Progress-monitoring data from classroom assessments are collected at frequent intervals in each tier. The data are used to determine whether students are responding to instruction and interventions, and to then guide instructional decision making about tiers. Although there may be some variation in instruction and intervention services in each of the tiers (e.g., time, size of intervention group, resources), similar principles and characteristics should remain consistent across classrooms and schools.

A **classroom instructional decision-making process** is used to decide how the instruction and interventions should be maintained, increased, or ceased based on assessment data and responses to instruction/intervention. **Assessment** results help us guide important educational decisions about instruction, interventions, supplemental programs, and possibly determine eligibility for other services, such as exceptional student education. If students are not successful despite intensifying instruction, it may be necessary to complete **diagnostic assessments** to provide specific information about student knowledge and skills (e.g., mathematics). These are usually completed by specialized diagnosticians. **Outcome assessment** provides us with the student results of our instruction and interventions. Students are usually assessed at the end of the unit, course, or school year. Chapter 3 will provide additional information about these assessments as related to instruction and interventions within RTI. In this next section, our discussions will focus on the RTI tiers and the roles of teachers.

Tier 1: Core, Universal Instruction and Supports

At the very heart of the RTI framework are the teaching and learning processes within our classrooms, referred to as *core instruction*. The focus of Tier 1 is ensuring that the core curriculum instruction consists of **evidence-based practices** taught with **fidelity of implementation** so that all students are mastering the curriculum. Data from universal screening assessments, usually collected from all students by the school or district, provide initial assessment information that is important for instructional planning. Instruction during Tier 1 is generally whole-class instruction, which includes **flexible grouping** and differentiation (also known as **differentiated instruction**). This means that *all* students, including those with disabilities, are receiving well-differentiated core instruction with flexible grouping and differentiation. The mathematics teacher leads the Tier 1 instruction and support. Teachers use progress monitoring to evaluate students' learning, collecting frequent data to guide their instructional decision making.

Mathematics teachers and other educators are responsible for learning and coaching each other in order to continuously improve and enhance their use of evidence-based instructional practices. Collaboration is important to help identify, use, and interpret results of ongoing progress-monitoring assessments to ensure that all students are succeeding in the classroom. The purpose of ongoing progress-monitoring assessment is to determine which students may need intervention at Tier 2. Progress monitoring will include collecting, graphing, and interpreting the assessment data from curriculum-based assessments.

The Primary Characteristics of Tier 1 Instruction

- Instruction uses evidence-based practices taught with fidelity.
- Instruction includes effective teaching practices.
- Progress is monitored for all students to determine learning outcomes as a result of instruction.

Tier 2: Targeted, Supplemental Interventions and Supports

For students who are not learning or are not making adequate progress in the Tier 1 core curriculum (determined from progress-monitoring assessments), teachers then combine their core instruction with more **targeted instruction** and intense instruction/interventions. It is important to understand that tiers are additive; students who require more intensive intervention receive Tier 1 + Tier 2, and so forth. This additional support is called *Tier 2 intervention*. This level of service consists of targeted, supplemental interventions aligned with the core curriculum. Tier 2 supports can be provided by the classroom teacher, a special education teacher within the general education setting, or by school support faculty, such as mathematics interventionists, mathematics instructional coaches, or other professionals. These interventions are generally delivered in a small-group format using strategies known to be effective in addressing the content for struggling learners. Progress monitoring data are used to adjust instruction and intervention, as well as document learning progress toward academic goals. Based on students' results on the progress-monitoring assessments in Tier 2, students will receive more or less intense instruction.

During Tier 2, the **RTI team**—consisting of teachers, mathematics coaches, and other educators, or school-based personnel—will enhance and differentiate large- and small-group instruction and interventions to meet the diverse needs of students. Core instruction will be delivered by mathematics or grade-level teachers, while other teachers may assist in providing interventions to small groups of students. Mathematics interventionists, special education teachers, and/or mathematics coaches may also offer collaborative, consultative, or coaching services to the general educator to ensure the fidelity of differentiated instruction. Progress-monitoring assessments will be administered regularly within the classroom in order to determine whether progress is occurring (Mellard, McKnight, & Woods, 2009). Other school personnel may support the mathematics teachers in collecting, graphing, and interpreting the data to make decisions about instruction and interventions.

The Primary Characteristics of Tier 2 Interventions

- Interventions are delivered to smaller groups of students, either within or outside the general education classroom or mathematics class.
- Interventions are provided in addition to and in alignment with core instruction.
- Interventions focus on particular skill areas that need strengthening.

Tier 3: Intensive, Individualized Intervention and Supports

There is a small percentage of students who will not respond sufficiently to Tier 1 and 2 interventions. These students will require more support and intensive intervention, in which the duration and frequency are increased. In typical RTI models, Tier 3 provides the highest level of support. It is critical that Tier 3 instruction is potent and effective. Tier 3 interventions must be provided by highly effective interventionists who are experts in the area of need. Students who receive Tier 3 services are provided one-on-one and/or small-group instruction aligned with the core instructional program. Like Tier 2, Tier 3 instruction supports and *does not* replace the general, core curriculum—it is additional instruction in the core curriculum. To determine whether instruction and interventions have been successful, teachers and members of the RTI team continue to collect progress-monitoring assessment data. It is important to collect sufficient data to determine whether students are responding to the instruction and interventions delivered; the data can be used to further modify and guide mathematics instruction as necessary.

In Tier 3, some students may require additional specialized intensive intervention in a one-on-one or small-group setting. At times, the role of a special education teacher (also known as the Exceptional Special Education [ESE] teacher) will be expanded when providing more intense services. The ESE teacher may provide the specialized, intensive interventions. The specific knowledge and competencies of diagnostic assessment and diagnostic teaching by special education teachers are invaluable during this process. The implications of the diagnostic assessment may result in a specific, intensive intervention for the individual student (Mellard, McKnight, & Woods, 2009). In some states, these services are already under the auspices of special education services. In addition, the student assessment data collected by teachers within the RTI process are important to the determination of a learning disability (Spectrum, 2010), if this is warranted for an individual student. Tier 3 is the most intense level of intervention; therefore, a student who does not respond to Tier 3 may qualify for special education services or other school services.

The Primary Characteristics of Tier 3 Intensive, Individualized Interventions

- Interventions are delivered one-on-one or in very small group settings.
- Interventions are provided in addition to and in alignment with Tier 1 instruction and Tier 2 interventions. Tier 3 interventions should include the most instructional minutes. It is critical that Tier 3 instruction does not replace the core instruction.
- Interventions focus more narrowly on defined skill areas.

An RTI model is a prevention model in which the primary instruction and intervention occur in the classroom as soon as problems are identified. Most national research and resources refer to *intervention* as the I in RTI. However, because prevention and high-quality instruction are critical for improved student achievement within the mathematics classroom, we are purposely referring to both *instruction* and *interventions* in defining the I in RTI. High-quality instruction, additional resources, initial interventions, differentiation, and scaffolded support must be considered, planned, and implemented at the classroom level within the RTI model based on multiple sources of assessment data (Bender & Shores, 2007; Little, 2003). Classroom instruction in mathematics may be differentiated and intensified based on the instructional needs of the students. Available classroom assessments are the primary sources of information, and continued monitoring of the students' learning provides the basis for instructional decisions. The RTI model provides a coordinated, comprehensive, and sustained system of continuous problem solving related to the teaching–learning–assessment processes within the mathematics classroom. Therefore, the essential components of RTI within each mathematics classroom include:

- An integrated data collection and assessment system to inform decisions and potential solutions at each tier of service delivery
- Multiple tiers of instruction and interventions
- A method of instructional decision making and problem solving

These three components are integrated and implemented within a coordinated and comprehensive system. This encourages a different way of work to fulfill the intent of mathematics teachers, instructional coaches, parents, researchers, and legislators that the academic and instructional needs for all students in mathematics are met.

Instructional Decision-Making Processes for RTI Implementation

Effective teaching is adaptive teaching. This is critical when implementing RTI in your mathematics classroom. You must change and adapt familiar lessons and standard units in ways that make them fit students' needs. No two lessons or units will be the same because your knowledge and skills will help you adapt and enhance lessons based on what your students do and say (Allington, 2009).

The next important concept of RTI is continuous problem solving within classrooms and schools. We continuously use an instructional planning and decision-making process (i.e., instructional problem solving) to make these important instructional decisions to meet the needs of our students. This same process is used to make instructional decisions about student learning based on progress-monitoring assessments within the RTI process. Therefore, it is important for teachers to think about and analyze student assessment data to make decisions throughout the RTI tiers about the multiple variables of teaching and learning so that each student learns the curriculum.

Data from classroom progress-monitoring assessments are collected at each tier and used to maintain, increase, or cease instruction or interventions. By observing and listening to students while teaching, effective teachers are continuously monitoring and adapting daily instructional decisions. These differences may require something as simple as an added example or as complex as re-teaching the skills using a completely different method. An effective teacher must consistently consider and plan using the following questions:

1. Problem identification: What is the problem? What are the variables to consider?
2. Analysis of the problem: Why is the problem occurring? Consider the possible variables (e.g., teacher, student, curriculum, instruction) for lesson planning and solutions.
3. Instruction/intervention planning and implementation: What are we going to do about it?
4. Response to instruction/intervention: Is it working?

Figure 2.2 portrays the continuous nature of the instructional decision making and problem solving as they are used throughout the RTI process. This is a continuous

FIGURE 2.2   Instructional Data-Based Decision-Making Process within RTI

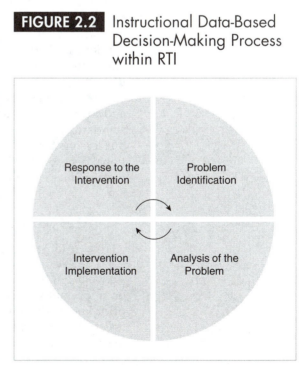

Response to the Intervention

Problem Identification

Intervention Implementation

Analysis of the Problem

FIGURE 2.3 Guiding Questions: Lesson Planning within RTI Tiers of Instruction

Guiding Questions
What are the critical concepts and skills to be learned by ALL students?
How do the current resources in my classroom address the selected lesson concepts and skills of this standard?
What prior knowledge do students need to master content standard?
What may be sources of difficulty and confusion for the students?
How can this lesson build on students' prior knowledge and experiences?
What will students think and do in response to the instructional lesson?
What scaffolding and support can I provide to meet the needs of ALL learners through differentiating instruction and accommodating individuals?
What questions, resources, examples, and so forth will clarify and/or extend conceptual learning by students?
What grouping arrangements, accommodations, adaptations, cognitive/metacognitive strategies, and/or technologies are needed for small groups of students?
How can I make the learning task less complex without changing the goal?
What kinds of data are available and will help us assess student progress toward the goal?
How will I check for conceptual understanding and depth of knowledge?

improvement cycle. We use data to guide instruction and take shared responsibility to ensure that instruction and supports are effective. If assessment data indicate that some of the students are not learning the curriculum, then we expand the circle of instructional decision making to include other school professionals (e.g., interventionists, instructional coaches, curriculum specialists, special education teachers). This will aid in problem solving as you work with the members of the RTI team to develop plans including more intense resources and services for students.

As we plan, there are questions that can guide our choices about instruction and interventions based on the needs of our students as related to mathematics standards. Figure 2.3 identifies the questions we need to ask ourselves as we plan our lessons for RTI. Answering these questions will help us focus on the instructional decision-making process for developing lessons that will be effective in our mathematics classrooms.

Instructional Variables in the Mathematics Classroom

As we begin to plan lessons in mathematics within our classrooms, we can focus on important instructional variables based on our students' interests, skills, and prior knowledge (*whom* to teach), the outcomes and standards of the curriculum (*what* to teach), and the instructional methods, resources, and models we will use (*how* to teach). Reflect on the following important variables: teacher, students, curriculum, and instruction (see Figure 2.4); then, visualize their importance as the main components and connections for learning mathematics. Let's look briefly at each of these variables.

Teachers

We believe there are several keys to effective teaching for all students. Teachers exhibit positive expectations for students' mathematical success. They are extremely good at managing their classrooms, and they know how to design mathematics lessons for student mastery. In addition, they offer emotional support and a sense of confidence to students who are nervous about or show anxiety toward the mathematical content being taught.

Positive Expectations

What type of expectations do you set in your classroom each day? This is an important question to ask ourselves because we hold the key to influencing our students. Our expectations set the tone for what our students think about mathematics, be it positive or negative. We know students learn more in classrooms and schools that are positive, caring, structured, and supportive (Sternberg & Subotnik, 2006). It is our expectations, encouragements, evaluations, attentiveness, and organizational procedures that motivate our students to feel both comfortable and productive in classrooms. Having positive expectations simply means that we believe in our students and believe that they can learn. When we believe that students can learn, students believe they can learn. The enthusiasm exhibited during teaching can yield increased academic achievement and decrease off-task behavior among students (Little, 2009c).

Teaching mathematics with enthusiasm is especially important for struggling learners. Our interactions not only create a climate of acceptance and learning, but also can motivate student learning. The more we know about our students, the more motivated and engaged our students will be. No matter what our personality styles, we must know the importance of planning and using various motivational strategies for successful mathematical achievement in the classroom.

Good Classroom Management within the Mathematics Learning Environment

Effective teachers are also managers of classroom procedures more than disciplinarians. Classroom management refers to all of the things that teachers do to organize students, classrooms, time, and materials so teaching and learning can occur (Wong & Wong, 1998). This is especially important when classroom teachers differentiate instruction through the use of manipulatives, learning styles, student centers, technology centers, and individualized study centers. Managing additional personnel, resources, and materials needed to adapt and intensify lessons and units is important when implementing RTI in mathematics. Classroom management, then, includes all of the things that teachers must do toward two end results:

1. To foster student involvement and cooperation in all classroom activities
2. To establish a positive, productive learning environment

Lesson Design for Student Mastery

Mastery is the student's demonstration that he or she comprehends a concept or can perform a skill at a level of proficiency determined by the teacher. To teach to mastery, an effective teacher must do two things:

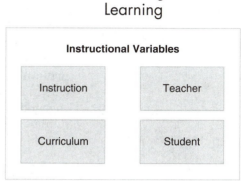

FIGURE 2.4 Variables within Teaching and Learning

Instructional Variables

Instruction	Teacher
Curriculum	Student

1. Know how to design mathematics lessons in which a student will learn a concept or a skill
2. Know how to evaluate mathematical learning to determine if the student has mastered the concept of the skill

Effective teachers plan, design, implement, reflect, and adapt lessons and units to ensure that *all* of their students master the concepts and skills of the curriculum. To increase student learning and achievement throughout the various tiers of instruction, it is important to increase the amount of time the student is engaged in learning the established objectives of the mathematics curriculum (Little, 2009b).

Students

Specific knowledge of students' academic performance will be important when planning lessons and units. For example, student data from mandated state assessments are often provided to school district personnel, school administrators, and classroom teachers as a basis for the school improvement process and for program planning. It is important to collect the assessment data as part of the universal screening and decision-making process of RTI so we know where our students stand academically. Other factors should be considered as well when planning for students. We should also know and recognize the interests, attitudes, knowledge, and skills of our students in our lesson planning. These are key components for both establishing positive and supportive classroom environments and increasing student motivation. This knowledge helps us connect with our students and their learning within the mathematics classroom. We can use interest inventories, observations, teacher–student discussions, and other interactions to gain valuable information that can be used for instructional planning. We can include topics of students' interests into lessons, learning centers, and units (see Figure 2.5 for an example).

As we think about instructional planning for students we also want to specifically address students' attitudes regarding mathematics. We can't talk about mathematics without talking about mathematics anxiety! You and I can probably list many students who have exhibited signs of nervousness or anxiety when we have taught mathematics lessons in our classrooms. We have witnessed many students who show very little courage and confidence when asked to perform mathematical tasks. We observe the pressure they feel and their unpreparedness for the content we are teaching. We hear cries of "I can't do this stuff!" and "When will I ever use this?" We also have students who will avoid the subject at all costs. Often, students will have behavior problems during math class. These include coming to class unprepared (without materials, books, pencils, etc.), playing with objects, leaving their seats without permission, refusing to open their books or do their class work or homework, daydreaming, exhibiting off-task behaviors, or asking to go to the bathroom or do other activities during math class (Gresham, 2004).

This anxiety is considered to be specific to mathematics instruction and mathematics-related activities, and can be so debilitative that it can interfere with mathematics performance and inhibit subsequent learning (Gresham, 2009; Hembree, 1990). Mathematics anxiety is a feeling of helplessness, tension, or panic when asked to perform mathematics operations or problems. It has been described as an *I can't syndrome*—a feeling of uncertainty and of not being able to perform well in mathematics or with numbers (Tobias, 1998). This anxiety is rooted in teachers and teaching, and it has been tied to poor academic performance. It is an emotional reaction toward mathematics that interferes with future mathematical learning. We recognize students' negative experiences with mathematics. These experiences can include but are not limited to:

FIGURE 2.5   Student Initial Mathematics Interview

Student Name: _____ Grade: _____ Date: _____

Interview

1. When I hear the word *math* I . . . ?

2. Do you enjoy learning math? Why or why not?

3. I like learning math because . . .

4. How does math make you feel?

5. What is your favorite thing to do in math? Why did you choose this as your favorite thing to do?

6. What types of math problems do you like to solve? Why did you choose those?

7. When is your favorite time to do math?

8. Do you enjoy doing math homework? Why or why not?

9. In math, I want to learn more about . . .

- Receiving a bad grade in mathematics or receiving poor instruction
- Lacking role models or encouragement from parents or teachers
- Being stereotyped by gender or ethnicity
- Having mathematics used as punishment in school
- Having a fear of looking or feeling stupid in front of peers
- Feeling pressure from timed tests
- Lacking preparedness
- Being placed in the wrong mathematics course for their ability level

You may be able to think of others. Students can mentally shut down as a direct result of mathematics anxiety, thus creating a void in the mathematical learning process.

We know that mathematics is a subject that carries an emotional stigma that often creates a negative reaction (Gresham, 2004). We also know that the instruction of mathematics plays a critical role in shaping one's attitudes toward mathematics (Gresham, 2007). Within the RTI framework, effective practices are crucial to helping struggling learners be successful in the mathematics classroom and changing negative attitudes toward mathematics to positive ones. To do so, we place emphasis on manipulative use, nontraditional approaches (see the sidebar entitled Ideas for Preventing and Reducing Mathematics Anxiety below), and authentic learning practices that mimic situations of dealing with mathematics anxiety. In addition, we want to offer students emotional support and genuinely recognize their feelings and emotions in regard to mathematics. See the sidebar for a checklist you can use to identify mathematics anxiety in your students.

Knowing that mathematics anxiety exists in our students is important. Addressing it with our students is critical to help lessen or alleviate the anxiety altogether. Incorporating journal writing about students' feelings is a good way to help them address their emotions regarding mathematics. Open communication between teacher and student is also important. We have provided you with a sample of a student journal writing page and an interest inventory for use in your classroom. In addition to these, we have also provided a mathematics anxiety rating scale you can administer to your students to determine the levels of mathematics anxiety in your students. (These can be found in the Teachers Resources section in the back of this book). Understanding the level of mathematics anxiety

A TIME TO REFLECT

How do you learn about your students' skills, interests, attitudes toward mathematics, and current knowledge of mathematics? How do you use this information when planning for instruction in your classroom?

Ideas for Preventing and Reducing Mathematics Anxiety

- Know your mathematics content! Teachers who are uncomfortable teaching mathematics due to lack of knowledge or self-confidence pass their anxiety on to their students.

- Do not limit yourself to traditional methods of teaching (e.g., worksheets, excessive drill and practice, board work, lectures, and rote memorization activities).

- Allow your students to get actively involved in the learning process by playing games and incorporating other hands-on activities that transcend from the concrete level to the abstract level.

- Expand your repertoire of teaching strategies to include problem-solving activities, discoveries, challenges, and simulations by organizing activities that relate to real-world applications. This can help students make sense of the mathematics they are learning.

- Use modeling, small groups, cooperative learning strategies, and peer tutoring.

- Establish open communication lines with your students by allowing them to talk about their feelings and attitudes toward mathematics. Provide props that invite reflection and stimulation. Facilitate conversation and communication through journal writing sessions, teacher–student talk times and small-group and peer-to-peer chats. Do not criticize or embarrass students for their thoughts or anxiety.

- Encourage students to ask questions. Empower and encourage your students as learners and increase their self-confidence in the mathematics classroom. All students can become successful mathematics learners if we teach them how to do so.

- Use technology such as calculators, computers, video, graphing calculators, and other tools.

- Be enthusiastic and positive about mathematics. Have a caring attitude and realistic expectations. Avoid negative self-talk and the myth that you need a "math mind" to excel.

- Teach to the learning style of the student. Teachers tend to teach just as they were taught or teach to their way of learning. Take into account the different interests and learning styles of students and incorporate activities that reflect these variations.

- Incorporate the Common Core Standards, NCTM standards, and state or district standards into your daily teaching practices.

in your classroom will help guide your instruction and the emotional supports you can offer students within the RTI framework.

Curriculum

Curriculum is the content to be taught and learned by the students, and is usually categorized by subject area (e.g., mathematics, reading) and grade level. Research informs the curriculum standards developed and adopted by states and professional organizations (e.g., NCTM standards, Common Core Standards). The curriculum standards may also be included in policies set forth by state departments of education. Each state department of education will have their curriculum standards, as well as related resources, available to educators within the state. It is important for teachers to be aware of the state curriculum standards, available resources, professional development opportunities, and content-area materials for students in specific grades, as well as for students with disabilities and those who speak other languages. State education departments often offer free current and accurate resources for teachers to use for instruction.

Many states and school districts review and adopt textbooks and programs to meet the established curriculum standards. Curriculum experts review the content of these resources to ensure that they have a research base that documents student mastery, referred to as evidence-based practice. Curriculum specialists and coordinators are important in further enhancing, revising, aligning, and providing resources and professional development for teachers related to the state and district standards. These resources are quite beneficial to teachers during the lesson- and unit-planning processes. Related resources may include annual mapping and pacing charts, calendars, and unit-planning forms for teachers within grade levels to facilitate planning that is aligned with the curricular standards.

Checklist for Identifying Mathematics Anxiety

Students with mathematics anxiety:

- Are more commonly female than male
- Will do whatever it takes to avoid the subject of mathematics
- Will show a lack of understanding mathematics (especially at-risk, struggling learners)
- Experience failure and frustration, and will receive or have received below-average or failing grades in mathematics
- May cry or become irritable when asked to do mathematics problems

---

READ MORE ABOUT IT!

Check the following websites for additional information:

What Works Clearinghouse: www.whatworks.ed.gov

Best Evidence Encyclopedia: www.bestevidence.org

Intervention Central: www.interventioncentral.org

The Access Center: Improving Outcomes for All Students K–8: www.k8accesscenter.org

---

Once annual outcomes, prerequisite skills, assessments, and core, intervention, and supplemental resources and materials are identified by the teaching team members, it is important to think about and plan your units and lessons using **curriculum mapping**. During this process, you will reflect on and document assessment of ongoing student progress as a way to determine if a student or small group of students require additional support through the tiers of instruction and supports prior to considering additional testing for services.

Instruction

If curriculum is *what* to teach, then instruction is *how* to teach. There are multiple theories of instruction and evidence-based instructional practices and programs that teachers use when planning for instruction. Differentiated instruction is a philosophy or approach to planning and teaching based on the premise that teachers must consider whom they are teaching (students) as well as what they are teaching (curricular content). The principles of differentiation include ongoing assessment and adjustment, clarity of the standards and learning goals of the curriculum, use of flexible grouping, tasks that are respectful of each learner, and instruction that stretches the learners (Tomlinson, 2003). Differentiating the content refers to what is being taught, as well as how students gain access to a body of knowledge.

Differentiating the content starts with the teacher having clarity about the essential understandings and goals of the curriculum for the lesson or unit. Differentiating the process refers to how a student makes sense of the information or content. Differentiating the product refers to assessments or demonstrations of what the student knows, understands, or is able to do. Differentiating the learning environment considers both the operation of the classroom as well as the more abstract climate of the classroom. Differentiating is based on a set of beliefs, guided by principles, and may be implemented in a variety of ways.

Development of a differentiated classroom occurs along a continuum. A lesson may be differentiated or a unit maybe be differentiated as teachers gain proficiency toward a broader use of differentiation. Differentiating instruction to meet targeted smaller groups of students, or the entire class, is a key component of lesson planning within an RTI classroom. We will further discuss the three tiers of instruction and intervention within RTI, provide examples, and reflect on how to differentiate instruction and interventions to meet the needs of students in our classes in Chapters 4 through 6.

Beginning and Delivering an Intervention Plan for Students

FIGURE 2.6 Multiple Variables with Instructional Decision Making

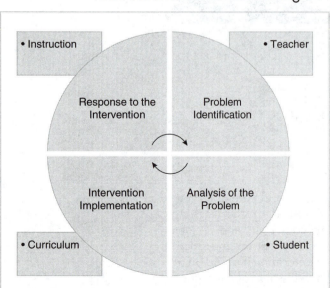

As we prepare for beginning and delivering an intervention plan in our classroom, the first question we must ask ourselves is "Are all of my students learning?" We know we must continuously observe, think about, and analyze student learning relative to mastery of grade-level curricular standards and expectations. (Use Reproducible #5, found in Appendix A, to record observations of student learning.) We have provided you with samples, checklists, and guiding questions to help you pinpoint a concern or issue on which to focus. Observing and interviewing students while they are engaged in learning, analyzing their work samples, and collecting classroom assessments are necessary at this stage. If learning is not occurring, we want to learn why. What is the goal for student improvement? What can we do to improve the learning process? We continuously make instructional decisions about all of the instructional variables to improve student learning based on assessment data (see Figure 2.6).

Coordinating Interventions with Core Classroom Instruction

Allington (2009) describes four characteristics of good teachers needed for RTI implementation:

1. *Expert* teachers have extensive knowledge of teaching and subject matter.
2. *Effective* teachers bring about higher student achievement.
3. *Analytic* teachers use observational techniques to record how well they meet their instructional intentions and goals.
4. *Reflective* teachers examine their teaching to become more thoughtful teachers.

Each of these teacher characteristics is necessary to improve academic and behavioral achievement for each student. RTI begins and continues with the teacher. We continuously observe, analyze, implement, and reflect using instructional decision making throughout the tiers of instruction and interventions, to ensure that the lesson and unit plans are meeting the academic and behavioral needs of all students in our classes. When considering the multiple instructional variables to enhance, adapt, and intensify instruction, we use our extensive skills and knowledge of teaching and the subject matter. We analyze the results of ongoing progress-monitoring assessments and observations to adapt and enhance the lessons as needed for the entire class and/or for small groups and individual students. This process is continuous and critical to ensure student success. Effective teachers continuously reflect on their teaching to bring about higher student achievement.

A TIME TO REFLECT

What should my students know and be able to do with what they know as a result of this lesson or this unit? How are my objectives related to national, state, and/or district standards or proficiencies?

How will students demonstrate what they know and what they can do? What forms of assessment, including observations and questioning, can I use? What will be the assessment criteria and what form will it take?

How will new knowledge, concepts, and skills be introduced? Given the diversity of my students and my task analysis, what are the best ways for me to instruct using various models of instruction and presentation modes of new material?

As you consider the information you just read, we want to refer back to Ms. Holly to see how the instructional decision-making processes within RTI comes into play in the classroom.

Teacher's Voice Revisited

Although state and school-wide assessment results were provided to each teacher at the beginning of the school year, Ms. Holly administered various curriculum-based informal assessments related to fourth grade–level curriculum benchmarks to determine students' mathematical strengths and weaknesses. (See Figure 2.7 for a sample of a fourth-grade math curriculum.)

In addition, Ms. Holly carefully observed, took notes, and talked to students to gain additional information about their knowledge in mathematics. Using the data she compiled, Ms. Holly identified that place value, addition,

FIGURE 2.7 Sample of Fourth-Grade Math Curriculum

Represent verbal statements of multiplicative comparisons as multiplication equations.

Multiply or divide to solve word problems involving multiplicative comparison.

Solve multi-step word problems posed with whole numbers and having whole-number answers using the four operations, including problems in which remainders must be interpreted.

Find all factor pairs for a whole number in the range from 1 to 100.

Recognize that a whole number is a multiple of each of its factors.

Generate a number or shape pattern that follows a given rule.

Compare two multi-digit numbers based on meanings of the digits in each place, using >, =, and <.

Use place value understanding to round multi-digit whole numbers to any place.

Fluently add and subtract multi-digit whole numbers using the standard algorithm.

Multiply a whole number of up to four digits by a one-digit whole number, and multiply two two-digit numbers using strategies based on place value and the properties of operations. Illustrate and explain the calculation by using equations, rectangular arrays, and/or area models.

Explain why a fraction a/b is equivalent to a fraction $(n \times a)/(n \times b)$ by using visual fraction models, with attention to how the number and size of the parts differ even though the two fractions themselves are the same size.

Understand a fraction a/b with $a > 1$ as a sum of fractions $1/b$.

Add and subtract mixed numbers with like denominators.

Compare two decimals to hundredths by reasoning about their size.

Know relative sizes of measurement units within one system of units.

Use the four operations to solve word problems about measurement.

Measure angles in whole-number degrees using a protractor.

Draw points, lines, line segments, rays, angles (right, acute, obtuse), and perpendicular and parallel lines. Identify these in two-dimensional figures.

Classify two-dimensional figures.

and multiplication were skills that should be retaught, reinforced, and mastered in order for several of the students to be successful with the problem presented. Clearly there were gaps in mathematical knowledge that affected students' ability to master the grade-level mathematics and additional mathematical support was needed.

Ms. Holly knew from her notes that the students of concern were able to memorize some but not all of their facts. It was through teacher–student conferencing that she realized the students did not know what it means to multiply or the situations in which multiplication is the appropriate thing to do. Students had not fully developed or mastered the language for thinking about and describing multiplicative situations and their quantities, units, and equal groups, and therefore lacked a basic understanding of multiplication. Ms. Holly knew that lack of multiplicative understanding was preventing students from being able to solve the problem presented. She knew an intervention plan was needed in order for them to be mathematically successful. Ms. Holly immediately referred back to some of the resources and materials from RTI websites to help with students' instructional needs.

Next, Ms. Holly met with the RTI support team in her school to discuss her concerns based on the instructional data. She wanted to find a solution to this problem using various instructional methods and resources, and develop a plan of action to target efforts to improve mastery for the selected students. The RTI support team in her school consisted of the curriculum mathematics specialist (mathematics instructional coach), two grade-level teachers, a mathematics interventionist, and the school psychologist. Ms. Holly then described the instructional processes and strategies that she had been using in her classroom to teach mathematics during the first six weeks of school. She also explained that she had been using small-group instruction in math fact knowledge and manipulatives, and had used an interactive computer software program focused on addition and subtraction. During the RTI team meeting, the following critical questions were addressed in order to formulate an action plan:

- What would indicate that these particular students have needs beyond the general mathematics instruction?
- How do we know that this is not a classroom or school-wide issue?
- How does the teacher organize for instruction?
- What considerations does Ms. Holly need to address when planning for instruction?
- What resources may be needed to help students?

The RTI team decided that Ms. Holly would continue teaching the identified students during the general mathematics instructional time and an interventionist would also work with the students who were experiencing the same problems for twenty to thirty additional minutes, three to five days per week. This ensured that while those students received mathematics instruction during the regularly scheduled math time (Tier 1), additional intensive instruction and support would be offered as Tier 2 services. Intensive instruction did not focus only on rote memorization and drill and practice, but included additional concrete, authentic, hands-on, research-based activities and strategies to help students develop a conceptual understanding of place value, addition, and multiplication. The RTI team was quick to develop an intervention plan to address students' academic difficulties using collaborative, school-wide, problem-solving approaches.

As evidenced in the case study, Ms. Holly identified an issue of concern in the mathematics classroom. Her observations revealed that the level of learning for some of her students fell below academic expectations. She took the time to investigate the areas of concern by collecting and analyzing information about the students' learning needs relative to mastery of grade-level curricular standards and expectations. Next, we will take a more in-depth look at the classroom considerations of RTI (planning and teaching in mathematics content), and how she is going to structure this in her classroom.

The primary focus of Ms. Holly's mathematics instruction is teaching students how to effectively develop conceptual meanings and explanations for multiplying and using grouping and regrouping for place value. Students use various strategies including invented and standard algorithms for multiplication and understanding the position and place value of numbers. Most recently, she has been teaching the importance of using multiplication concepts for solution of particular types of problems. While her students must ultimately develop fluency with a balance between conceptual understanding and computational proficiency, Ms. Holly has found it is most beneficial to focus on just one or two techniques at a time. She is now teaching students how to make connections between the numbers involved and the meaning of the symbolism, showing representations of the arithmetic operations for expressing unioning (multiple addition), making predictions and estimations, habituating the facts, and understanding place value.

In the full-class group, Ms. Holly asks students to draw and represent objects, helps students connect numerals to those figures, and shows them how to make notations to help with the content they are learning. Students also work with nonproportional and proportional materials to build collections of tens to trade and represent with numerals. Nonproportional manipulatives include coins, popsicle sticks, buttons, and other objects. She is also using place-value blocks (base-10 blocks), number cubes, beans, counters, and place-value charts. She encourages students to draw on their prior knowledge to make drawings and representations, to think about and write predictions on a whiteboard, and to use paper-and-pencil work if needed. She also encourages students to think about the answer before solving the problem and to discover alternative algorithms for solving the problem. In addition, she has students complete a few problems at a time and has them do simpler problems before moving to more difficult ones. She has students discuss their findings and how they generated the facts by using materials and manipulatives. Following the group discussion, she has students partner with math buddies or get into groups. These math buddies or groups have been determined by Ms. Holly based on assessment data from students' educational profiles, student interests, and her own in-class assessments.

The twenty-four students in the class are organized in various groupings that were established based on student needs and lesson goals:

- The entire class is taught by Ms. Holly from 10:00 to 11:00. She uses direct instruction to provide anticipatory set (i.e., motivates students, activates student's background knowledge, and introduces the lesson), demonstrates the skills of making predictions and solving problems, and provides opportunities for students to practice in the large classroom group. She uses multiple methods to model multiplication and place-value skills and uses the whiteboards and various signals (thumbs-up/thumbs-down, etc.) to both actively engage the students and continuously assess their learning.

- At 10:10, twelve pairs of students practice solving multiplication problems with specific resources provided by Ms. Holly. Corrective feedback and responses from the teacher and from partners occur throughout this guided practice.

- At 10:30, student grouping consists of four mixed-ability groups of six children who share similar areas of interest. Groups independently practice their multiplication skills through problems of their choice using number cubes. Ms. Holly meets with student groups for feedback and to continuously assess learning. She carries a clipboard with various answer keys and a student record sheet to continuously record observations, student responses, and accuracy.

FIGURE 2.8 Sample of Initial Lesson Plan

Lesson Planning in the RTI Classroom

Teacher Name: *Ms. Holly*   Content Area: *Fourth-Grade Math*   Dates: *September 3–5*

Curricular Goal: M.A. 4.2: *When given five word problems, compute using multi-digit multiplication with fluency by using a variety of strategies, including invented and standard algorithms, and provide explanations.*

Prior knowledge (preskills): Fluency in multiplication facts, reading at grade level, number sense operations.

Differentiation of core instruction: Word problems with computation at various skill levels, cooperative groups (reading ability), manipulatives, whiteboards.

Tier 1—Classroom/student considerations: Predetermined mixed-ability, cooperative groups established with student skills of grade-level reading and multiplication skills. Various levels of math problems provided.

Tier 2—Small student groups (use student initials): Use of vocabulary cards (operations), whiteboards, and concrete manipulatives. Additional practice: Multiplication facts on computer (program:_____).

Tier 3—Individual (use initials): Specific word problems with minimal reading, use peer tutor, and intensive practice with multiplication fluency on computer (program: _____).

Instruction/Intervention Summary

	Instruction/Intervention	Lead Teacher	Materials/ Resources	Classroom Assessments	Student Results	Teacher Notes
Tier 1	**Core Instruction** –Introduce high-interest lesson –Review vocabulary with examples –Organize cooperative groups; review group expectations –Provide one word problem –After ten minutes, review student responses –Guided practice: Provide five word problem cards to each group –After twenty-five minutes, review problems orally –Independent practice/ informal assessment: Provide one word problem (various reading/math levels) for each student to complete Curriculum Based Measurement (CBM)	Ms. H	Word problems from textbook and additional resources	–CBM from textbook –Teacher observation using rubric of task analyses	–Number of items mastered: –90% (multiple components of rubric) on CBM Tasks not mastered (list):	–Date to report data of results with RTI: Support team: Data sources: –District benchmark: –CBM: –Observation rubric: –Computer: –Other:

- At 10:50, six homogeneous groups of four students each are organized by mathematical strengths and deficits. Each group works on skills needed, from enrichment and independent practice to more intense instruction and intervention. Formative and curriculum-based assessments are continued and recorded throughout this lesson and subsequent lessons related to multiplication and place value. In addition, software has been included on student computers for more intensive instruction and interventions, as needed.

During the one-hour mathematics block, Ms. Holly has used multiple grouping arrangements, high-interest materials, various cognitive strategies, active engagement techniques, differentiated instruction, and intensified instruction, and has provided interventions and continuously collected formative assessment data. All of these components are necessary variables when implementing RTI in classrooms. Based on the results of student learning, Ms. Holly will continue to use various techniques and technologies to teach and intensify instruction and intervention through the tiers of RTI.

Curriculum, instruction, and assessment are integral and interrelated components within the RTI framework. We want you to be able to articulate classroom expectations, focus on your instructional practices, and teach to the curricular expectations. Therefore, we have included a sample lesson plan to help you visualize what Ms. Holly's lesson plan may be as she works with her struggling learners (see Figure 2.8).

With increasing emphasis on assessments, evaluation, and accountability in mathematics and RTI, there is a unique and immediate need to learn more about the use of assessments to improve student learning within the RTI framework. We have provided the specifics of RTI in preparation for its delivery. The next chapter will discuss various types of assessment that will deepen your professional knowledge, expertise, and skills, and will help you focus on applying important information about your students in your mathematics classroom.

TEACHERS' CORNER

Keys to Getting You Started with RTI

- Complete the self-reflection checklist, Considerations for Effective Teaching Practices (Reproducible #2 in Appendix A). Discuss your responses with colleagues or with your school-based RTI team if already in place.
- Complete the Student Demographics within RTI Universal Screening to collect and organize assessment information for instructional planning (Reproducible #3 in Appendix A).
- Begin completing the Curriculum Mapping and Pacing Chart to Use with RTI to identify, locate, and plan using multiple curricular resources and variables (e.g., annual goals, objectives, grade-level benchmarks, state standards if applicable) (Reproducible #4 in Appendix A). Once these are identified, think about and plan your units and lessons within the curriculum maps. Reflect on and document assessment data of ongoing student progress to determine whether a student or small groups of students require additional support through the tiers of instruction and support. If you already have these in place, reevaluate your units and lessons for effectiveness and make any needed changes.
- Complete the Student Observation Form (Reproducible #5 in Appendix A) to record observations of student learning.
- Complete Professional Learning Community Chapter 2 activities.
- Complete the book study questions for Chapter 2 (see Appendix B).

Chapter 3

Knowing the Students Are Learning: Use of Assessment Data

"Data provide the power to . . . make good decisions, work intelligently, work effectively and efficiently, change things in better ways, know the impact of our hard work, help us prepare for the future, and make our work benefit all children."

—*Victoria L. Bernhardt*

What You Will Find in This Chapter

- Multiple types and purposes of assessment
- Assessments within RTI: Universal screening, formative assessment, progress monitoring, diagnostic assessment, and summative assessment
- Multiple assessments for instructional planning within tiers of RTI
- Sample assessments and resources

Teacher's Voice

During our faculty meeting yesterday, the discussion quickly turned to assessment. We broke into grade-level teams to discuss our thoughts for universal screening, progress monitoring, curriculum-based measurements, and so forth. We know we need to determine where our students are mathematically before we begin the school year. I realize that doing so will help me prepare my lessons and help my students learn the math effectively. No problem, I thought. I can do that! I do understand the importance of assessing my students with universal screening, using the data to work on my lesson planning and delivery, and working with students to achieve mastery of the mathematical content. I know I should use assessment as a way to assist me in my teaching practices and help my students. I do use some assessment practices in my classroom now, but not as frequently as I think I should or need to in order to assist my students. My goal for this year is to gain a better understanding of all the purposes for and types of assessment and get it all organized so I can be much more effective in the classroom.

Ms. Holly, fourth-grade teacher

We use assessment data every day to learn about our students, just as Ms. Holly has indicated she is doing in her classroom. We closely monitor our students during instruction to ensure that progress is made by all students to meet the standards and benchmarks in mathematics. Gathering formative assessment data from many sources builds a complete picture of our students' abilities, skills, dispositions, and learning. We analyze the data to adjust our practices for improved student learning. The goal of this chapter is to describe assessment practices within the RTI framework through an overview of the types and uses of assessments. We will share multiple resources of evidenced-based progress-monitoring assessments for use with groups and individual students within mathematics.

Understanding the Purposes and Types of Assessment

There has been much national discussion regarding the purposes of assessments, especially with the increased focus on standardized assessments in mathematics (National Research Council, 2001). We all want our students to know and be able to use mathematics. However, high-stakes testing has placed such an emphasis on students being able to complete choice tests that the larger goal of teaching our students to be independent thinkers and educating them mathematically sometimes gets lost. Much concern has been expressed regarding students' inability to think for themselves, solve problems, demonstrate number sense, and reason creatively (National Research Council, 1993). In response, NCTM (2000) revised their standards to promote the active involvement of students in their learning to pose and solve mathematical problems; develop reasoning ability; communicate about mathematics through written, oral, symbolic, and visual means; create and use multiple representations to learn and communicate mathematical ideas; and recognize and make connections among mathematical ideas. The changes in standards also created changes in assessment and evaluation of student learning. Major shifts are recommended to meet these revised standards. Figure 3.1 provides an overview of the shifts necessary for assessment in mathematics; these are aligned with the NCTM standards and Core Curriculum Standards.

Assessment tasks continuously provide us with information about students' prior knowledge, competencies, and skills aligned with mathematics curriculum and instructional strategies. In other words, we should not teach one way and assess another way. Assessment should be viewed as a tool to assist us in designing and revising instruction for our students. All of the information that we learn about our students throughout our teaching must align with our objectives as well as connect their learning with the standards in mathematics in a continuous improvement cycle of learning (see Figure 3.2).

As we continue the discussion on assessment we want to address both formative and summative assessments because understanding the difference between the two is sometimes difficult. First, let's look at summative assessment. In general, **summative assessment** typically documents how much learning has

FIGURE 3.1 Major Shifts in Mathematical Assessment Practices

Decreased Attention on . . .	Increased Attention on . . .
Using only written tests	Using multiple formative assessment techniques including written, oral, and demonstrative
Using standardized achievement tests as the only indicator of outcomes	Using standardized achievement tests as one of many indicators of outcomes
Excluding calculators, computers, and manipulatives from the assessment process	Using calculators, computers, and manipulatives in the assessment process
Using exercise or word problems requiring only one or two skills and moving away from memorizing and repeating	Developing problem situations that require the application of multiple skills in mathematics through investigations and a variety of mathematical topics
Assessing what students do not know	Assessing what students do know and how they think about mathematics

occurred at a point in time through measurement of students' understanding of a subject by determining what they know and do not know. Many teachers associate summative assessments only with standardized tests such as state testing, but they are also used as a part of district and classroom programs. These can include state assessments, district benchmarks assessments, chapter or unit tests, end-of-term or semester exams, or scores that are used for accountability purposes such as Adequate Yearly Progress (AYP). The purpose of summative assessment is to measure the level of student, program, or school success. It is important to note that summative assessment cannot reflect the efficiency of teaching because it is carried out only *after* the instruction.

Formative assessment, on the other hand, delivers information *during* and *throughout* the instructional process, *before* the summative assessment. Formative assessments are used as ongoing diagnostic tools, and the results are solely used to modify and/or adjust our teaching practices. They are usually embedded within the instructional process. Both the teacher and the student use formative assessment results to make decisions about what actions to take to promote further learning. (Students need to be involved in assessing their own learning as well as each other's learning. If students are not involved in the formative assessment process, then it is not practiced or implemented to its full effectiveness.) It is an ongoing, dynamic process that involves far more than frequent testing, and measurement of student learning is just one of its components (Chappuis, 2005).

There are numerous types of assessments that we use to learn as much as we can about our students. Assessments may be used in isolation or in combination with other students for the purpose of providing important information to use in instructional planning. Assessments can range from classroom observation to standardized tests. The increased attention on using multiple, problem-based assessments to assess what students know and how they think about mathematics encourages us to deepen our knowledge about and use of various types of assessments. The list of types of assessments in Figure 3.3 provides a brief description of each one.

FIGURE 3.2 Continuous Cycle

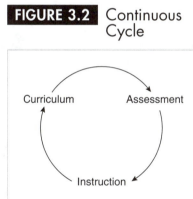

FIGURE 3.3 Types of Assessments

Objective	Includes true–false responses, yes–no answers, and multiple-choice questions
Alternative	Includes portfolios, journals, notebooks, projects, and presentations
Authentic	Incorporates real-life functions and applications
Performance	Requires completion of a task, project, or investigation; communication of information; or construction of a response
Naturalistic	Observation of students' performance and behavior in an informal context
Achievement Test Battery	Subtests of mathematics concepts and skills that usually include technical aspects
Standardized	Formal, standardized samples to establish norms and make inferences
Diagnostic	Teacher- or commercially made instructional models

A TIME TO REFLECT

As you reflect on the shift in standards and assessments in mathematics, what types of assessments are you already using in your classroom? How could you use these assessments to implement RTI? Also consider other professionals in your school with knowledge in this area for collaboration and discussion.

Assessments Used within RTI

The intent of RTI in mathematics is to ensure that students receive rich experiences and differentiated instruction to improve learning for all students. Therefore, as we implement RTI we need to use multiple sources of assessment data to determine student learning. This information is the basis for us to continuously analyze, revise, and enhance our instruction within our classroom. There are four types of assessments that are important in analyzing our instruction in mathematics: universal screening, progress monitoring, diagnostic, and outcome. We will take a closer look at each of these assessments with definitions, examples, and resources.

Universal Screening

Universal screening assessments are an important means of collecting student performance data that focus on curriculum standards. They provide important preliminary or baseline information about our students' strengths and weaknesses. One source of universal screening data is often part of the state or district benchmark assessments of mandated curriculum standards. These **standardized assessments** are provided at the initiation of a school year or beginning of a unit of study. These screening measures are generally used by district- or school-based administrators as a broad indicator of student knowledge, skills, and abilities for the purpose of program planning for instructional services. For example, student summative assessment data from mandated state assessments are often the **baseline data** for the school improvement plan and program planning. In addition, numerous school districts develop and administer multiple benchmark assessments several times during a school year. These assessments are aligned with the state curriculum standards to provide continuous assessment data related to student learning using a standardized assessment measure. Therefore, these assessments should also become part of the initial, universal screening assessment that impacts the instructional decision-making and lesson-planning processes within our mathematics classrooms.

These assessment data become an integral part of the teaching and learning processes because they provide information about our students' learning aligned to state and district curriculum standards and benchmarks. A **review of previous records** will provide important assessment information about students' skills and competencies, especially if trends or inconsistencies in student learning are noticed. This information will be useful when considering instructional goals, student groups, and necessary resources, and can be added to student demographic information (Reproducible #3 in Appendix A). The guiding questions in Figure 3.4 will guide your review of records.

Three other informal assessments provide important information when planning for instruction and completing universal screening for RTI: observations, work-sample analyses, and initial curriculum-based inventories.

■ **Observations**—Students should be observed while they are working on mathematics tasks, during instructional lessons, while working independently and in small groups, and during large-group instruction. Observations can and should be completed throughout instruction during all of the tiers because they provide initial and continuous information about student learning.

Guiding Questions to Consider

- Does the student appear interested and engaged in the learning?
- How often does the student answer questions and need assistance?
- Does the student use calculators, manipulatives, etc.? Does the student use them often and accurately?

FIGURE 3.4 Guiding Questions

Source of Data	Guiding Questions to Consider
Previous standardized test results	• What are the areas of strength? • What are the areas of need? • Are the areas of strength and need consistent? • Do the areas impact mathematical performance? • Are the data consistent? Do they show a trend with previous years' scores?
Past summative assessments	• Are the summative assessments from prior units of study consistent? • Are results of the summative assessments reflective of mathematical performance that is consistent with peers? For instance, did most students do very well or very poorly on a specific assessment?
Universal screening (such as a grade-level assessment)	• Do the screening data reflect consistencies with the standardized test data? • Are there areas that seem to be consistent? • Are there areas that are not consistent? • What specific content standards in mathematics appear to be areas of strength and areas that need additional instruction?

- Does the student accurately represent the math problem?
- What are the student's strengths?
- In what areas does the student need additional help?
- Are the observations consistent? Do they follow a trend with other sources of assessment data?

■ **Work-sample analyses**—A critical aspect of comprehensive assessment in mathematics includes careful analysis of students' work products. These products can include performance tasks such in-class assignments, board work, and problem-based learning assignments.

Guiding Questions to Consider

- Does the student follow the directions (oral or written) about the task?
- Does the student accurately represent the math problem?
- Does the student complete all sections of the task? Are the responses accurate? Is the task completed independently?
- Does the student use appropriate skills when completing the task?
- What are the student's strengths?
- In what areas does the student need additional help?
- Are the observations consistent? Do they follow a trend with other sources of assessment data?

■ **Curriculum-based inventories**—These inventories and assessments are used to evaluate students' performance on a particular level of mastery in the curriculum. This form of evaluation identifies skills that students have mastered and those that need to be mastered. These assessments can be developed using the scope and sequence charts from the curriculum in mathematics (as aligned with district and state standards and benchmarks). Some are also packaged and published commercially (see websites listed in the Math Probes section for more information).

Guiding Questions to Consider

- Does the inventory align with state and district standards and benchmarks?
- Does the curriculum have inventories available?
- Were student results consistent with other assessments?
- What are the student's strengths?
- In what areas does the student need additional help?
- How will I use this information when planning for instruction?

Progress Monitoring

There are a variety of purposes for continuous formative assessment as we teach. One is to monitor the instructional engagement, understanding, and progress of our students' learning related to the curricular goal in mathematics. Another purpose is to diagnose and guide any necessary changes to the curriculum or instructional processes. Progress-monitoring assessments are usually short and frequent skill-based assessments that provide a snapshot of student learning related to the instructional objective. The following list includes several samples of ongoing progress monitoring. Instructionally relevant assessment data come from broad categories of progress-monitoring instruments, including:

■ Published program assessments in mathematics (in conjunction with published curriculum programs)
■ Published content assessments and inventories

- Informal classroom assessments that are teacher-created measures of student ability as aligned with predetermined benchmarks or individuals students' prior performance
- Curriculum-based measurements (CBM) of specific skills in the content areas aligned with curriculum benchmarks (Adapted with permission from Mellard et al., 2009.)

Curriculum-based measurement (CBM) is an effective and efficient means of assessing and monitoring students' ongoing progress in the curriculum. This powerful assessment tool measures mastery of mathematics skills and allows us to learn how our students are *progressing* in the core academic areas. CBM can specifically address the mathematical skills sets (benchmarks) we teach and target students' increments of growth over time. We can use CBM to assess areas of need on a weekly basis for a period of one to five minutes, depending on the mathematical skills being measured. Students are given brief, timed exercises (probes) to complete, using the mathematical skills and materials that are drawn directly from the school curriculum. See Figure 3.5 for CBM sample.

This frequent sampling of student knowledge provides current information of mathematical progression within our classrooms. In other words, it tells us how well our students are performing or understanding mathematics. Students' are scored on accuracy of performance, mathematical fluency and skill knowledge, and speed. CBM provides a clearer view of the rate of learning over time and determines whether we need to continue the instruction the same way or if we need to change it. In essence, CBM helps *guide and inform* our instruction. Based on student's correct and incorrect responses, we can change and/or modify our teaching practices by finding the amount and type of instruction our students' need to make sufficient mathematical progress to meet the academic goals we set for them. We can change the instructional time (increase), change the grouping arrangement (individual instruction instead of small-group), or change our teaching techniques or way of presenting the mathematical material.

The results of these CBM assessments are then recorded and graphed to visually display learning progress within a particular time frame (see Figure 3.6). We use CBM to view students' mathematical strengths and weaknesses and to determine the error patterns they are making. CBM was developed to be an efficient, valid, and reliable opportunity to help us monitor student growth, inform instruction, and tie our instruction to the curriculum. This ongoing method is easily accessible for classroom application and implementation and is an analysis of student learning from instruction and interventions within our classrooms.

Results from progress-monitoring assessments indicate whether our students are experiencing success in learning or need additional supports. When looking at students' results from progress-monitoring assessments, consider these important questions:

- Are the students showing progress?
- Is the rate of progress keeping up with pacing of instruction?
- Is student progress similar to that of their peers?

FIGURE 3.5   CBM Sample

1) 23	2) 315	3) 524	4) 657	5) 345
+ 15	+ 24	+ 238	+ 455	+123
6) 27	7) 182	8) 543	9) 974	10) 876
− 15	− 35	− 56	− 352	− 345

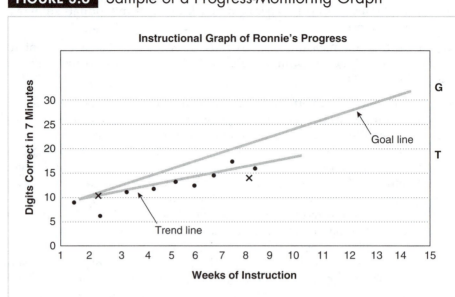

FIGURE 3.6 Sample of a Progress-Monitoring Graph

If the answer to any of these questions is no, then we must respond and provide differentiated instruction through the use additional supports and accommodations. We must also provide additional support in the form of reteaching or reinforcement to increase the levels of prerequisite skills needed for success.

Guiding Questions to Consider

- Do the assessments align with state and district standards and benchmarks?
- Does the curriculum have assessments available?
- Were student results consistent with other assessments?
- What are the student's areas of strength?
- In what areas does student need additional help?
- How will I use this information when planning for instruction?

Math probes, used in association with curriculum-based assessments, are quick and efficient ways of measuring and monitoring students' progress in their math curriculum. Probes are timed samples (generally one to six minutes) of skills in areas of mathematics that assess students' accuracy and fluency. Accuracy, which is used to identify whether a student has acquired a skill, is generally the area that is stressed in evaluation. Fluency is based on how quickly students are able to perform or recall a math fact, process, or procedure. When students are more fluent in completing mathematics processes, they are more likely to remember the skills used and will be better able to master more advanced skills. When using or creating math probes, teachers should include at least three items per target skill so that careless mistakes are noticeable.

Guiding Questions to Consider

- Does the assessment have a match to the instruction? For instance, if the students learn a skill with a specific procedure, is the same procedure assessed?
- Does the assessment reflect errors in common within multiple trials?
- Does the assessment reflect errors in common with many peers?
- Does the assessment reflect complete mastery and lack of need for further instruction?

- Are the CBM and math probes comparing the same indicators of a desired learning outcome over time?
- Do the data show clear trends of progress or lack of progress?
- Is the rate of progress appropriate to maintain grade-level performance expectations?

Diagnostic Assessment

Diagnostic assessments are intended to support us in planning focused, standards-based instruction for our students. They are often conducted with individual students to identify specific skill deficits in the curricular content or domain. Generally, they are made up of four components: (1) screening measures, (2) observational measures, (3) diagnostic measures, and (4) short screening measures. Screening measures provide an analysis of our students' understandings of the fundamental concepts and skills and help identify students who may be at risk and need intervention. Observational measures are embedded in our daily instruction and provide us with mechanisms for collecting information and monitoring our students' progress and intervention needs. Diagnostic measures provide student profiles that we can use for both formative and summative assessment at key checkpoints throughout the school year or to determine student progress as a result of our instruction. These measures do not have to be administered at one time and can be broken up into multiple sessions. Short screening measures will quickly tell us if our students are on track or in need of further assessment.

> **Progress-Monitoring Resources and Probes for Mathematics**
>
> AIMSweb Progress Monitoring and RTI System www.aimsweb.com
>
> easyCBM http://easycbm.com
>
> Intervention Central www.interventioncentral.org
>
> National Center on Student Progress Monitoring www.studentprogress.org
>
> Monitoring Basic Skills Progress/Pro-Ed, Inc. (Curriculum-Based Measurement Computer Software) www.proedinc.com/store/index.php?mode=product_detail&id=0840

The data from diagnostic assessments provide us with more in-depth and specific information on the strengths of deficits of individual students related to mastery of curriculum. The purpose of diagnostic assessments is to evaluate the underlying knowledge and skills of students; this way we can ascertain, prior to instruction, our students' mathematical strengths, weaknesses, knowledge, and skills. This diagnostic assessment data will provide specific skills and abilities to target for intense intervention, possibly through aligned, but different curriculum resources using high-quality instruction. In other words, it allows us to remediate students and adjust our curriculum to their specific mathematical needs. Diagnostic assessment often focuses on one area or domain of knowledge and can be administered before and/or during instruction within a school or classroom setting. For example, during the first week of the year, a school may administer a diagnostic test to all fifth-grade students specifically aimed at multiplying and dividing fractions. Another example is a teacher who wishes to teach students how to multiply double-digit numbers but must first check for student understanding of place values and their mastery of basic multiplication facts. The use of early screening tests means students who are experiencing problems in mathematics can be identified at an early stage so appropriate remediation can be planned and provided at that point.

As we teach, we must also consider that diagnostic assessment calls for continual assessment of our students' abilities. We can carefully examine the actual work samples of individual students to identify error patterns, deficits in conceptual understandings, and/or better identify specific skill weaknesses in prior knowledge. This type of analysis also indicates the students' strengths, and the results can be used by the teacher in lesson planning, providing differentiated instruction, and extension work. Checking for understanding (diagnostic teaching) is tailored to our particular lessons so we may quickly assess our students' progress. Asking students to do a "thumbs-up" or "thumbs-down" and/or calling on students to answer questions can gauge for mathematical understanding. We may also have students write answers on a small whiteboard as we walk around checking for understanding. In order to use diagnostic methods effectively in the classroom, we must provide valid feedback to students. This should be done quickly to ensure students recognize areas of need or to correct error patterns and misconceptions. Students may also be allowed time to explore why their answers are right or wrong through one-on-one discussion with the teacher, peer chats, and small-group discussions. This information from diagnostic teaching and diagnostic assessment assists us in better individualizing instruction for our students who continue to struggle. Often your colleagues in special education can also assist with diagnostic assessment and diagnostic teaching skills.

Guiding Questions to Consider

- Does the assessment target specific areas of concern?
- Do the results answer questions about ability, motivators, triggers for negative behavior, or areas of strength?
- Do the results seem consistent with other assessment measures?
- Are the data specific enough to create a statement to be used to design a plan of action?

Outcome Assessment

Outcome assessment (also called summative assessment) provides data related to a student's comprehensive learning at an established period of final assessment. This can occur at the end of units of study, the end of the school year, and/or during state and district assessments. The purpose of outcome assessments and evaluation is usually related to decisions regarding programs for students to meet their instructional needs. These outcome summative assessments provide a summary of learning by all students in a class, program, or special service. As previously mentioned, numerous state departments of education and school districts use the results of summative state assessments aligned with the state curriculum standards to make decisions related to promotion and subsequent student programs. Administration and actions from summative outcome assessments are often high stakes, with implications set in state and school district policies. It is imperative that we (and other instructional personnel) are knowledgeable about the high-stakes summative assessments that directly impact our students. Student assessment data from these summative assessments can and should be used by us as part of the universal screening assessment data within unit and lesson planning processes. This cycle of teachers' instructional decision making uses the multiple sources of assessment, aligned with national and state curriculum standards and benchmarks, to meet the instructional needs of our students through effective unit and lesson planning within the RTI classroom. Table 3.1 provides an overview of the types of assessments used when implementing RTI by teachers.

A TIME TO REFLECT

What does it mean to say, "Assessment guides instruction"? What are some ways to make this happen? What are the benefits of using a variety of assessments? Are there any disadvantages?

How do you fit assessment into your own classroom instructional time? Are any changes needed to make it more effective for your students?

TABLE 3.1 Types of Assessments Used by Teachers in RTI

	Universal Screening	**Progress Monitoring**	**Diagnostic**	**Outcome**
Definition	Initial determination of broad base of student performance	Skill-based, ongoing, sensitive to small changes in student learning	In-depth, specific information regarding knowledge and skills	Final determination of broad base of student performance
Uses	Broad benchmark attainment index (initial)	Specific academic or behavioral target	Specific academic domain of knowledge, skills, or abilities	Broad benchmark attainment index (final)
Student Focus	School-wide	Class or small group	Individual student	School-wide
Frequency	Annually/3 to 4 times per year	Every 3 weeks/ weekly	Annually (or as needed) for in-depth evaluation	Annually
Instruction	Class or school curricular or program decisions	Effectiveness of instruction and interventions	Selecting appropriate programs and/or educational placements	Align with curriculum goals and instructional planning process
Implication	First step in instruction and intervention planning	Continue or revise instruction and/or interventions	Program or curriculum planning	High stakes, based on state and school district policies

Using Assessment to Plan Instruction within RTI in Mathematics

As we think of assessment we must ask ourselves a few questions: How are all my students performing (screening)? How are all students responding to intervention and additional supports (progress monitoring)? What additional information do I need to meet the needs of some of the students who do not appear to be mastering the mathematics content (diagnostic)? Student learning depends on two key factors. The first factor is the knowledge we have about the unique characteristics and needs of our students, the mathematics content we teach, how students are grouped for instruction, and how their learning and mastery of critical content is progressing. The second factor is the degree to which we effectively integrate validated and evidence-based instructional practices and interventions within our classrooms. Teachers who regularly collect assessment data about student learning will gain valuable information to make subsequent instructional decisions. In order for student data to have a positive influence on our students' learning, we need to locate, analyze, and interpret data to help guide us in lesson planning, and provide differentiated instruction through techniques such as individualized learning plans, flexile grouping strategies, and alternative instructional approaches that are geared to different student profiles. It is important to remember that it is an ongoing cycle of curriculum, instruction, and assessment as informed by multiple, ongoing assessments. Next we'll consider the student test scores in Table 3.2 to determine how data can be used to inform or guide our instruction.

TABLE 3.2 Student Test Scores on Class Measurement Test (Hypothetical Data)

Student number	Multiplying Fractions (% correct)	Dividing Fractions (% correct)	Multiplying Decimals (% correct)	Dividing Decimals (% correct)	Total score (% correct)
1	99	95	89	100	96
2	89	77	60	45	68
3	100	100	72	97	92
4	87	91	56	32	67
5	97	78	100	83	90
6	92	95	73	43	76
7	100	100	100	100	100
8	100	100	92	74	92
9	80	80	60	56	69
10	87	100	75	50	78

As you look at the item-level analysis for each student we can use the data to adjust our teaching practices in ways that would enhance these students' learning. What do the numbers represent to the class as a whole? What do you know about individual students? Is the current curriculum and instruction appropriate for all students or only some? Are the diverse needs of all students being met? Can differentiated instruction be provided based on the data? Could targeted instruction through small groups or individual meetings help in specific areas? Would pairing students and letting students who are strong in one area help those who need more practice work? Would a review of the concepts, such as providing supporting materials that could enable students to acquire the concepts, be beneficial to them? What about offering instruction through different learning modalities? Would one-on-one tutoring be helpful? How about intensive instruction or enrichment or extension activities? Could students also benefit from integrating subject or skills knowledge? What about engaging them in problem-solving activities? What is each student ready for next? How do the data support this?

The data allow us to determine whether we should give greater or lesser emphasis on certain topics or should plan individualized instruction for students. The goal is to decide what the data reveal and to generate new strategies to reach students, make practical educational decisions, meet the needs of individual students' learning styles, determine and reevaluate our decisions for instructional effectiveness, and be more effective and productive in the mathematics classroom. In other words, the data determine our students' needs, interests, and needed supports so we may develop a plan to target instruction and change or improve our current instructional practices.

Ongoing assessments are used to understand how well students are responding to the core program (standards-based curriculum and high-quality, differentiated Tier 1 core instruction), which may help identify students in need of additional supports or interventions. We know that formative and summative assessments are interconnected as they seldom stand alone in effect or construction. Often assessments are embedded into classroom lessons to assist students in mastering the necessary content and skills we are teaching them. Our goal is that we have a balanced assessment system (see Figure 3.7) by using a continuum of

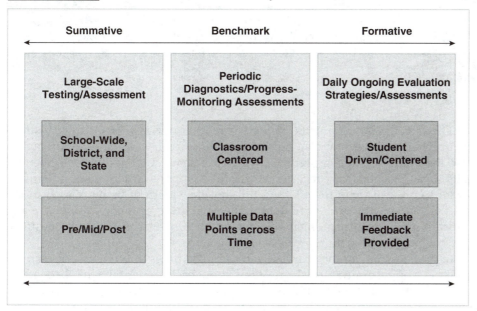

FIGURE 3.7 Balanced Assessment System

assessments, having a primary purpose for each assessment type, using multiple information resources to create a complete picture of student progress, and having multiple users.

The multiple sources of assessment data provide the necessary feedback to teachers, parents, and students. Teachers, along with other instructional personnel, use the results from the assessments during lessons and planning, while continuing to provide information to RTI support team members, as needed. In addition, these data can be very motivating for students and can facilitate communication between teachers and parents. When we learn that students are having problems learning, action must be taken to address the problems. Sometimes this instructional planning and decision-making process is carried out by teachers; at other times it is carried out in collaboration with parents and other professionals on the school-wide RTI team. Student performance will be improved if the process is informed by assessment data that are aligned with the curriculum benchmarks and the specific needs of the students.

It has been established that previous assessments and screening assessments provide initial information about our students and contribute to the planning of instruction. Formative assessments are part of the instructional process and assist in appropriate implementation of instruction. Progress-monitoring assessments reflect the rate and growth of a student or students in response to the instruction. In some cases, diagnostic assessment information may also be available and can contribute to the picture. Each of these assessments provides valuable information as well as opportunities for further questions. The questions that may be generated differ for each of these sources of information. For any data source there are also some general questions to ask. These are:

- Do the data reflect a level of motivation that is exceedingly high or low?
- Do the data reflect a level of ability that is exceedingly high or low?
- Do the data reflect the need for more attention, supports, or services to be provided immediately?
- Are the data inconsistent and need further investigation or more specific data?

A TIME TO REFLECT

As you reflect on RTI and the tiers of instruction/intervention, how do the assessment results impact the tiers? Also consider the opportunities presented when implementing the tiers of RTI and describe the changing roles for teachers and other educators in your school.

The screening assessments, as well as teacher observations during instruction, provide an overview of a student's abilities or performance, allowing us to use the information as a platform. There are some students whose screening results raise questions or concerns. When this happens, students are identified in order to prevent them from falling through the cracks or being missed in the system. A student who is identified through universal screening may not have any significant mathematical problems. However, there is a reason to ask questions and to monitor the student more closely than others.

In the beginning of the year and at designated times throughout the year, we should have opportunities to ask questions about each student that has been identified. Each student should have assessment data and these should be reviewed. A review may determine that the student had a difficult time with a specific assessment, but demonstrates competency on all other assessments. These reviews may also indicate significant reasons for concern. For any student who has been determined to be of concern, we should gather and collect more information and data. These students of concern should have frequent progress-monitoring indicators that are recorded and tracked. The progress-monitoring data should indicate whether the student is experiencing success in learning or if the student needs additional supports.

In many classrooms and schools, teachers and administrators develop annual goals and pacing calendars based on state and district curriculum standards and benchmarks. The intent is to provide guidance when planning units and lessons to ensure content coverage. In addition, the use of progress-monitoring assessments, including curriculum-based measures, provides frequent and important feedback to teachers, as well as other educators, about student learning of the state and district curriculum standards and benchmarks. Expectations for student performance, including mastery of content and adherence with learning timelines, provide intermittent achievement goals within the school year. These expectations are called **trend lines** when implementing RTI. Within RTI, these data are displayed in graphs to provide visual representations of student achievement (learning) related to the expectations (trend line), especially when collecting progress-monitoring data for students receiving Tier 2 and Tier 3 interventions. These progress-monitoring measures should be sensitive to measure the effects of both instruction and intervention.

The frequency of progress monitoring depends on the complexity of the skill or the knowledge to be mastered and demonstrated. For example, the frequency of collecting progress-monitoring data of early number fluency may require a shorter period of time to see evidence of results than division computation. More frequent measures would be taken when collecting progress-monitoring data for early number naming interventions than for mathematics computation interventions. While providing these additional supports for struggling students, progress-monitoring data should continue to be collected frequently. Specific data collection within the small-group setting, data collection within the classroom, and individual data collection samples are appropriate. As you consider the above information, let's revisit Ms. Holly's class to see what has taken place and how she has arrived at her conclusions to continue with the assessment process.

As we indicated in the scenario in Chapter 1, Ms. Holly knew that several of her students had gaps in mathematical knowledge that affected their ability to master fourth grade–level mathematics. She had already used information from the universal screening assessments delivered at the beginning of the school year to organize students with mixed abilities into cooperative groups. One day, Ms. Holly taught a lesson on solving two-digit multiplication within a word problem. After a few minutes of teacher-led instruction with examples, students began working in groups on the problems presented. Ms. Holly invited students to discuss their thinking about the questions presented in pairs, and asked representatives to share their thinking with their larger cooperative group members (**Think-Pair-Share**). Each group was asked to present several possible answers to a question and then discuss each one through student-focused feedback. In addition, students were to write and discuss their understanding of the vocabulary and concepts presented during the lesson and summarize the main ideas and important items they took away from the lesson that day. As students worked, Ms. Holly walked around observing each group, then observed each group member individually to monitor student learning. These observation checks were intentional, systematic, and focused on the desired instructional outcomes intended for students in her lesson planning. It is through these observations that Ms. Holly quickly noticed five students struggling with the content. These five students had already been identified as per the initial universal screening at the beginning of the school year and were on her watch list. She used teacher questioning, teacher feedback, and class discussions to determine whether concepts were clear and to understand students' thoughts about and knowledge of multiplication. She clearly identified and communicated to students the learning goals and criteria for success. She knew from the results of the student questioning and analysis of student work (non graded) that further diagnosis was needed to identify specific deficits in mathematical content areas. The identity of these students through universal screening allowed Ms. Holly to continue closer monitoring as needed in the Tier 1 classroom.

As we consider the process and uses of assessment to plan our instruction through curriculum and classroom evaluations in Ms. Holly's classroom, we can see that she purposefully directed formative assessment toward the students, particularly those who were indentified during instruction. Formative assessment seems to have the greatest impact on students' learning because it does not emphasize how we deliver content and information but, rather, how our students' *receive* it, how well the instruction is *understood,* and how well they can *apply* what is given. Formative assessment is informal, with interactive timely feedback and response. It is intended to monitor student learning and to inform teacher practice. The purpose is to organize individual student target-setting goals that build on previous skills and encourage higher achievement levels. It is an intentional, systematic process that provides feedback and adjustments to instruction through ongoing instructional outcomes. Formative assessment aims to encourage students and raise their mathematical self-esteem and self-assessment through the celebration of effective and appropriate questioning. As we focus on the particular learning outcomes of lessons and tasks, we want to share the learning outcomes with students and focus on the oral and written feedback provided to them. As we look at the benchmarks we are required to teach, our goal is to determine to what extent all students are progressing, determine how well additional supports or services are working, and consider what learning comes next for our students through alignment. It is very important that we rely on various formative assessments to provide us the clarity we need to determine and evaluate our students' mathematical successes. It is equally important to be able to respond effectively to their mathematical difficulties as warranted. We want the collection of high-quality, relevant data to be expedient and in a manner that will help us quickly respond to our particular students' mathematical instructional needs. Figure 3.8 illustrates how it all fits together.

FIGURE 3.8 How Does It Fit Together?

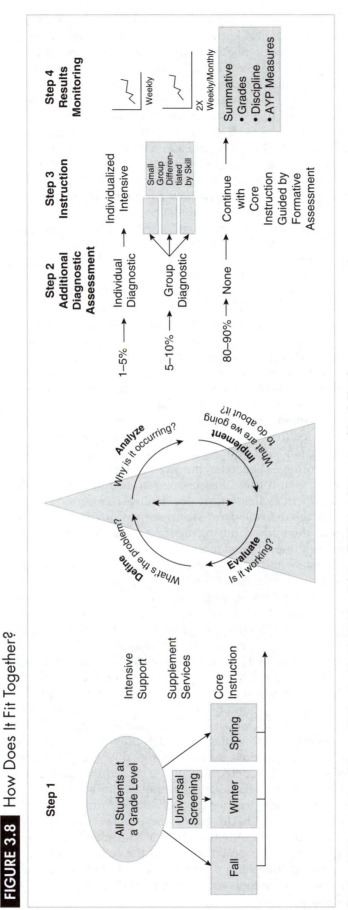

A TIME TO REFLECT

How well do you share learning goals with students? How do you involve your students in self-assessment? Do you provide timely feedback to students? In what capacity—oral and/or written? Do you offer a review of student progress through constant inquiry of students' academic and behavioral progress?

No one piece of data can fully communicate about a student, but any one piece can raise questions or provide important information. Universal screening includes information from the past. Sources such as previous summative assessments, standardized testing results, and records from prior years provide information to examine. Preassessments and screening data may also add to the picture for a more accurate view. While instruction occurs, formative assessments (e.g., curriculum-based assessments, math probes) and progress monitoring all contribute to information about the student. In some cases, diagnostic assessment data contribute even more information about the needs of a student. Together all of these pieces play a significant role when planning for instruction. The data are used to make decisions and determine if additional supports and services are needed. The data also serve to raise questions, confirm or deny the effectiveness of instruction, or determine approaches to instruction. All of these actions are part of the process of differentiated instruction and responsive teaching.

In the next chapter, we will go into detail on the continuous formative assessment, progress monitoring, and curriculum-based measurement to inform instructional decision making in Tier 1. We will also feature the decision-making process in Ms. Holly's classroom and the use of assessments to diagnose her students' strengths and weaknesses in regard to content areas within the mathematics classroom and how she addresses them through her lesson planning and teaching practices. Essential components of assessing effective instruction, curriculum enhancement, and differentiated instructional practices (including the levels of support offered to learners) will be the focus of the chapter. In addition, we will feature learning and multiple representations, and the intensity and scaffolding of lesson components.

TEACHERS' CORNER
Keys to Getting You Started with RTI

- Familiarize yourself with the types of assessments used within RTI. Write down the currents assessment practices used within your classroom and school.

- If you do not already have a universal screening tool or progress-monitoring resources in place in your school, visit the websites we have provided within this chapter. Discuss with colleagues those that will benefit your students most effectively. If you already have those tools in place, evaluate the benefits of their use and determine their significance with your students.

- Review your instructional decision-making processes and identify how they align with your current benchmarks and standards.

- Determine which students may be "identified" as per the universal screening data. This identification will help guide you in planning for additional supports within the tiers.

- Begin identifying how you purposefully use assessment practices in your classroom. This will help you determine how effective your current teaching practices are. It will also help you consider what additional learning will be necessary so students' mathematical understanding and success become more evident.

- Complete Professional Learning Community Chapter 3 activities.

Chapter 4

Teaching All Students in My Classroom: Tier 1

"Teaching our students mathematics is one thing. Teaching students to think mathematically with understanding is another."

—Dr. Gina Harwood Gresham

What You Will Find in This Chapter

- Universal screening and the instructional variables within Tier 1
- Using differentiated instruction in the mathematics classroom
- Using concrete manipulatives and multiple representations
- Scaffolding instruction for improved mathematical learning
- Using curriculum-based assessments for instructional decision making

Teacher's Voice

I awaken each school day morning wondering if this will be the day my students understand what I am teaching them. I get so anxious to see that "aha" moment on their faces and witness the opportunity of discovery when they are able make the connections in math. I know something will have clicked inside their heads and I will become proud of the lesson I taught them that day! I know that these days aren't as often as I would like them to be, but as I continue to learn more about RTI in mathematics and how to provide lessons to enhance mathematical understanding, I become more excited to know that my students will only benefit more and more from what I am learning. I know that instruction rests on evidence-based effective teaching practices and high-fidelity implementation, and that progress monitoring occurs for all students to determine their learning as a result of my instruction. I know I have the challenge of managing everything that goes on in my classroom and I need to work to find ways to draw my students into mathematics to help them make connections by scaffolding my instruction. I want my lessons to truly serve all students in my classroom and I feel I'm up to that challenge!

Ms. Holly, fourth-grade teacher

An Overview of Tier 1

Tier 1 is the driving force of our instruction within RTI. It is the tier in which students receive core, universal instruction and supports as we teach with fidelity so that all students are mastering the curriculum. As evidenced by Ms. Holly's words, she understands the need to have students interact with and deepen their understanding of the mathematics content. It is important that we provide opportunities to immerse our students in the mathematical information, skills, and strategies we present and that we "immerse" them in the mathematics vocabulary. Tier 1 places emphasis on a high-quality general curriculum in which specific interventions are implemented for students who may be at risk for achieving grade-level tasks. Therefore, it is important for us to use differentiated instruction and scaffolding, whole-class instruction, flexible grouping, and evidence-based practices and strategies within our teaching practices. The use of ongoing assessment, both formally and informally, takes place within this tier to determine the level of intervention impact and to decide what instructional changes may be needed for our students' mathematical success.

The regular classroom teacher is the integral part of this tier. We offer in-class assistance and we have the opportunity to meet the needs of all students rather than referring them to other intervention tiers within the RTI framework. Tier 1 interventions generally occur within the general education setting either with or without additional support from other RTI team members. In other words, Tier 1 is the foundation of the mathematics program. We know that 80 to 90 percent of our students will find mathematics success within Tier 1 if instruction is broad enough to meet their mathematics needs within *and* beyond the grade-level curriculum.

Universal Screening and Instructional Variables

High-quality instruction is effective teaching. The universal screening of our students in the mathematics classroom is important because it is the first step in determining the effectiveness of our instruction within Tier 1. It should be brief, repeatable, and easy to administer and score. As we look to begin monitoring of our effectiveness in teaching through universal screening, we always want to ask ourselves a few questions:

- Are most students in our classroom improving at an adequate rate?
- Is the targeted group improving at an adequate rate?
- Are individual students improving at an adequate rate?

Universal screening focuses on the critical grade-level skills and provides accountability because it screens all students for progress toward the curricular standards we are required to teach. Early in the school year we want to identify those students who are showing signs of struggling with the mathematical content or are otherwise not making adequate progress toward the grade-level mathematics benchmarks so we can provide them the instruction they need.

Universal screening helps us with our instructional planning (including resource allocation with planning and supports) because the results can show us that a student's progress shows a significant gap between what is expected and the actual classroom performance of their peers. It works to identify students' level of proficiency and progress in target areas. We then use this information to adjust instructional models or intervention delivery, to assist in goal setting, and to address the instructional variables (instruction, teacher, student, and curriculum). Even though we identified instructional variables in Chapter 2, we bring them to the forefront in this chapter because they are critical components of Tier 1 instruction. Instructional variables play an essential role in lesson planning and delivery as determined by universal screening.

It is extremely important for us to plan the mathematical focus of our lessons based on the outcomes of universal screening and the instructional variables (see Figure 4.1) because this helps us identify how to teach, what to teach, and whom to teach.

As we work to reach all students, we want to help them reflect on what is experienced and learned through recoding, rehearsing, reviewing, and retrieving the mathematical material (Sprenger, 2005). As we prepare activities, whole- and small-group discussions, or interventions we must preplan what mathematical skills, concepts, and strategies we are trying to develop in our students. Struggling learners are most affected by poor preplanning. We want our lessons to be focused with provisions for different activities, strategies, and ideas that follow clean trains of thought, and we want them to be geared toward helping students make clear connections with mathematics.

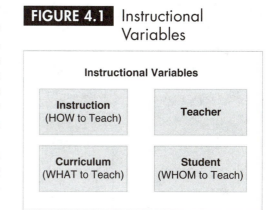

FIGURE 4.1 Instructional Variables

Effective Instruction in the Mathematics Classroom

"An effective and coherent mathematics program should be guided by a clear set of content standards, but it must be grounded in a clear and shared vision of teaching and learning—the two critical reciprocal actions that link teachers and students and largely determine education impact" (Leinwand, 2009, p. 90). Effective planning and instruction reaches all students. We all know that when we teach students we are striving to promote the growth and learning of mathematical knowledge. Planting the seed of knowledge is always at the forefront of our lesson planning and watching that knowledge grow and prosper is what we as educators hope for. At the root of this knowledge and learning we find instruction, curriculum, and assessment. We want our instructional contributions to be sufficient in that we provide students the necessary skills to have mathematical understanding and proficiency and that their mathematical growth and learning are evident.

We must assist our students with mathematical understanding by helping them make connections with the new information we provide through previously developed mathematical ideas and problem solving (see Figure 4.2). The goal is to help guide our students and teach them to reflect on the thinking that occurs in mathematical learning. Therefore, as we consider what understanding mathematics really means (helping students make connections), we help students develop understanding when they figure out how each new idea is related to the other mathematical ideas they already know (Heibert & Carpenter, 1992). Learning mathematics with understanding is best supported by engaging our students in the problem-solving process (NCTM, 2000). In addition, it promotes the development of autonomous learners, enhances the transfer of mathematical knowledge, influences students' attitudes and beliefs, helps with memory, and provides motivation (Gresham, 2005).

In preparing mathematics lessons for our students, we must remember that engaging them in the instructional learning process will help them acquire the knowledge that we will later assess. We engage students by creating clear expectations. It is through our expectations that we help students understand and know the learning goals and the criteria for reaching them. The adoption of the Common Core State Standards has changed the depth of the concepts we are required to

FIGURE 4.2   Developing Mathematical Connections

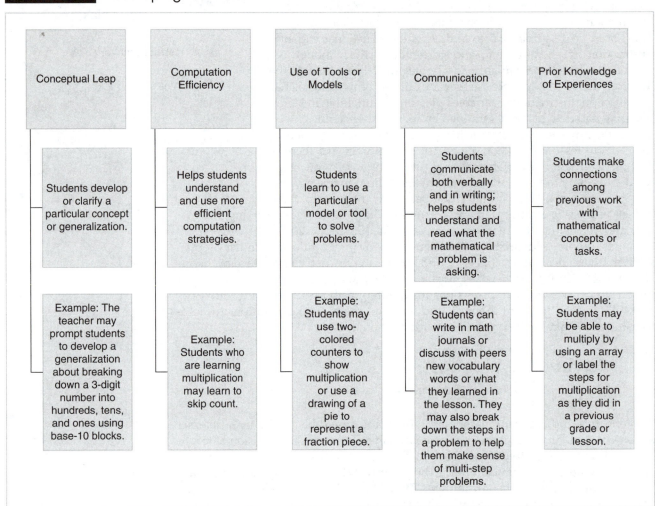

Conceptual Leap	Computation Efficiency	Use of Tools or Models	Communication	Prior Knowledge of Experiences
Students develop or clarify a particular concept or generalization.	Helps students understand and use more efficient computation strategies.	Students learn to use a particular model or tool to solve problems.	Students communicate both verbally and in writing; helps students understand and read what the mathematical problem is asking.	Students make connections among previous work with mathematical concepts or tasks.
Example: The teacher may prompt students to develop a generalization about breaking down a 3-digit number into hundreds, tens, and ones using base-10 blocks.	Example: Students who are learning multiplication may learn to skip count.	Example: Students may use two-colored counters to show multiplication or use a drawing of a pie to represent a fraction piece.	Example: Students can write in math journals or discuss with peers new vocabulary words or what they learned in the lesson. They may also break down the steps in a problem to help them make sense of multi-step problems.	Example: Students may be able to multiply by using an array or label the steps for multiplication as they did in a previous grade or lesson.

Source: Adapted in part from the Delaware Department of Education, 2011.

teach and how we teach mathematics to our students. These standards specifically outline that our mathematics instruction must:

- Help students make sense of problems and persevere in solving them
- Help them reason abstractly and quantitatively
- Teach them to construct viable arguments and critiques
- Use modeling strategies
- Choose appropriate tools strategically while attending to mathematics precision

We help make mathematics meaningful for our students when we have included these standards as well as offering instructional activities and practices within our lessons to help students grasp what we teach. We want to provide varied situations for students to *use* the mathematics they learn. We can accomplish this through effective lesson planning within the RTI in mathematics framework. "As we ground and guide students' mathematical development, we envision a highly effective school mathematics program for all students that focuses on effective instruction that:

- Is thoughtfully planned;
- Has an emphasis on problem-solving;

- Balances and blends both procedural skills and conceptual understanding;
- Relies on alternative approaches and multiple representations;
- Uses context and connections to engage students and increase the relevance of what is being learned;
- Provides for frequent opportunities for students to communicate their reasoning and engage in productive recourse;
- Incorporates ongoing cumulative review;
- Employs technology to enhance learning;
- Maximizes instructional time on task;
- Uses multiple forms of assessment and uses those results to adjust instruction;
- Integrates curriculum and ensures student mastery of grade-level standards;
- Encourages teachers to reflect on their teaching, individually, collaboratively, and makes revisions to enhance student learning" (Leinwand, 2009).

As educators, we must gauge the pulse of our own teaching. Employing multiple teaching practices and instructional resources as identified above is important. We must consider both the content and instructional methods and identify the evidence-based instructional approaches (e.g., direct instruction, whole/small group, peer tutoring, computer-assisted instruction) in order to positively impact our students. In addition, we need to be alert to students' mathematical misconceptions and the specific error patterns, and to understand why they may be making these errors or using the certain procedures. As we focus on this, as well as our teaching practices and instructional resources for effective instruction, we are able to help students who are experiencing mathematical difficulties. We must be aware of both conceptual learning and procedural learning in mathematics and tie the two together. When we create lessons for effective instruction we should build concepts on top of one another (**scaffolding**) and weave ideas together so students better understand and make reasonable connections within mathematics. As we consider this, our instructional delivery of effective practices is critical in helping students make connections. We do this by offering students the important instructional delivery components of appropriate pacing and adequate processing time, allowing for frequent student responses, monitoring those responses, and providing feedback (Hall, 2002).

Lesson planning is also a critical component of effective mathematics teaching. Table 4.1 provides a sample of OPTIONS lesson plan elements for your consideration when you are planning for effective instruction. When designing lessons for delivery and implementation, our goal is to carefully think about the crucial elements needed to help students clarify information, make generalizations about the content being learned, and provide opportunities for establishing a foundation of the mathematics they are learning through communication, representations, computations, and connections.

As you consider the elements of effective lesson planning in Table 4.1, we also want to familiarize you with that we call the "OPTIONS Lesson Planning Process." We want to bring mathematics alive in our classrooms through our lesson planning, implementation, and delivery so students can create, learn, and become engaged in and excited about mathematics because they are learning in ways that work for them. Therefore, we have created a lesson planning packet for you to use in your classroom. The purpose of the lesson planning packet (see Reproducibles #6 through 9 in Appendix A) is to provide scaffolded resources you can use to enhance high-fidelity implementation of evidence-based techniques, active student engagement techniques, instructional and assistive technology, and accommodations to meet the learning outcomes for your students within an RTI in mathematics framework. The initial pages provide an overview of critical lesson components and reflective questions to enhance the conversations during lesson study and/or professional learning community (PLC) collaborations. The

FIGURE 4.3 OPTIONS Lesson Plan

Lesson Planning in the RTI Classroom Using OPTIONS

Teacher Name: *Ms. Holly*   **Content Area:** *Fourth-Grade Math*   **Dates:**

O—Outcome/Objective:

Curricular Goal: M.A. 4.2: When given three to five word problems, compute using single and multi-digit multiplication facts with fluency by using a variety of strategies, including invented and standard algorithms and provide explanations.

P—Prior Knowledge (preskills):

Fluency: Addition and subtraction facts with regrouping, basic multiplication facts, reading at grade level, number sense operations, place value.

T—Teaching/Tiers:

Differentiation of core instruction: Word problems with computation at various skill levels, cooperative groups (mathematical and reading ability), manipulatives (e.g.,

Unifix cubes, abacus, beans, numeral cards, dice, base-10 blocks, number cubes, two-colored counters, ten frames, dominoes, Cuisenaire rods, spinners, money, number line, whiteboards, choice boards, learning contract, and interest centers).

Tier 1:

Classroom/student considerations: Prior knowledge and experience, predetermined mixed ability, strategic partnering of students, cooperative groups established with student skills (both grade-level mathematics and reading), addition/subtraction skills, multiplication skills, place-value skills, number sense skills, various levels of math problems provided, choice boards as per student

interest inventory, independent practice, mathematics anxiety levels.

Tier 2:

Small group: Student groups (use initials): Use of vocabulary cards (operations), whiteboards, and concrete manipulatives (see above for examples). Additional practice: Addition/subtraction facts with regrouping on computer (program: Fast Math Tracker) and multiplication facts.

Tier 3:

Individual (use initials): Specific word problems with minimal reading, peer tutoring, and intensive practice with addition/subtraction fluency on computer (program: APlusMath).

I—Instruction/Intervention Summary

	Instruction/Intervention	Lead Teacher	Materials/ Resources	O—Ongoing Assessments	Student Results	Teacher Notes
Tier 1	**Core Instruction** ■ Introduce lesson—high interest ■ Set clear expectations and the learning/target goal and the criteria for reaching it ■ Discuss learning contract ■ Review vocabulary with examples ■ Organize cooperative groups; review group expectations ■ Provide one word problem and allow opportunities/provide encouragement for students to invent algorithms ■ After five minutes, review student responses ■ Allow for self- and peer assessment ■ Use teacher observation and questioning strategies ■ Guided Practice: provide three to five word problem cards to each group ■ After ten to fifteen minutes, review problems orally ■ Independent practice/informal assessment: Provide one word problem (various reading/ math levels) for each student to complete. (CBM)Choice boards, centers, extension menu ■ Student record keeping—write in journals/exit card question (s)	Ms. H.	Word problems from textbook and additional resources	■ CBM from textbook and/ or Intervention central.com ■ Teacher observation using rubric of task analyses	Number of items mastered: 90% (multiple components of rubric) on CBM Tasks not mastered (list):	Date to report data of results with RTI: Support team: Data sources: ■ District benchmark: ■ CBM: ■ Observation rubric: ■ Computer: ■ Other:

Tier 2	**Small Groups** ■ Guided, small-group station teaching to reinforce and enhance concepts ■ Groups arranged from results of universal screening ■ Resource teacher will work directly with Tier 2 students	Math resource teacher Ms. H.	Use of vocabulary cards, whiteboards, and concrete manipulatives	■ CBM from textbook ■ Teacher observation using rubric of task analyses	MBSP Computation: Results:	
Tier 3	**Individual** ■ During computer time, student will practice addition/subtraction fluency using aligned computer program	Peer tutor Ms. H.	Intensive practice with addition/ subtraction fluency on computer	■ Computer scores ■ MBSP Computation:	Results:	

N—Needs of All Students: Considerations to intensify instruction and interventions

Instructional Component	Tier 1	Tier 2	Tier 3
Dosage: instructional time	Forty-five minutes	Thirty additional minutes	Fifteen additional minutes
Group size	Thirty students	Small groups of six	One-on-one
Immediate, positive feedback	Teacher, peers per rubric	Resource teacher	Computer feedback
Response opportunities	One to six response ratio	One to six response ratio	100 percent each time

S—Summarize/Strategize:

OPTIONS Lesson Plan may serve as a guide to help you incorporate the multiple and complex components of lesson design into the three-tiered framework. This plan includes components of lesson design for us to consider during planning, implementing, and reflecting. We want you to have an option to choose from when designing and implementing effective lessons within the RTI in mathematics framework.

The intention of a lesson plan is not to substitute thoughtful, and careful preplanning activities. Lessons should be planned to positively and properly impact students' learning and development, as well as to meet students' mathematical needs, strengths, backgrounds, attitudes, and interests. As you view Figure 4.3, you will see how Ms. Holly is using the OPTIONS Lesson Plan to guide delivery of instruction to Heather and four other students identified as having difficulties after determining their mathematical needs through CBM. She has taken into account prior knowledge experiences and what Heather and others need to know before accomplishing the problems delivered within the lesson. Ms. Holly has also identified both classroom and student considerations and how she will use formative assessment and differentiate her instruction throughout the lesson. (Differentiated instruction is discussed in further detail later in this chapter.) In order to determine differentiated instruction within her lesson planning, she administered a student interest inventory and used the data from the universal screening to develop instructional target goals for students. She also developed choice boards and extension menus, and prepared

TABLE 4.1 OPTIONS Lesson Plan

OPTIONS for Lesson Planning within RTI Classrooms		
Letter	**Lesson Component**	**Description**
O	Outcomes, objectives	Curriculum outcomes and unit/lesson objectives described by the state departments of education, school district curriculum specialists, and/or a student's individual education plan (IEP) or Section 504 plan.
P	Prior knowledge; prerequisite skills, pretest assessment	Necessary foundational skills and knowledge sets for completeness and accuracy to build on during the learning of curricular outcomes.
T	Teaching within tiers; techniques; technology	The content (what to teach) and process (how to teach) of instruction using multiple techniques, differentiation, and technology to ensure all students master outcomes and objectives.
I	Intensify instruction/ intervention	Through the various tiers, increasing instructional time (dosage), response opportunities, corrective feedback, and decreasing group size provide additional support for learning.
O	Ongoing progress monitoring	Continuous assessment procedures that collect samples of student learning through multiple curriculum-based assessments, progress-monitoring probes, observations, and/or other informal classroom assessments. Data are used to inform and/or intensify instruction/interventions.
N	Needs of group and individuals	Revising any of the following instructional conditions: Instructional groupings or arrangements, teaching style or delivery of instruction, environmental conditions, and/or instructional materials to meet needs.
S	Summarize, share, and strategize	Formative assessment data collected through ongoing progress monitoring will assist the teacher in determining the next actions to take and whether to continue with current practices, revise the instructional plan to more specific and intensive interventions, or report the results of student successes.

exit card questions. Lastly, she has listed her grouping and individual practice strategies and how those will take place within her lesson.

When planning for effective instruction we also want to consider as many opportunities, strategies, and ideas as possible to attract our students' attention and stimulate them to learn. We want to ask several questions as we consider our lesson planning. Is the lesson interesting? Is the presentation clearly defined? Are the examples appropriate? Are the students involved in the lesson as it unfolds? Will the students have ample opportunity to seek clarification of the points presented? These questions and their analysis will help you construct a more effective mathematical learning environment for all students. When we consider Tier 1 instruction within our classroom practice and as we prepare for effective instruction, our goal is to help our struggling learners be the best they can be in mathematics. That is, we want them to be able to develop, clarify, generalize, understand, use more efficient computation, use a particular tool or model to solve problems, communicate their thinking both verbally and in writing, and make connections among work they did earlier with particular mathematical concepts or tasks. It is equally important that we provide students opportunities to develop/invent algorithms for solving problems, and not just show them how to solve a problem or show only one way to solve it. Let us illustrate how this might happen in the classroom.

Teaching that involves the use of multiple representations caters to a wider range of learners and learning styles and allows students to construct bridges between different representations. This provides a more complete understanding of the concepts under investigation. Suppose a student needs to discover the relation between a square area and that of a new square after the length of the side is altered. Typically, teachers tell the student that when the side length of a square is doubled, the area is quadrupled; if the side length is tripled, the area is increased by a factor of nine; and so forth. We could have students use an interactive geometry program to complete the following:

Draw segment $\overline{AB}$.

Mark endpoint B of the segment as rotation center.

Rotate segment $\overline{AB}$ 90 degrees (see Scene 1 of Figure 4.4).

Mark vector BA.

Translate $\overline{BC}$ along vector BA, naming the new endpoint D (see Scene 2 of Figure 4.4).

Construct segment $\overline{CD}$ (see Scene 3 of Figure 4.4).

In the following dialogue, we illustrate the possible communication between teacher and student as learning occurs:

T: How can the side length of the square be doubled?

S: Duplicate the square beside itself.

T: How can that be accomplished?

S: Use one side of the square as the mirror and then reflect the rest of the square over it (see Scene 4 of Figure 4.4).

T: Is that adequate?

S: No. You need to double the other side too.

T: Why?

S: To make a new square.

T: How can I do that?

S: Mark one long side of the rectangle as the mirror. Then reflect the two squares over it (see Scene 5 of Figure 4.4).

T: What has doubling the side of the square done to the original area?

S: The new area is four times that of the original.

T: How do you know that?

FIGURE 4.4 Presentation of a Square

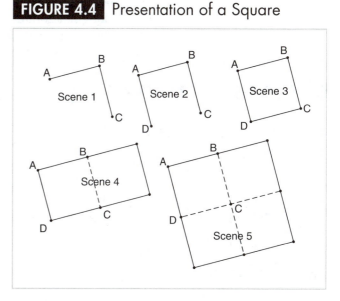

This lesson could be extended to tripling the length of the side of the square, or even more as needed. The advantage is that the students can see what is being discussed. Creating a mental image here will help

FIGURE 4.5 Solving Individual
Income

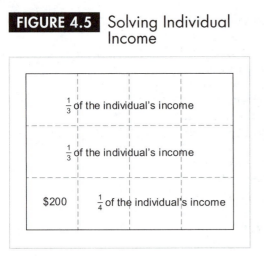

$\frac{1}{3}$ of the individual's income

$\frac{1}{3}$ of the individual's income

$200 $\frac{1}{4}$ of the individual's income

students formulate responses (conjectures and generalizations) to similar future problems. Indirect instruction (guided discovery or hands-on learning) promotes an increase incritical thinking and problem-solving skills. Students are encouraged to explore and discover information through the use of open-ended questions, group discussions and activities, experiments, and hands-on exercises. Indirect instruction has been shown to improve attitudes toward subject matter, especially for those students with a low success rate with direct instruction (Brumbaugh, Ortiz, & Gresham, 2006).

Now let's consider the classical way of having a class deal with learning a new concept. The formula is given and a few examples done. Then, practice problems are assigned. The problems are all essentially the same, they just use different counting numbers, fractions, decimals, or a combination of elements of the real numbers. How much better it would be if, rather than assigning twenty similar problems only five were given, with the expectation that they be solved more than one way. For example, suppose one-third of an individual's income is spent on housing, another third is spent on transportation and education, and 25 percent is spent on food and entertainment. The individual has $200 left for saving, giving, investing, and shopping. How much does the individual make per month? Algebraically, a solution could be determined through the equation $\frac{x}{3} + \frac{x}{3} + \frac{x}{4} = x - \$200$, where x represents the monthly income. Solving $\$200 = \frac{x}{12}$ indicates that $x = \$2400$.

Figure 4.5 shows how that same problem could be done geometrically. The total income (big rectangle), is divided into thirds horizontally, and fourths vertically. The net result is a total of twelve congruent squares, four of which represent thirds and three of which represent fourths. There is one square left after the fourth and both thirds are represented. But, we know that the left over money is $200. Since there are 12 congruent squares, the total income must be $12 \times \$200 = \$2400$. Solving the problem a second way enhances the students' versatility.

Consider another problem that can be done more than one way. Nine playing cards are arranged as shown in Figure 4.6. Five are side by side with the longer edge vertical and four are side by side with the longer edge horizontal. The large rectangle, formed by the nine cards, has an area of 180 square units. What are the dimensions of the cards, assuming they are all congruent?

The rectangle is $5a$ long and $(a + b)$ high. The area is $5a(a + b)$. It must be the case, then, that $5a(a + b) = 180$ square units. But it is also true that $5a = 4b$ from the two long horizontal dimensions, giving $b = \frac{5a}{4}$. Substituting in $5a(a + b)$ gives $5a\left(a + \frac{5a}{4}\right) = 5a\left(\frac{9a}{4}\right)$. So $180 = \frac{45a^2}{4}$, which yields $a = \pm 4$ units. Because a card side cannot be negative, the width of the card is 4 units. Substituting in $b = \frac{5a}{4}$, $b = 5$ units, the length of the card. This same problem could be solved by initially dividing 180 by 9 since it is known that the cards are congruent. The area has to be 20 square units $= ab$. The ratio of length to width would still be $b = \frac{5a}{4}$, and the rest of the solution would be the same.

In both examples, one problem is solved in two different ways. Having students do the same routines over and over can create narrow, inflexible thinking. Conversely, asking students to solve a problem more than one way helps create divergent thinkers.

Take a look at the next example. A surf shop sells black, red, and blue surfboards. The black surfboards are sold four times as often as the red

FIGURE 4.6 Arrangement of Playing Cards

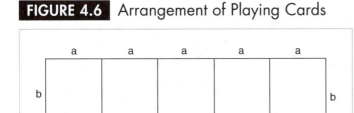

FIGURE 4.7 Surfboard Illustration

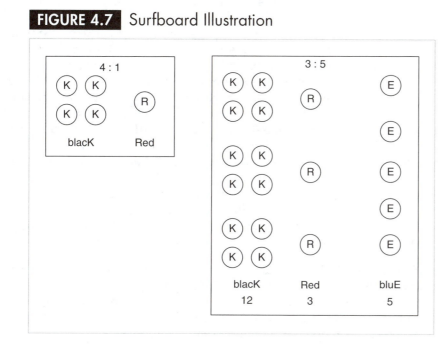

ones. During the time in which three red surfboards sell, five blue surfboards sell. How could the potential surfboard sales situations be shown? Students can use a variety of approaches to represent and solve this problem. Figure 4.7 shows a discrete model that could be used. It is a merging of the information from the two ratios in the problem statement.

Students could also consider making their own representation to illustrate what ratio of the surfboard sales are black. They could also make a model to show what percent of the surfboard sales are blue. Or students may make a representation to show this number: "If 60 black surfboards were sold in a month, what is the total number of red and blue surfboards sold in that month, assuming the described ratios hold?" The representation for the surfboard sales combines visual and numerical information, which can be appreciated in solving many problems involving ratios, proportions, and percents.

Consider another problem. Several students go to the local pizza parlor for dinner. They have $60 to spend. If the tax plus tip is 25 percent more than the food prices shown on the menu, how much can they spend on the food so that the total cost will be $60? Figure 4.8 illustrates one way to solve this problem. Four sections represent the price of the food and one section represents the tax and tip. Because there are five equal parts and the total is $60, each part must be $12. Therefore, the total price allowed for food is $48 (Bennett, Maier, & Nelson, 1988). This particular representation could also help students understand that when one quantity is 125 percent of a second quantity, then the second is 80 percent of the first. Furthermore, this same figure can help students understand that a situation like this can be interpreted more than one way. Either one segment (the shaded part of Figure 4.8) is 80 percent of the whole, or the whole is 125 percent of the shaded segment.

We realize that this food problem has limitations. Many students would react to it by saying it is a silly problem. Assuming the students are sensitive

FIGURE 4.8 Tax and Tip Illustration

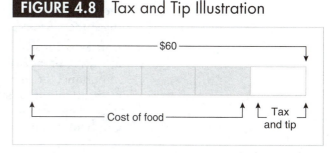

to tipping, it is likely that someone would solve it saying that the food should total about $50, add tax to that, and the difference between that sum and $60 is the tip. Still, problems such as this are quite common. It is important to note that there are alternate methods for solving this problem. Guess and check, for example, could be seen when the students say spend about $50 for food. A tremendous follow-up question to the student would be "How do you know?" Here, the request is for evidence to support the response. We encourage you to be judicious as you select problems for your examples, assign problems to be worked, or create problems. The desirable setting would be for the students to work with problems that they find intriguing, interesting, and challenging. This enhances communication, mathematical and representational connections, and discussion.

As we think of opportunities to show students how to invent algorithms, we should also focus on students' readiness to complete a mathematical learning task. Therefore, we have provided the following as an elaboration of readiness levels for your consideration.

1. **Mathematical readiness** is defined as the level of total development that enables a student to learn a behavior, comprehend a concept, or perform a given way with ease. This definition implies that readiness occurs on a continuum and involves students' individual differences influenced strongly by biological development and environmental experiences.

2. **Content readiness** involves a student's ability to work with ease on a specific mathematics area. For example, a student who counts objects meaningfully and accurately, effectively demonstrates "take-away" subtraction situation with cubes, knows all or most of the 100 subtraction facts, and understands place value for numbers 9 through 999, has a high degree of content readiness for learning subtraction computation involving two- and three-digit numbers.

3. **Pedagogical readiness** considers students' understanding and appropriate use of materials including objects, pictures, representations of objects, symbols, models, manipulatives, technology, and other instructional materials used to facilitate students' learning of mathematics. For example, in using an algebraic equation to generalize a numerical pattern, some students may not understand the generalization represented by the equation and not be pedagogically ready for this type of abstraction. They may also need to work with the pattern involving other types of pedagogical materials.

4. **Maturational readiness** considers students' natural developmental and cognitive stages and mental abilities. For example, it is not appropriate to assume that all sixth-grade students are ready to begin subtracting integers at the same time. As teachers, we might expect students to know certain mathematical or algebraic concepts and skills, but all students do not have the same level of maturational readiness. In some cases, students might need concrete objects to think with and about.

5. **Affective readiness** considers a student's mathematical disposition or motivation and attitudes toward mathematics. Affective readiness influences the student's success in learning and using mathematics.

6. **Contextual readiness** refers to students' awareness of the ways mathematics are used or applied in real-life problem solving, and realization of the importance of mathematics. This aspect of readiness also involves paying close attention to students' backgrounds and interests, and incorporating these elements into the teaching and learning activities (Brumbaugh, Ortiz, & Gresham, 2006).

We must allow time for students to develop their own strategies and processes for solving problems so they can make sense of what they are doing. When planning for instruction we look at many different aspects to help our students be mathematically successful. As we work with our students, particularly struggling learners, we must ask ourselves: What readiness levels do my students exhibit? Do they need intervention in their mathematical learning? If so, when would interventions need to occur? What would an intervention look like? We will help answer these questions as we discuss differentiated instruction, the use of concrete manipulatives and multiple representations, and scaffolding instruction for mathematical learning.

Differentiating Instruction

Differentiating instruction is the heart and soul of Tier 1 (Howard, 2009). It is an invaluable opportunity in which a wide range of mathematics instruction can occur. It allows us to have a deeper understanding of how our students think, and provides us with ways to engage our students in order to capitalize on their particular mathematical strengths. To differentiate instruction in your classroom, you need to be knowledgeable and efficient at four research types or models of instruction. The four models of instruction are direct, cognitive, social, and information processing (schema theory). Table 4.2 provides a brief overview.

We know that differentiation is not a strategy, but rather a commitment to motivating our students by meeting them where they are mathematically

TABLE 4.2 Overview of Models of Instruction

Model of Instruction	Definition	Characteristics	Types
Direct (explicit)	Concentrates on observable behavior and clearly defined tasks and methods for communicating progress to the student.	■ Clearly defined tasks ■ Directions ■ Reinforcement schedules	■ Direct instruction ■ Differential reinforcement of other behaviors (DROB)
Cognitive	An efficient method for presenting organized information from a wide range of topics to students at every stage of development.	■ Teacher thinking out loud ■ Modeling ■ Self-regulation ■ Scaffolded instruction	■ Strategy instruction ■ Metacognitive strategy instruction ■ Self-regulation
Social	The development of positive school cultures is a process of developing integrative and productive ways of interacting and norms that support vigorous learning activity.	■ Positive interdependence ■ Individual accountability ■ Group processing ■ Social skills ■ Face-to-face interactions	■ Cooperative learning (e.g., jigsaw, Think-Pair-Share) ■ Peer tutoring ■ Group investigation
Information Processing	Models provide the learner with information and concepts, some emphasize concept formation and hypothesis testing, and others generate creative thinking or enhance general intellectual ability.	■ Student choice ■ Student centered ■ Whole-part-whole approach ■ Authentic purpose for learning ■ Immersion in language and print	■ Case-based learning ■ Optimal learning environment ■ Critical thinking ■ Problem solving

and moving them forward to where we want them to be, even if they are struggling learners, advanced learners, or students from different cultures or backgrounds. We believe differentiation within the RTI in mathematics framework is the key to meeting our students' diverse mathematical needs. In order to successfully differentiate mathematics instruction within our classrooms, we must first recognize the *need* for us to differentiate. The goal is to build a community of learners that strengthens our understanding of students' individual needs and differences and helps us become proficient at identifying and understanding what needs our students may have. As we identify the key concepts, skills, and principles to be learned within our classrooms, we become proficient at implementing the different strategies and managing differentiation within our lessons. We also want to familiarize you with a glossary of terms as used with differentiated instruction, shown in Table 4.3. This will help you understand differentiated instruction and how it is used within our classrooms. As you use the OPTIONS Lesson Plan, knowledge of these strategies will help guide you in planning for effective instruction.

One question that we must answer is, How do we know we are differentiating our instruction? We know we are differentiating when we are providing flexible grouping (e.g., cooperative learning, peer-tutoring pairs at same or different grade level, and mixed-ability groups); small-group activities; flexible activities based on a variety of preassessment strategies; and increasing individual alternatives that consist of learning contracts, learning centers, independent and peer study times, anchor activities, compacting, tiered assignments, choice boards, and extension menus as related to learning styles and interests. We know we are successful at differentiation when we begin to see ourselves as organizers of the learning practices and opportunities that are taking place as we implement our lessons on a daily basis. We no longer separate our instruction and assessment but rather incorporate those practices together and throughout our lesson delivery. We create a learning community in mathematics that respects all learning differences and styles, and have working conditions that are conducive to student learning whether they are at, above, or below grade level. In other words, we are maximizing our students' mathematical learning potential to the fullest capacity by offering learning in new, exciting, meaningful, and essential ways.

Differentiation should be an integral part of instruction, rather than an adjunct to the core or grade-level curriculum. That is, we want to modify what students will know (content), how students will think (creative, critical, and problem-solving processes or skills), how they will access and use the resources we provide to them (research skills), and how students will be able to summarize and share the learning as presented (products).

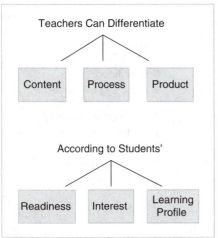

Teachers Can Differentiate

Content   Process   Product

According to Students'

Readiness   Interest   Learning Profile

We know that differentiation should be provided consistently with teacher instruction and should not be self-taught by students. It should be accompanied by high standards of performance and be based on the state content standards at each grade level. We want our students to venture further and deeper into the curriculum (depth), and broaden their understanding of the area of study through connections, relationships, and associations between, within, and across subjects (complexity). We also want to deliver to them the ability to construct the meaning of mathematical knowledge in an individualized manner (novelty) through the concept of altering the pace or speed of the learning process (acceleration or pacing). It is the individual growth that is central to the success of our students in the mathematics classroom. As we involve our students in the nature of the mathematics classroom, we allow them to grow academically and significantly. We want to prepare our

TABLE 4.3 Glossary of Differentiated Instruction Terms

Strategy	Focus of Differentiation	Definition	Example
Tiered assignments	Readiness	Tiered assignments are designed to instruct students on essential skills that are provided at different levels of complexity, abstractness, and open-endedness. The curricular content and objectives are the same, but the processes and/or products are varied according to the student's level of readiness.	In a unit on measurement, some students are taught basic measurement skills, including using a ruler to measure the length of objects. Other students can apply measurement skills to problems involving perimeter.
Compacting	Readiness	Compacting is the process of adjusting instruction to account for prior student mastery of learning objectives. Compacting involves a three-step process: (1) assess the student to determine his or her level of knowledge on the material to be studied and determine what the student still needs to master; (2) create plans for what the student needs to know and excuse the student from studying what the student already knows; and (3) create plans for free time to be spent in enriched or accelerated study.	A third-grade class is learning to identify the parts of fractions. Diagnostics indicate that two students already know the parts of fractions. These students are excused from completing the identifying activities and are taught to add and subtract fractions.
Interest centers or interest groups	Readiness Interest	Interest centers (usually used with younger students) and interest groups (usually used with older students) are set up so that learning experiences are directed toward a specific learner interest. Allowing students to choose a topic can be motivating to them.	Interest centers can focus on specific math skills, such as addition, and provide activities that are high interest, such as counting jelly beans or adding the number of eyes on two aliens. Interest-group students can work in small groups to research a math topic of interest, such as how geometry applies to architecture or how math is used in art.
Flexible grouping	Readiness Interest Learning Profile	Students work as part of many different groups depending on the task and/or content. Sometimes students are placed in groups based on readiness, other times they are placed based on interest and/or learning profile. Groups can either be assigned by the teacher or chosen by the students. Students can be assigned purposefully to a group or assigned randomly. This strategy allows students to work with a wide variety of peers and keeps them from being labeled as advanced or struggling.	The teacher may assign groups based on readiness for direct instruction on algebraic concepts, and allow students to choose their own groups for projects that investigate famous mathematicians.

(continued)

TABLE 4.3 (continued)

Strategy	Focus of Differentiation	Definition	Example
Learning contracts	Readiness Learning profile	A learning contract begins with an agreement between the teacher and the student. The teacher specifies the necessary skills expectations and the required components of the assignment, while the student identifies methods for completing the tasks. This strategy (1) allows students to work at an appropriate pace; (2) can target learning styles; and (3) helps students work independently, learn planning skills, and eliminate unnecessary skill practice.	A student decides to follow a football team over a two-month period and make inferences about players' performances based on their scoring patterns and physical characteristics. The student, with the teacher's guidance, develops a plan for collecting and analyzing the data and conducting research about football. The student decides to create a PowerPoint presentation to present his findings to the class.
Choice boards	Readiness Interest Learning profile	Choice boards are organizers that contain a variety of activities. Students can choose one or several activities to complete as they learn a skill or develop a product. Choice boards can be organized so that students are required to choose options that focus on several different skills.	Students are given a choice board that contains a list of possible activities they can complete to learn about volume. For example, students can choose to complete an inquiry lesson in which they measure volume using various containers, use a textbook to read about measuring volume, or watch a video in which the steps are explained. The activities are based on the following learning styles: visual, auditory, kinesthetic, and tactile. Students must complete two activities from the board and must choose these activities from two different learning styles.
Anchoring activity independent study	Readiness Interest Learning profile	Students are given a meaningful activity that is meant to be done independently in order to allow the teacher to work with the student individually or with small groups.	Students are given activities that may include reading, journal writing, exit card questions, working on a portfolio or task cards, practicing skills, or working on an extension menu or cubing activity.
Cubing and extension menus	Readiness Interest Learning profile	Students are provided alternative activities when work is completed, or they are allowed to participate in the learning and interests centers.	Cubing requires students to look at a topic from six different angles such as: describe it, compare it, associate it, apply It, analyze it, argue for or against it. These can be placed on dice. Students roll the dice and perform the task either through writing or orally within small-group discussion. Extension menus offer possibilities organized around a topic of study to provide an extension of the skills currently being taught.
Assessment	Readiness Mastery	Both diagnostic and formative assessments are embedded within the curriculum or lesson structure and implementation.	Preassessment checks for understanding along the way, such as thumbs-up, exit cards, asking "why" and "explain" questions, teacher observation and questioning, on going assessment, peer and self-assessment, quizzes, tests, and performance and alternative assessments.

Source: Adapted in part from Hall, Strangman, & Meyer (2003) and Tomlinson (1999).

Differentiated instruction is	Differentiated instruction is not
■ Using assessment data to plan instruction and group students	■ Using only whole-group instruction
■ Teaching targeted small groups (three to five students)	■ Using small groups that never change
■ Using flexible grouping (changing group membership based on student progress, interests, and needs)	■ Using the same text with all students
■ Matching instructional materials to student ability	■ Using the same independent seatwork assignments for the entire class

students (readiness) to work with a prescribed set of knowledge, understandings, and skills (Tomlinson, 2003).

Differentiated instruction is something we should already be doing. Good instruction is effective instruction. We want to provide you with as many tools as possible for using differentiated instruction and making RTI in mathematics implementation in your classroom as easy as possible. We have provided you with several teacher resources (reproducibles) in Appendix A to help you with differentiated instruction within your classroom. These include learning contracts, extension menus, choice boards, personal learning journal prompts, exit card questions, independent and group study forms, problem-solving strategies, progress reports, and manipulative choices. Feel free to pick and choose and use what works best for you and your students in your mathematics classroom.

Using Concrete Manipulatives and Multiple Representations

Classrooms have long come from an era of teaching in which teachers would expect that all students did with their hands was fold them (DeGeorge, 2004). Traditionally, teachers have relied on workbooks, drills, and memorization to present mathematical concepts. Research indicates children have more positive experiences learning mathematics if the instruction moves from concrete to abstract, and when they have many experiences in problem situations and in working with physical objects to develop understanding about mathematical operations (Gresham, 2005). Studies using manipulatives in the classroom have shown that students who are using them outperform those who do not. The use of manipulatives or hands-on learning helps students readily understand mathematical concepts and boosts their self-efficacy within mathematical learning (Gresham, 2005). Therefore, it is very important that we make manipulatives available for students to use at all times. Such availability offers the students the opportunities to devise their own solution strategies and promotes autonomous thinking and confidence in learning mathematics. In addition, manipulatives help students construct, link, and connect to real-world mathematical problem-solving situations.

We want to help students prepare strong foundations for understanding mathematics skills and concepts. We should encourage them to translate mathematics ideas from one mode to another and represent them in more than one mode (see Figure 4.9). Therefore, we must emphasize the building or recognizing of relationships between and within representations. For example, a student

FIGURE 4.9 Chart of Teacher Moves

		Teacher Moves			
		Concrete	Pictorial	Symbolic (representation)	Verbal
Child's Response	Concrete	C → C Teacher shows concrete representation; student manipulates concrete objects.	P → C Teacher shows picture; student manipulates concrete objects.	S → C Teacher writes; student manipulates concrete objects.	V → C Teacher talks; student manipulates concrete objects.
	Pictorial	C → P Teacher shows concrete representation; student chooses or draws picture.	P → P	S → P	V → P
	Symbolic	C → S Teacher shows concrete representation; student writes symbol.	P → S	S → S	V → S
	Verbal	C → V Teacher shows concrete representation; student discusses/talks.	P → V	S → V	V → V

Note: C = concrete; P = pictorial; S = symbolic; V = verbal.

may recognize patterns while using base-10 blocks by noticing the corresponding decreasing size of the blocks (looking at the cubes, longs, flats, and units). Students may also transform an idea from one form and represent it as another by constructing a graph or drawing a diagram to illustrate a concept.

Students may also be able to listen to a description of a problem and represent it with blocks (concrete manipulatives) and then write a response or solution to the problem (written symbols). Using different manipulatives and pictorials can aid in the effectiveness in establishing this foundation as we begin at the concrete-manipulative level then move toward more efficient methods and mathematical processes. Students will experience greater mathematics understanding if they can relate to the mathematical facts and symbols with visual experiences. As we prepare our lessons, we must focus on providing students many experiences in problem situations and working with physical objects (manipulatives) to develop an understanding of the mathematical concepts and operations we are teaching to them. For example, if we want to teach integers, equations, inequalities, factoring, polynomials, or estimation, we may consider introducing students to algebra tiles to help guide them find alternative algorithms for solving problems. Teaching number concepts using number cubes, two-colored counters, spinners, calculators, number cards, dominoes, decimals squares, base-10 blocks, Cuisenaire rods, and fractional models may be beneficial to students. However, sometimes we know it can be a daunting task to identify what manipulative to use in order to help students understand the concepts or skills we are required to teach. Therefore, we have provided a list that consists of mathematical manipulatives used to teach specific mathematics concepts and to engage students in the learning process (see Teacher Resources-Manipulatives to Concepts-Concepts to Manipulatives) (Gresham, 2009). We hope you will find this helpful as you prepare for the use of concrete manipulatives in your mathematics classroom.

As we consider the use of concrete manipulatives, we must also focus on the use of representation. Representation refers both to process and product and is central to the study of mathematics. It is the act of capturing a concept or relation in some form (process) and connecting it to the final mathematics model (product). Some representations are externally observable (such as manipulating base-10 blocks to represent a certain quantity), or a student attempting to draw a model of fractional pieces to illustrate their knowledge of $\frac{3}{8} + \frac{4}{16}$ (making abstractions or connections to new learning). Throughout elementary and middle school, student mathematics representations are usually about objects and actions in using those objects to solve problems. Students are learning to create, compare, and use mathematical representations to work toward more abstract ideas, or to identify, portray, clarify, or extend a mathematical skill or concept. They are also beginning to communicate their thinking through the use of physical objects, drawings, charts, graphs, and symbols.

Representation encourages students to organize their thinking and helps them make mathematical ideas more available for thought and reflection (Brumbaugh, Ortiz, & Gresham, 2006). Multiple representations should be treated as essential in supporting students' understanding of mathematical concepts and relations; in communicating approaches, arguments, and understandings of one problem to another; in recognizing connections among related concepts; and in applying mathematics to realistic problem situations through modeling and demonstrations (Brumbaugh, Ortiz, & Gresham, 2006). We can provide students many opportunities through our effective instructional practices by using representations for mathematics concepts. We do so by using the different learning levels (concrete, pictorial or representations, and abstract levels) and related modes of representation; real-world situations (concrete level); manipulatives models (concrete level); pictures of manipulative models (pictorial or representations level); oral language (abstract level); and written symbols (abstract level) (Berh, Lesh, Post, & Silver, 1983) (see Figure 4.10).

For example, a student can represent the concept of "six" with six fingers (real-world application), with six cubes (manipulative model), with six balls (pictures), by saying the word (oral), and by writing the word *six* or the numeral *6* (written symbols). Modes of representation can take on many forms.

FIGURE 4.10 Modes of Representation and Possible Interconnections

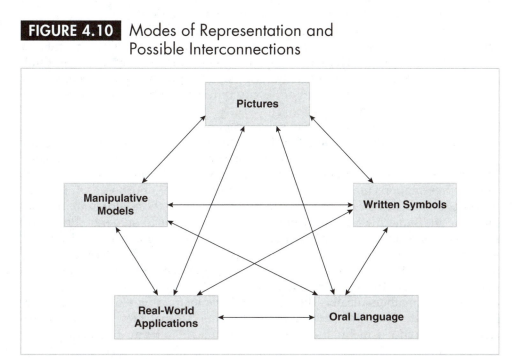

Source: Brumbaugh, Ortiz, & Gresham, 2006

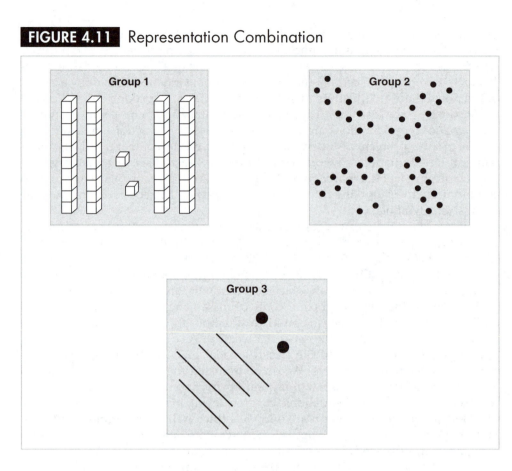

FIGURE 4.11 Representation Combination

Figure 4.11 shows three different representations for the number forty-two. Group 1 illustrates using base-10 blocks at the concrete level. This group used longs and units to show four groups of ten and two ones. Group 2 modeled their understanding using dot arrays at the pictorial or representation level. Group 3 used dots and segments, also at the representation level.

Representations are also used to convey numbers and operations. Not only can we represent specific numbers and operations, but you can also represent and preserve relationships, such as a + b = c (Troutman & Lichtenberg, 2003). To think algebraically, we must know how the symbols of representation are combined. Figure 4.12 shows three examples of how to reflect the combination of using the power of representation.

Students will be better able to solve problems if they can easily move from one type of representation to another. This flexibility can emerge as your students gain experience with multiple ways of representing a contextualized problem. Mathematical ideas can often be represented in very different ways, and each of those representations may be appropriate for very different purposes within your lesson plan structure. You may elect to use a variety of these representations to illustrate the same mathematical ideas you are teaching to students. Providing students opportunities to use different representations for a mathematical idea can lead them to different ways of understanding and using that idea. Representations help students think about the mathematics presented to them. Mathematics offers a broad selection of representations that help students solve problems and communicate mathematically. The goal is to have instruction that helps students build bridges to form their own ways of thinking so that they come to understand, value, and use the mathematical tools available to them. This is the power of representation!

FIGURE 4.12 Tile Presentation

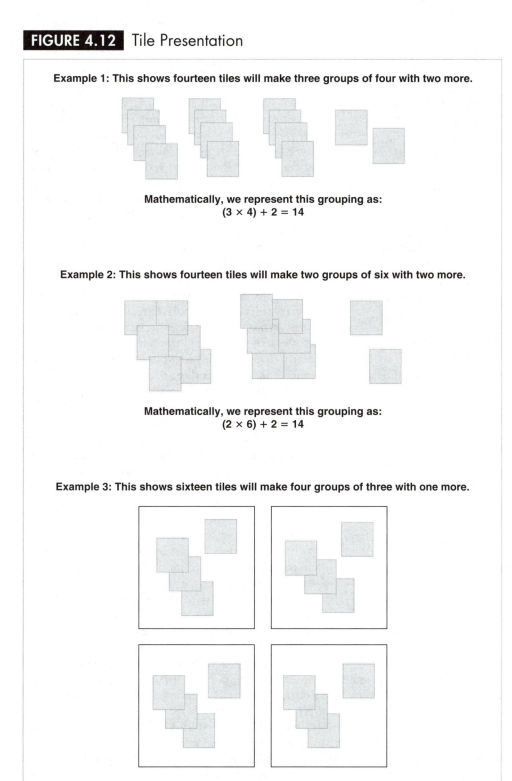

Example 1: This shows fourteen tiles will make three groups of four with two more.

Mathematically, we represent this grouping as:
(3 × 4) + 2 = 14

Example 2: This shows fourteen tiles will make two groups of six with two more.

Mathematically, we represent this grouping as:
(2 × 6) + 2 = 14

Example 3: This shows sixteen tiles will make four groups of three with one more.

Mathematically, we represent this grouping as:
4 × (3 + 1) = 16

Scaffolding Instruction for Mathematical Learning

When we see a tall skyscraper we see the height and beauty of a magnificent structure. Builders use scaffolds to work their way up to the top for its final completion as each beam and piece is carefully put together using supports to hold it in place. A variety of nuts and bolts, mortar, and metal pieces are welded together to create a strong foundation and sturdy structure that will withstand many elements and the test of time. When we think of mathematics we must think of the tall skyscraper. It is very important for us to provide our students with the tools and materials they need to be mathematically successfully. These tools may include guidance, self-confidence, strategies, activities, manipulatives, feedback, reinforcement, support, and many opportunities for them to develop a strong mathematical foundation and structure that is filled with a variety of mathematical content and skills. We can accomplish this task by scaffolding instruction for mathematical learning.

Scaffolding is one of the primary principles of effective instruction and one that enables us to accommodate each of our students' individual mathematical needs. Scaffolding is best described as specialized teaching strategies geared to support learning when students are introduced to a new concept or subject. Scaffolding allows us to provide a context, foundation, or motivation to help students understand the new information we are introducing within our lessons.

Scaffolding is formulated from Vygotsky's concept of the **zone of proximal development**, which is described as "the distance between what children can do by themselves and the next learning that they can be helped to achieve with competent assistance" (Vygotsky, 1978, p. 176). It is a systematic sequencing of prompted content, materials, tasks, and teacher and peer support that optimize learning until students can apply new skills and strategies independently (Dickson, Chard, & Simmons, 1993). It provides our students the crucial learning supports they need to move from initial acquisition of a mathematics skill or concept toward independent mathematical performance of those skills or concepts and is employed in problem-based learning environments. This type of instruction can positively impact students, reduce mathematics anxiety, and will afford us the opportunity to constantly evaluate student learning and understanding within the lesson. We also refer to this type of instruction (scaffolding) as **guided practice**. Why? Because scaffolding—guided practice through supports—allows the teacher to begin the lesson by modeling the skills to be learned while providing a high level of direction (including questioning, additional modeling if necessary, student demonstration of skill performance, and immediate teacher feedback) to help students obtain mastery of mathematical content.

Scaffolding Strategies May Include

- Activating prior knowledge
- Piquing student interest/curiosity by offering a motivational context to the topic at hand
- Breaking a complex task into steps to facilitate student achievement
- Showing students an example of the desired outcome before they complete the task
- Modeling the thought process for students through "think aloud" talk
- Offering hints or partial solutions to problems and using verbal cues to prompt student answers
- Teaching student chants or mnemonic devices to ease memorization of key facts or procedures
- Facilitating student engagement and participation
- Using graphic organizers to offer a visual framework for assimilating new information
- Teaching key mathematical vocabulary terms before reading
- Guiding the students in making predictions for what they expect will occur in a story, experiment, or other course of action
- Asking questions to encourage deeper investigation of concepts
- Suggesting possible strategies for the students to use during independent practice
- Modeling an activity for the students before they are asked to complete the same or similar activity
- Asking students to contribute their own experiences that relate to the subject at hand

(Tomlinson, 2003)

In order to incorporate scaffolding throughout the lesson, teachers may find the following framework outlined by Ellis & Larkin (1998) helpful:

1. **The teacher does it:** In other words, the teacher models how to perform a new or difficult task, such as how to use a graphic organizer. For example, the teacher may have a partially completed graphic organizer on an overhead transparency and will "think aloud" as he or she describes how the graphic organizer illustrates the relationships among the information contained on it.

2. **The class does it:** The teacher and students work together to perform the task. For example, the students may suggest information to be added to the graphic organizer. As the teacher writes the suggestions on the transparency, students fill in their own copies of the organizer.

3. **The group does it:** Students work with a partner or a small cooperative group to complete a graphic organizer (either a partially completed or blank).

4. **The individual does it:** This is the independent practice stage in which individual students can demonstrate their task mastery (e.g., successfully completing a graphic organizer to demonstrate appropriate relationships among information) and receive the necessary practice to help them perform the task automatically and quickly.

With lesson planning, the activities presented during scaffolding are provided to build on our students' prior knowledge so they may internalize the mathematical information we are giving them. One aspect to remember is that we want the supports (scaffolding) to be temporary. That is, we want to provide students with as much assistance as needed, but to ultimately have them work independently of the teacher and be self-regulating learners. Our goal is to help them link and connect old information with the new information we are introducing in our daily mathematics lessons. When preparing lessons for scaffolding we want activities and tasks that

- Motivate or enlist the student's interest related to the task
- Reduce frustration and risk
- Simplify the task to make it more manageable and achievable for a student
- Provide some direction in order to help the student focus on achieving the goal
- Clearly indicate differences between the student's work and the standard or desired solution
- Model and clearly define the expectations of the activity to be performed (Bransford, Brown, & Cocking, 2000)

We want to offer students engaging activities that provide cues, prompts, partial solutions, think-aloud opportunities, direct instruction, hints, and peer, small, and cooperative group learning activities. How then can you implement scaffolding instruction in your mathematics classroom? We have provided a sample lesson plan from Ms. Holly's classroom so you can visualize what scaffolding might look like in the mathematics classroom on a day-to-day or weekly basis (see Figure 4.13). Ms. Holly prepared her OPTIONS Lesson Plan (Figure 4.3) and has now divided her instructional practices to show evidence of how this will take place in her classroom for weekly planning. She indentifies her group placements, concepts for knowing and learning, technology (websites), independent learning stations for students, and questions she may ask. We have also included the blank template (Reproducible #9 in Appendix A) and several guided math teacher resource pages in the back of this book.

One of the primary benefits of scaffolding is that our students will become engaged in the learning process whether it is within small groups or one-on-one learning. As we learn more about our students, we gain invaluable insight into our their mathematical standing and where we can take them to enhance their

FIGURE 4.13 Guided Math Plan (Scaffolding)

Differentiating Instruction/Interventions Using Targeted OPTIONS: Tier 1

OUTCOME (Standard in mathematics): M4N4 Number and Operations: Division

PROGRESS-MONITORING DATA:

TIER 1 Objective: Students will develop understanding of division of whole numbers within problem-solving situations.

Essential Questions: What are the different ways students can show understanding of multiplication and division? How are remainders and divisors related?

Length of Time: Five days

INSTRUCTIONAL PERSONNEL (circle all that apply):

MT: Math teacher (Ms. Holly)

IC: Instructional coach

SP: School psychologist

IRT: Instructional resource teacher

CT: Co-teacher

INTERVENTIONS	**ONGOING PROGRESS MONITORING (OPM)**
Record intervention, method to intensify, other professionals, and other classroom/student considerations used.	Record OPM assessment, results, and dates. Be sure to attach charts and graph results.

Group 1	**Group 2**	**Group 3**	**Group 4**
Jennifer	Kevin	Corey	Justin
Tyler	Alecean	Meredith	Roderick
Tameka	Tawana	Mae	Heather
Brian	Ronnie	Kirby	Amelio
Mary	Shaun	Anaya	Chloe
Carlos	Julio	Chase	Riley

Day 1	Day 2	Day 3	Day 4	Day 5
Math rap

Whole-group lesson: Introduce division with modeling Students will use base-10 blocks to model two digit by two digit division problems. Guided practice: Students will solve division problems as the teacher observes and takes notes. Diagnostic | Homework check

Mini-lesson: Review division of two digits by two digits. Review long division steps.

Homework check

Independent learning station groups: | Homework check

Mini-lesson: Review division of two digits by two digits.

Independent learning station groups:

Group 1— Target Day | Homework check

Mini-lesson: Mental math division patterns

Independent learning station groups:

S6—Group 1 S5—Group 2 | Summative assessment:

Students will explain the steps of long division in finding the quotients of given numbers: Division quiz #1.

Students will calculate quotients of division problems. |

assessment: Pretest— two digit by two digit division (six problems) **Introduce independent learning stations** (see below)	S6—Group 1 S7/S2—Group 2 S1—Group 3 guided math S3—Group 4 guided math	S4—Group 2 guided math S5/S7—Group 3 S5—Group 4 guided math	S3—Group 3 guided math S4/S7—Group 4 guided math	Students will retell the procedure and steps of a long division problem.

Concepts for Knowing	**Concepts for Learning**	**Websites**
Division facts Dividing two digits by one digit, and three digits by one digit Estimate quotients (mental math)	Develop skill and accuracy in estimating (mental math) quotients and writing quotients when dividing by two and by two-digit numbers and two digit numbers by three digit numbers	www.mathwire.com http://cemc2.math.uwaterloo.ca/ mathfrog/english/kidz/div4.shtml www.hbschool.com/activity/cityblocks www.ikeepbookmarks.com

NEEDS OF INDIVIDUAL STUDENTS

Independent learning stations:

Computer stations

S1 (low): <u>Divvy It Up!</u>—Students will apply knowledge of division facts to solve two digit by two digit division problems (step-by-step interactive game)

S2 (average/high): <u>Tile It</u>—Students will arrange digits in a multiplication problem to create the given product

Skill/drill stations

S3 (low): <u>Division Game</u>—Students will apply knowledge of long division with remainders by using a game to reinforce the skills taught.

S4 (average/high): <u>Remainder Reminder</u>—When given a quotient, students will formulate a division problem using 2- and 3-digit by 1-digit factors that equal the quotient. Next, student will explain in a journal the steps used to generate the problems.

Journal junction

S5 (low): <u>When the Doorbell Rings: Reading Comprehension</u>—Students will explain how division works in their journal.

S6 (average/high): <u>Wally's World</u>—Students will research costs of supplies for school store, create a store and stay within budget, and predict profit to be made. (Students must make enough money to pay for supplies needed.)

S7 (average/high): <u>Slap it!</u>—Students will play a card game relating inverse operations with fact families.

Questions to ask: What is this problem about? What does the information in the problem mean? What did you do? Why did you do it? What do you notice? What questions do you have? What did you figure out? Why does it work or not work? What does your result mean? What is the meaning of _____? How did you check your answer? Did you use a different approach or line of reasoning from your main solution path? Does the solution make sense? Are there new problems that this one makes you think of? What other types of problems or situations does this remind you of? What parts of the problem-solving process were the most and least satisfying or interesting?

Summarize

Date to review instruction/intervention and assessment data: _____

Team meeting members: _____   Location: _____

mathematical independence. We will create mathematical momentum through the structure provided with scaffolding as students spend less time searching and more time learning and discovering (which results in quicker learning). We want to guide and support our students with learning strategies and activities that serve as bridges to get help them construct new understandings and have them reach the next level in mathematics. Remember, our ultimate goal is to teach students in their "zone"!

A TIME TO REFLECT

What strategies, activities, and provisions do you currently implement in your classroom that relate to differentiated instruction and scaffolding? Provide your own examples of each and share and discuss these with colleagues.

Curriculum-Based Assessments for Instructional Decision Making

Differentiated instruction and scaffolding are practices we must address through our instructional decision-making processes. As we implement these practices within our classrooms, we must determine whether *what* we are doing and *how* we are doing it is working. The curriculum-based measurements we implement with our students will aid in determining this as we continue to move forward with RTI. We know that curriculum-based measurement (CBM) is a specialized form of measurement characterized by standardized, direct, and frequent measures of skills based on the mathematical content of the particular curriculum being used within our classrooms. We use it to create both long- and short-term individualized goals and objectives for our students, and it is a simple way to monitor student progress. If we see our students are not making adequate progress based on the CBM measure, we use the data to alter or change our instructional practices and programming to best meet our students' rate of growth and learning to a more acceptable level. We use the feedback to make day-to-day changes within our mathematics instruction. We can assess addition, subtraction, multiplication, and division and add additional skills to assess depending on the curriculum and the grade level (e.g., fractions, geometry, algebra, measurement).

We use CBM as a sampling assessment of items from the classroom curriculum, administer it to one or more students under the same or similar conditions, summarize the information graphically, and use the assessment information in our instructional decision making (Fuchs & Fuchs, 2001). Once the data is collected, students are rank ordered from highest to lowest. Students who score at or below the tenth percentile should be considered at severe risk of math failure. Students scoring between the tenth and the twenty-fifth percentile should be considered at risk (Fuchs & Fuchs, 2008). The next step in the problem-solving process is intervention plan development. Students with low skill levels will likely require acquisition and mathematical fluency instruction. This could take the form of additional practice, changes in the

So What Should We See in an Effective Mathematics Classroom?

- A curriculum of skills, concepts, and applications that are reasonable to expect all students to master, and not those skills, concepts, and applications that have gradually been moved to an earlier grade on the basis of inappropriately raising standards.

- Implementation of a district and state curriculum that includes essential skills and understandings for a world of calculators and computers, and not what many recognize as to much content to cover at each grade level.

- A deliberate questioning of the appropriateness of the mathematical content, regardless of what may or may not be on the high-stakes test, in every grade or course. (Source: Leinwand, 2009, p. 59) current curriculum, or supplementing the curriculum with additional instruction. CBM should be used in conjunction with a problem-solving approach. There are five process steps for using CBM in problem solving: (1) problem identification, (2) problem analysis, (3) intervention plan development, (4) intervention plan implementation, and (5) intervention plan evaluation.

As you think of CBM and its use, let's revisit Ms. Holly's classroom to view how she has implemented CBM in her instructional decision making with the RTI in mathematics framework. As we described in Chapter 2, Ms. Holly had several students who appeared to be struggling with the curriculum. Based on the universal screening at the beginning of the school year, Ms. Holly utilized the information from the data and from teacher observations, field notes, and student conferencing to identify mathematical problem areas in five students, in particular a student named Heather. Ms. Holly completed the Student Observation Forms (Reproducible #5 in Appendix A) and Classroom Problem Identification Plan (Reproducible #10 in Appendix A) to aid in further investigating her five students' areas of concern. After she received the information from the benchmark assessment data, she followed through by administering additional screening measures (progress monitoring) to determine the students' strengths and weaknesses. However, for this particular scenario, we will focus only on Heather's progress as identified by Ms. Holly.

As you recall, Ms. Holly identified that place value, addition, and multiplication were skills that needed to be retaught, reinforced, and mastered as Heather's level of learning fell below expectations based on other students in the classroom. As Ms. Holly worked with Heather, she continued to administer various curriculum-based informal assessments related to fourth grade–level curriculum benchmarks to determine Heather's mathematical strengths and weaknesses and to further diagnose her problem areas. Figure 4.14 is an illustration of a CBM Ms. Holly administered to Heather.

As seen from the scoring, Heather does understand how to multiply a two-digit number by a one-digit number and does show mastery of the ones and twos. There is only one problem that includes the threes, so analysis of mastery of the three facts cannot be determined with this CBM probe. Figure 4.15 shows how Ms. Holly listed Heather's strengths and weaknesses and indicates the analysis of the probe. Ms. Holly indicated that Heather does not exhibit any significant error patterns when multiplying a two-digit number with a one-digit number. However, Ms. Holly does denote comments about one specific problem but was corrected by Heather (see the error pattern comments in Figure 4.15).

Ms. Holly continued with the curriculum benchmarks as the mathematical skills became harder, and Heather's problems became evident when Ms. Holly administered another CBM probe with harder multiplication facts including the sixes, sevens, eights, and nines (see Figure 4.16).

The scoring results show that Heather does have an understanding of some but not all of her multiplication facts. Ms. Holly analyzed the probe and wrote Heather's strengths and weaknesses (see Figure 4.17). As you view this particular CMB probe, notice the error patterns that have occurred in the first problem as Heather tried to solve 65×8. She does have mastery of her fives and placed the 40 to show her answer. However, she did not carry the 4 to the tens column above the 6 when she multiplied 5×8. Instead she placed the 4 beside the 0 in the tens column in the answer section. She does not have mastery of the six multiplication facts and attempts to solve 6×8 by writing tally marks to determine the answer. Even though she did write the correct number of tallies next to the problem, Heather placed an X with her pencil near the top of the tallies and crossed out the problem without completing it. Ms. Holly conferenced with Heather and asked her why she did not continue to work the problem. Heather indicated she got frustrated when writing so many tallies and just gave up. She said the second problem looked easier and she wanted to move on.

FIGURE 4.14 Heather's CBM

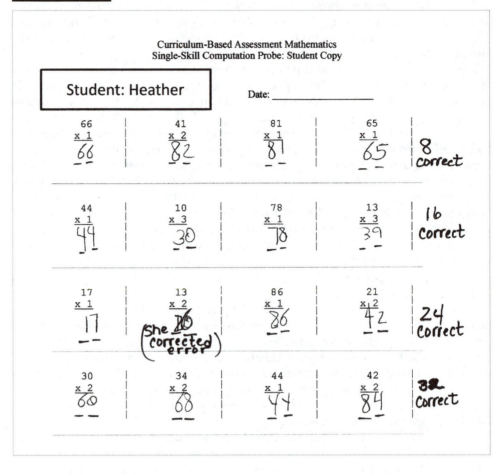

Curriculum-Based Assessment Mathematics
Single-Skill Computation Probe: Student Copy

Student: Heather   Date: _____

66 x 1 66	41 x 2 82	81 x 1 81	65 x 1 65 — 8 correct
44 x 1 44	10 x 3 30	78 x 1 78	13 x 3 39 — 16 correct
17 x 1 17	13 x 2 (she corrected error)	86 x 1 86	21 x 2 42 — 24 correct
30 x 2 60	34 x 2 68	44 x 1 44	42 x 2 84 — 32 correct

FIGURE 4.15 Analysis of Heather's Curriculum-Based Assessment: Single-Skill Computation Probe

Strengths

1. Has mastery of multiplication facts using twos. (She gets all of these correct.)
2. Heather knows the column format for multiplication and knows that she should begin multiplying by the ones digit of the multiplier.
3. Multiplication knowledge when zero or one are involved.

Error Patterns

1. Heather initially wrote that $13 \times 2 = 16$ (third column, second problem), but corrected her answer before she moved to the next problem. She did not erase but wrote over the incorrect number. (I questioned her after the probe time ended about why she did not erase the one in the tens column. She indicated that she was still not sure of the answer and hoped either would be scored correctly. When she thought about it she said she chose not to erase the 1 and wrote the 2 over it instead.)

FIGURE 4.16 Heather's CBM

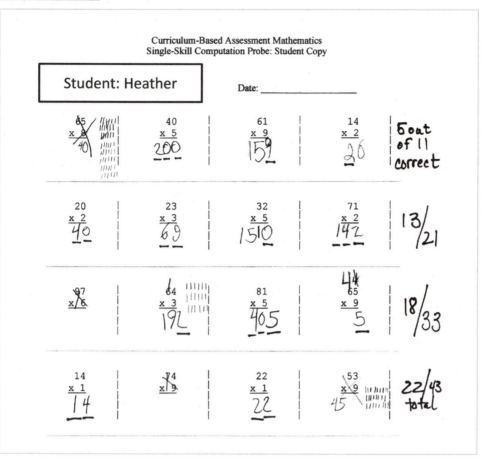

FIGURE 4.17 Analysis of Heather's Curriculum-Based Assessment:
Single-Skill Computation Probe

Strengths

1. Has mastery of multiplication facts using twos, threes, fives, and some sixes. (She gets all of the twos, threes, and fives correct, and one of the sixes—6 × 3.)

2. Heather knows the column format for multiplication and that she should begin multiplying by the ones digit of the multiplier.

3. Multiplication knowledge when zero or one are involved.

Error Patterns

1. Fails to record regrouped digit to tens column when multiplying numbers from ones column.

2. Adds numbers presented on some problems instead of multiplying.

3. Placed regrouped number in ones column instead of tens column. (Heather corrected this and crossed out the number instead of erasing it. She wrote the correct number above the tens column. However, she still failed to complete the problem so unable to check for understanding of adding the regrouped number. There is no indication she understands how to add because she does not know her sixes or nines.)

The third problem in the first row reveals another common error pattern. Heather does multiply 1×9 correctly and does show knowledge of multiplication when zero and one are involved. However, instead of writing tallies as she did in the first problem to solve 6×8, she added $6 + 9$ and placed her answer of 15 in the appropriate column. Heather does not indicate strong knowledge of regrouping, the adding of regrouped numbers, or where they should be placed within the problem. In the second row, third problem, there is evidence that she lacks this skill as she attempted to solve 32×5. Heather made a common error pattern when multiplying the ones column. She multiplied 2×5 and indicated 10 as the answer, but she did not place the number one above the multiplier so that it may be added when the numbers in the tens column are multiplied. She tried to correct this within another problem (third row, fourth problem) when she multiplied 65×9. Heather seemed to indicate some knowledge of place value and regrouping when she placed the 4 above the 5 in the ones column. She corrected herself by crossing out the 4 and placing it in the appropriate column. She did indicate knowledge of her fives but she did not complete the problem. In the very last problem, Heather once again used tally marks to attempt to solve the problem. Her mastery of the fives is evident and she knows to place the answer in the tens column in the appropriate place-value holder, but she did not complete the answer.

As evidenced from each analysis done by Ms. Holly, she was able to identify and document Heather's strengths and weaknesses after each CBM probe. This allowed Ms. Holly to realign and adjust Heather's intervention strategies within Tier 1 based on her findings.

Throughout this chapter, we have discussed differentiation, scaffolding, manipulatives, and multiple representations and how each can work for you within the RTI in mathematics framework. We have also provided resources to utilize these practices and begin your lesson planning and effective instruction. You have learned about effective instruction and how it works in the mathematics classroom. Now we want you to put this knowledge into practice and begin the instructional decision-making process. Read the upcoming scenarios and consider the following:

- Determining the starting point for instruction
- Selecting outcomes and content
- Teaching strategies for the learning experiences and assessment opportunities
- Learning experiences and assessment opportunities
- Providing feedback
- Noting evidence of learning
- Evaluating

You will also want to address the following important questions:

- What hypothesis can you make as to why the student is struggling?
- What indicators do you have to identify that the student may need additional support?
- What error patterns can you immediately identify?
- Are other error patterns seen as you work with the student and analyze his or her work samples?
- What remediation should be offered to the student?
- How will you differentiate and scaffold instruction?
- What resources may be needed?
- What concrete manipulatives and multiple representations can be included in the lesson?
- What assessment will be provided to monitor student progress?

Scenario 1

Student: Justin Nicolas

Age: $10\frac{1}{2}$

Grade: 4

Justin is $10\frac{1}{2}$ years old and in the fourth grade. He loves tools and machines and working with his hands to build things. He has some difficulty with mathematics vocabulary skills, but likes to read books above his grade level. His writing is difficult to read and when he does computation in math it is usually not legible. However, when questioned about the problems he is working on he does explain his answers correctly.

Justin seems to be a good problem solver. He does need extra support with mathematics, particularly long division, fractions, and geometry. However, he does respond well to having material explained by teacher examples and those that are demonstrated on the whiteboard or projector. He listens well and does better when material is discussed with him individually rather then presented to him in written form or with the whole class. He stays on task for minimal time lengths (four to five minutes), then becomes sidetracked. He gets very frustrated and angry if he does not know the answer right away, gives up easily, and can be physically aggressive when he does not understand the mathematical material presented. He does prefer physical movement when learning. Justin likes to work with his peers and in groups.

Scenario 2

Student: Chase Norton

Age: 13

Grade: 8

Chase is a handful! He is usually up out of his seat during math class, wants to be the center of attention, exhibits off-task behaviors, and refuses to do tasks. He tries his best to avoid doing math and is the class clown when the mathematial task is too difficult. He likes to spend time with others and enjoys listening to and telling stories, music, writing activities, and using his vivid imagination. He struggles with most mathematics content and needs prodding to complete his assignments when he works independently. He likes to work with others, but generally gets them off task with his disruptive behavior. When questioned about mathematics problems he can explain some but not all of his answers.

Written work is often difficult for Chase to follow and the text, workbooks, and work charts confuse him. He has a number of strengths including the formatting for division, multiplication, subtracting, addition, and regrouping. He knows how to work with fractions, but makes many errors in solving them. He is aware that a fraction represents part of a whole, but lacks fraction number sense because he is not able to represent the quantity as a connection to models. Chase also does not understand rational number interpretations, nor does he connect the drawings to the correct fractions notation. He counts the shaded part in relation to the unshaded rather than to the whole number unit.

Scenario 3

Student: Chloe Melisaah

Age: 7

Grade: 2

Chloe is very shy and timid. She does not like to be called on in class and generally does not like to raise her hand to participate in activities. She works better in smaller groups than larger ones. Her mathematics skills are at grade level, but her reading and vocabulary skills are above grade level. She enjoys reading, spending time by herself, and talking with the teacher as long as others are not around. She is inquisitive about mathematics, but does not like to take the initiative when working with peers. She is a fairly competent student.

Chloe seems to understand addition and the meaning for the operation and basic number sense. She is able to explain the appropriate addition steps for completing each problem, but she is having difficulty with subtraction. She seems to always subtract the smaller value from the larger value, regardless of whether the smaller value is the minuend or the subtrahend. She seems to have a good grasp on some subtraction facts, but is not recognizing the need to regroup.

As educators, we should constantly evaluate our own teaching practices and lessons for effectiveness. As we have indicated, taking the pulse of our own teaching practices allows us to reflect on the learning processes taking place within our classrooms, and provides us with opportunities to make changes as students' needs indicate. Below are considerations for you to keep in mind as you prepare for Tier 1 instruction in your classroom.

Tier 1 Considerations

1. How will the core instruction be delivered using evidence-based practices? How will this be verified?

2. What assessment tools or processes will be used to identify instructional needs and the students' responses to instruction/intervention?

3. Is the core instruction effective?

    a. What percent of students are achieving standards/benchmarks (approximately 80 percent or more)?

    b. What percent of students in subgroups are achieving standards/benchmarks (approximately 80 percent or more)? What percent of students in the subgroup to which the referred student belongs achieved benchmarks?

    c. If core instruction is not effective:

    • Is the curriculum appropriately matched to the needs of the students?

    • Is support provided for implementation fidelity?

    • How effectively has the school-based leadership team engaged in Tier 1 level problem solving in order to increase the effectiveness of core instruction?

4. How are parents and students informed, involved, or engaged in supporting and monitoring effective core instruction? Provide documentation.

When thinking about classroom concerns, we want you to think about what *you* are noticing in your classroom that is drawing your attention. The questioning of and reflection on what we are doing in our classrooms offers invaluable insight for further evaluation of our own teaching practices so that we may better prepare and equip our students mathematically. You may notice that student learning is not occurring as intended or planned. Can you reach them through differentiation or scaffolding their instruction? What changes can or should you make? Your expectations for your students' learning should be related to the grade-level curriculum standards and where they stand mathematically. As we evaluate the rate of learning over time, we learn to focus our instructional practices to be more student centered and effective. (Completing the Classroom Problem Identification Plan, Reproducible #10 in Appendix A, may assist you in this process.)

In the next chapter, we will provide information on how to intensify instruction for Tier 2 supports within the RTI in mathematics framework. We will offer tips for organizing instruction with grouping and scheduling, problem solving, and monitoring student progress for instructional decision making. We will also offer considerations and discussions of curriculum focus and alignment, in conjunction with supports, accommodations, and scaffolding to meet individual student needs in mathematics. We will offer discussions between Tiers 1 and 2 interventions and provide case studies and highlight the important aspects for implementation of RTI within classrooms and schools.

TEACHERS' CORNER
Keys to Getting You Started with RTI

- Review the Tier 1 considerations on page 78. These are important questions to answer as you prepare for RTI and Tier 1 instruction.
- Administer and review your universal screening data to establish criteria and goal setting. Set clear expectations as well as the target goal and the criteria for reaching it with your students within Tier 1 instruction.
- Gather evidence of student learning and use teacher anecdotal records, observations, diagnostic assessments, and so forth.
- Complete the Classroom Problem Identification Form (Reproducible #10 in Appendix A) to identify problems areas with students.
- Complete the Worksheet for Evaluating Explicit Instruction and Systematic Curriculum (Reproducible #11 in Appendix A) to evaluate explicit instruction and systematic curriculum for effectiveness in your classroom and school.
- Complete Professional Learning Community Chapter 4 activities.

Chapter 5

Interventions within Tier 2

"Both common sense and research support the concept of fidelity of implementation to ensure an intervention's successful outcome."

—*Gresham, Reschley, & Shinn, 2011*

What You Will Find in This Chapter

- Using data for the selection of interventions for students
- Standard protocol and problem solving
- Grouping, scheduling, and organizing instruction within the RTI framework
- Monitoring student progress for instructional decision making in the classroom

Teacher's Voice

We started RTI in mathematics in the fall of this year. While I was hesitant at first, I am so glad I got onboard! We have been having grade-level meetings, RTI team meetings, and school-wide faculty meetings. This week at our RTI team meeting, we discussed a group of five students that had much difficulty with the mathematics content I presented in my classroom, particularly with multiplication. I have realized that some students do not understand what I present and some seem to have more emotional, social, and academic skill needs than ever before. Discussions with my colleagues have offered great help and support. I have learned so much just from our talks about activities, strategies, and interventions that could work. The discussions also help me see that I am not alone in this process. I have definitely learned that we must work together as a team in order for RTI to be successful and we must plan, plan, and plan! For example, I talked to colleagues about some of the planned strategies and activities that I have been using and showed them the progress-monitoring results. I am concerned that my five "identified" students have not progressed as quickly as my other students and feel they need additional support. After viewing my progress-monitoring reports on each one, we decided that an intervention plan was certainly in order and a plan of action was developed for the group. I will continue teaching them during their regular math instructional time and the mathematics instructional coach will start taking them three days a week for fifteen to thirty minutes of *additional* instructional time. I am anxious to see how all this works out and how it will affect the overall learning in my classroom. We all agreed we want to make the most of every minute and design a range of approaches to help the students be successful with their mathematical learning. And not just with my students, but with all the students in our school. It is really great to see how we are all trying to make a difference through our involvement with teamwork, planning interventions, and supports.

Ms. Holly, fourth-grade teacher

An Overview of Tier 2

"You can't have a plan that works unless you plan your work, and work your plan." How fitting is this quote as we think of Tier 2 instruction and how it works for our students? We see the planning that is taking place within Ms. Holly's classroom and understand its importance, particularly through discussion with the RTI team. We must be committed to ensure that all students *will* learn mathematics. Therefore, we must plan our instruction, plan our interventions, and plan for assessment. We must do whatever is needed to ensure that our students are met with confidence from teachers who *can* and *will* deliver planned effective instruction, as well as provide as many opportunities and planned supports as needed by students in order for mathematical understanding to occur. It is a warranted plan of action, even if it means we must intervene with students in Tier 2 to help them become better equipped mathematically. As we identify the students that are falling below district benchmarks and need extra support, we initiate the problem-solving process within Tier 2. We begin gathering all relevant pieces of formative and classroom data so we may reference them during our RTI team (problem-solving) meetings. The RTI team works through the problem-solving process and determines whether the student will receive intervention through Tier 2 to meet the district benchmarks as established.

As we work with students in Tier 2, we must complete a **gap analysis** for each student at least monthly to determine whether the determined goal is being met. A gap analysis determines the difference between the student's current level of performance and benchmark expectations. If the goal is being met, we should consider raising the goal and continuing the intervention, stopping the intervention and moving the student back into Tier 1, or scaffolding away the support as determined by the student's needs. It is very important for us to decide whether the student needs to continue in Tier 2 for prolonged periods of time. If the set goal is not being met, we must review the problem-solving process, change the interventions, increase the frequency of the interventions, increase the intensity of the interventions, or decide whether the student will benefit from moving to Tier 3 support.

Within Tier 2, we are responding to the instructional supports that students need through more collaboration with colleagues, extra time to do mathematical tasks, and targeted, supplemental interventions based on student progress-monitoring assessments. We provide further coaching and teaching to students who may need additional levels of service within mathematical areas that are aligned with the core curriculum. This additional support is beyond the modifications or accommodations within our instruction, and outside the blocked or scheduled math time. Tier 2 is provided in addition to Tier 1 instruction and is focused on specific mathematical skills and content. It is not "drill and kill," but rather enhancing the mathematical script to actively engage, excite, and motivate the students. Tier 2 is the combined efforts of many that will ensure the likelihood that our students will be mathematically successful in the general education setting.

Using Data to Select Interventions for Students

We never want to waste our time, nor do we want to waste students' time with instructional strategies that are not working. Further, students do not want to be involved in a lesson that introduces material about which they have much knowledge or have already mastered. This becomes very important as we look at how we can use data to select instruction/interventions based on the results from the progress monitoring of our students. We want our data collection to reveal valuable information to help us determine what we need to do next in order to help our students learn the mathematics material. The assessment data in Tier 2 become more frequent and help us reflect and monitor students. It is through data collection that we are able to match students to appropriate targeted supports. The key to success is to define the problem, generate a functional hypothesis as to why the problem is occurring, and access a standard supplemental program or customize a targeted intervention that is linked to the hypothesis. Several factors are discussed and included in the Tier 2 framework (see Figure 5.1). Let's revisit Ms. Holly's classroom to see how these factors may come into play within RTI implementation and how they can work in your classroom.

In the last RTI team meeting, Ms. Holly described to colleagues how she monitored her planning and instruction; used the OPTIONS lesson plan

FIGURE 5.1 Tier 2 Framework

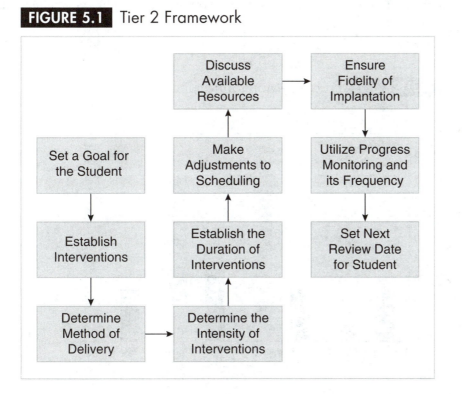

(see Chapter 4); maintained observational notes; used CBM analysis to identify strengths, mastery, and error patterns; and graphed student results from administered progress monitoring. After six weeks of Tier 1 instruction, the data revealed that even though nineteen students were progressing as expected with the grade-level benchmarks, five students identified for Tier 1 instructional supports were not progressing as expected (see Figure 5.2).

In response to the data, the RTI team decided that Heather (along with four other students who were experiencing some of the same mathematical difficulties) would benefit from additional supports within Tier 2 instruction. Through team discussions, goals and interventions were established, the methods of delivery were determined, and adjustments were made to daily scheduling to accommodate additional instruction. The delivery of Tier 2 instruction would be provided by the mathematics instructional coach *in addition to* the general classroom instruction provided by Ms. Holly. Available resources were discussed and organized. Progress monitoring would continue so students' mathematical strengths and weaknesses could be identified.

The mathematics instructional coach provided Heather and others with **explicit and systematic instruction**, with more opportunities to respond and verbalize their thought processes and to view models of proficient problem solving. They were engaged in "doing" mathematics through hands-on experiences that related to real-life situations, and multiple representations were incorporated to increase their interest in mathematics. As they worked on their problems, students were asked to explain their thinking and justify their work through verbal think-alouds. Journaling and writing activities were used to help them gauge their misunderstandings, misconceptions, and gaps in understanding the mathematical content that was presented to them. Opportunities for students to think about the material presented were extended and both Ms. Holly (Tier 1) and the mathematics instructional coach (Tier 2) communicated positive expectations and involved all students in goal setting. They also used progress charts to monitor individual student progress (see Figure 5.3). Group results were also graphed weekly in order to view progress and gaps in mathematical learning (see Figure 5.4).

The mathematics instructional coach prepared the OPTIONS lesson plan section for Tier 2. She used warm-up activities, pretaught the mathematical

FIGURE 5.2 Progress-Monitoring Chart

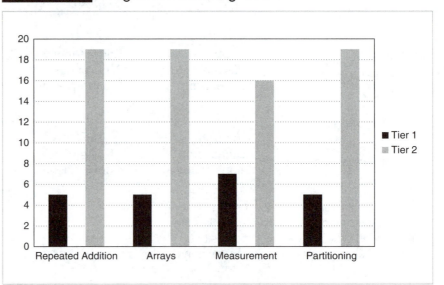

vocabulary, and provided opportunities to review content that the students had not previously mastered. She presented content using modeling and representations, guided practice, and independent practice, and she offered feedback (i.e., direct and explicit instruction) to help make connections among the mathematical ideas. She scaffolded approaches using graphic organizers, and used manipulatives (two-colored counters, base-10 blocks, beans, and ten frames) during instruction (see Teachers Resources-Manipulatives to Concepts-Concepts to Manipulatives for manipulative ideas and Intervention Strategies). She made an effort to identify students' mathematical insights, misconceptions, and error patterns as she probed students through conferencing and interviews, and she used self-assessment questioning to gauge understanding. More time was spent on difficult tasks, fewer transitions took place, and mastery of content was determined before moving on to other mathematical tasks. Brief assessments (five problems) provided continuous progress monitoring of student learning, with the results graphed for individual students. Corrective feedback of student accuracy was offered immediately. The OPTIONS lesson plan in Figure 5.5 illustrates a sample plan for the five students needing additional supports through Tier 2.

FIGURE 5.3 Sample of Individual Student Progress Chart

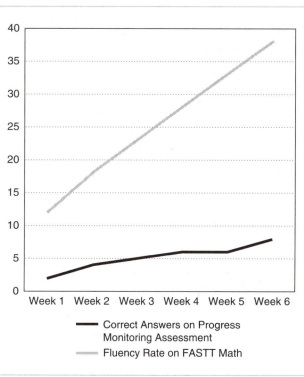

—— Correct Answers on Progress Monitoring Assessment
········ Fluency Rate on FASTT Math

All students, particular Heather, responded well when verbally praised for their efforts and each student was eager to become engaged in the problems and work through them to their completion. This proved to be a powerful

FIGURE 5.4 Sample of Group Monitoring Chart

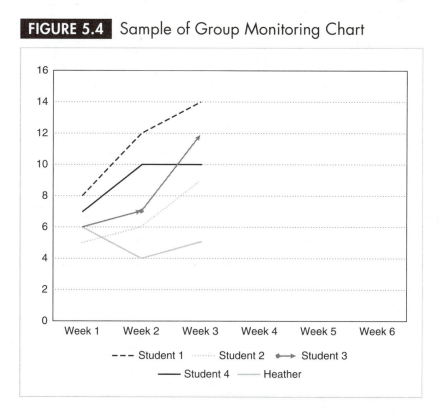

- - - Student 1   ········ Student 2   →→ Student 3
—— Student 4   —— Heather

FIGURE 5.5 Plan for Five Students

OPTIONS Lesson Plan

OUTCOME (Standard in mathematics):

PROGRESS-MONITORING DATA:

TIER 2/TIER 3 Objective:

Length of Time (days):

INSTRUCTIONAL PERSONNEL (circle all that apply):

MT: Math teacher

IC: Instructional coach

SP: School psychologist

IRT: Instructional resource teacher

CT: Co-teacher

INTERVENTIONS	ONGOING PROGRESS MONITORING (OPM)
Record intervention, method to intensify, other professionals, and other classroom/student considerations used.	Record OPM assessment, results, and dates. Be sure to attach charts and graph results.

Tier 2 Mathematics		
Students' names: Heather H. Ronnie H. Amelio C. Roderick K. Tawana M.	■ Utilize warm-up activities and preteach the mathematics vocabulary. ■ Review content not previously mastered by each student. ■ Use modeling, guided practice, independent practice, and offer immediate feedback. ■ Use sets of objects to practice the facts and relate to real world. Review daily abstract term; illustrate through graphs, drawings, charts, tables, models, and representations. ■ Question to check for understanding. ■ Use a peer tutor, then allow the student to be the peer tutor (learn and teach). ■ Chunk the information provided by mini-lessons on skill deficits while building and scaffolding learning on prior knowledge. ■ Use two-colored counters, base-10 blocks, beans, and ten frames.	Daily assessment and explicit feedback will be given to each student CBM will occur biweekly Student interviews/conferencing Observation and recording of student behavior Conceptual mapping and organizers Ongoing analysis of error patterns

Tier 3
Mathematics
Students' names:

NEEDS OF INDIVIDUAL STUDENTS

Remember to record all interventions, data from progress monitoring, and so forth for each individual student for possible referral.

INSTRUCTOR NOTES:_____

Summarize

Date to review instruction/intervention, and assessment data:_____

Team meeting members: _____   Location:_____

motivational tool to keep each student engaged in the word problems, particularly those that were difficult ones for them to understand. As determined in the initial action plan, the mathematics instructional coach and Ms. Holly met with the RTI team after one month to discuss student progress, analyze data, and determine necessary revisions to the RTI action plan. As seen from progress-monitoring data in Figure 5.6, Tier 2 instruction/interventions had a positive and significant impact on most of the students' mastery of the identified goals in mathematics.

Assessments Should:

- Match what students have been studying;
- Focus on important content rather than trivia;
- Yield useful information, not just scores;
- Use clear and helpful criteria; and
- Provide a complete picture of students' learning and abilities. (NCTM, 2000)

When students have reached the benchmark goal for Tier 2 they should be placed back into Tier 1 instruction. Remember the goal is to provide *temporary* Tier 2 supports. As you review the data you can see that Heather is not reaching the goal as set by the RTI team. She is still unable to master the concept or procedures of multiplication as evidenced by the graphed progress results (**goal and trend lines**). Heather's progress is shown in the individual student progress graph produced by the mathematics instruction as per the CBM administered (see Figure 5.7). The graph is broken down to show Heather's individual results compared to the goal line (**aimline** or target) and the trend line (rate of improvement) for students.

After six weeks of general classroom instruction by Ms. Holly and additional supports through Tier 2 instruction with the mathematics instructional coach, Heather's trend line becomes clearer and lack of progress is identified through the graphed results. We can determine from the data that even though intensive supports were offered through Tier 2 interventions, adequate progress has not been sufficiently made and the mathematical gap compared to others in her grade level is not closing. A change in instruction and supports may be needed in order for Heather to be mathematically successful.

FIGURE 5.6 Number of Multiplication Problems Soved Correctly

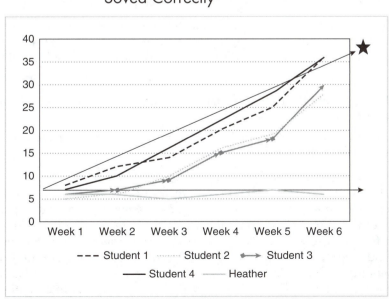

FIGURE 5.7   Heather's Graphed CBM Results

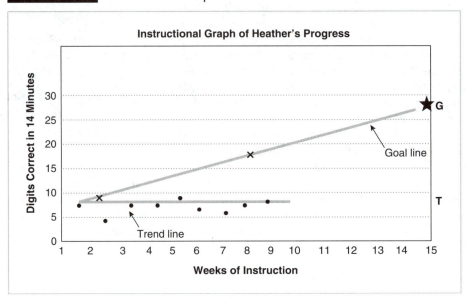

We must ask ourselves a few questions as we consider the existing data and determine whether additional data are needed to make a determination for further intensity of support:

1. What further modifications do we need to consider in order for Heather to be mathematically successful?

2. Will she benefit from an adjustment to group size?

3. Does she need more intervention time or a change in frequency of the intervention?

4. What other variables should be considered?

5. What do the progress-monitoring data, diagnostic/formative data, daily lesson data, curriculum assessments, and teacher-observation data during intervention and core instruction show?

6. What teacher and/or parent input has taken place?

As we think of the answers to these questions, we must consider other options if our students are not showing progress within a particular tier. If a change is needed, more questions should follow and be discussed by the RTI team:

1. Does the student need a different, more appropriately matched intervention?

2. Can we modify the current instruction/intervention to better accommodate the student?

3. If no, will the student benefit from a more intensive intervention with the same instructional focus (Tier 3)?

Gathering assessment data from many sources can help build a complete picture of student learning and abilities and measure progress related to the impact of classroom instruction. Using only one form of assessment can provide a misleading snapshot of individual ability on only one day, whereas gathering evidence from many different sources over a longer period of time yields a broader and deeper understanding of students' knowledge and learning. It is through multiple forms of assessment that we are able to better select interventions for students based on the data. How do we know what to change and select in regard to interventions when students are not making adequate progress? We follow the data!

A TIME TO REFLECT

Why is it important to determine error patterns within your students' mathematical work? How does this information help in determining what Tier 2 interventions and effective instruction will be needed? Describe what it means to "gather data" to help us discover students mathematics strengths/weaknesses and misconceptions.

Intensifying and Implementing Interventions: Standard Protocol and Problem Solving

If a student is not performing as expected, we will change what we are doing and continue problem solving until we find what works. This becomes very important as we intensify and implement interventions in mathematics for our struggling students. Tier 2 interventions serve as **standard intervention protocols** for students who require extended learning opportunities or for those who are not making adequate progress and need additional interventions. The goal for students receiving Tier 2 interventions is to determine their areas of need, with the intention of providing supplementary instruction and supports along with more intensive progress monitoring in order to increase the rate of learning. Standard protocols provide interventions that are chosen to address the most common student weaknesses within the school. Interventions are made readily available to students as soon as their mathematical needs are identified and are provided in small groups by a teacher or interventionist who has been thoroughly trained within the specific program or strategy. As you consider a standard protocol model for your school, you should begin by examining student data to determine the most significant areas of mathematical weakness as identified by universal screening. For example, data may reveal that in your school first graders have the most significant mathematical difficulties with number sense, while data for seventh graders reveal difficulties with multiplication and division of fractions and decimals. Once this is determined, you may choose one or two research-based interventions that specifically target those identified areas. The student would then be assigned to a group that matches that protocol. (For more information on interventions for standard protocol visit the websites listed in the Teacher's Corner at the end of this chapter.)

Because the steps of the intervention are well defined, the evaluation of the integrity of the implementation is straightforward as established through a checklist of the critical steps for intervention implementation (see Figure 5.8). A blank reproducible intervention form is provided in Appendix A (see Reproducible #12).

As we follow each step of the defined protocol we are ensuring that the intervention is delivered as it is designed. Some schools choose to do this during specific blocked times throughout the school day, five days per week (see Figures 6.8 and 6.9). Others choose to have blocked times less than five days per week or on alternate days. It is your school's choice, but it is very important to let the data be your guide.

Advantages of Standard Protocol

1. The intervention can be carried out with strong fidelity when proper training is provided by interventionists.

2. Once students are identified with mathematical deficits, they can receive immediate access to targeted interventions.

3. Students may receive this additional instruction as long as is necessary to erase the deficit or until it is decided that the student may need more intensive instruction through Tier 3. (Fuchs & Fuchs, 2005)

FIGURE 5.8 Intervention Implementation Form for Standard Protocol

Heather's Intervention Form A

Ms. Holly, Fourth-Grade Mathematics

Classroom Interventions and/or Standard Protocol Interventions

Tier 1

Primary Area of Concern	Classroom Intervention	Duration Start Date End Date	Intensity (Group Size/ Session Length)	Frequency (Number of Sessions/Week)	Student's Response to Intervention
■ Mastery of multiplication facts for fours, sixes, sevens, eights, nines ■ Mastery of multiplying one- and two-digit numbers ■ Regrouping when multiplying digits in tens column	■ Use of concrete manipulatives ■ Problem modeling and demonstrations ■ Peer tutoring and cooperative grouping ■ Word problems ■ Guided practice ■ Independent practice ■ Role playing and modeling	Sept. 25–Oct. 31	■ Whole group (twenty-six students): five to fifteen minutes of teacher-led instruction ■ Small group (two to four students): thirty to forty minutes	Daily instruction, forty-five minutes to one hour	■ Has high interest and attention in whole/small groups. ■ Responds well with teacher-directed instruction. Weakness with independent learning. ■ Progress monitoring indicates mathematical skill weaknesses. ■ Recommended for Tier 2.

Tier 2

Primary Area of Concern	Strategic Intervention	Duration Start Date End Date	Intensity (Group Size/ Session Length)	Frequency (Number of Sessions/Week)	Student's Response to Intervention
■ Multiplication facts ■ Fails to record regrouped digit to tens column when multiplying numbers from ones column. ■ Adds numbers presented instead of multiplying. ■ Place-value concerns—using 0 as place-value holder when multiplying.	■ Concrete manipulatives ■ Small groups (two to four students) ■ More time on task ■ Games to build fluency ■ Guided practice ■ Independent practice ■ Word problem demonstrations ■ Review expectations ■ Intensive fluency with multiplying ■ Scaffolding approaches ■ Graphic organizers ■ Immediate feedback	Nov. 1–Dec. 15 (Daily assessments given each week for review)	Two to four students	Fifteen to twenty minutes, three to four times per week	■ Responds well with groups and teacher-led instruction. ■ No recognition of using 0 as place-value holder. ■ Little mastery of multiplication facts. ■ No evidence of adding with regrouping in answer for multiplication process. ■ Responds well to verbal praise ■ Becomes engaged in the problem-solving process ■ Has not progressed with mastery of concepts or procedures of multiplication

Students need a deep, rich understanding of the mathematics they learn in school (NCTM, 2000). It is not enough that they can add and subtract whole numbers or fractional pieces, determine the area or perimeter of a rectangle, or even memorize their facts and procedural steps. Teaching them to *understand* is the goal. As we look at problem solving within the RTI in mathematics framework, we see an alternative to assessments and diagnostic categories to help identify students who need additional instruction and support. The **problem-solving model** is a systematic approach we can use to review our students' strengths and weaknesses, identify the evidenced-based instructional interventions to employ, frequently collect student progress-monitoring data, and evaluate the effectiveness of the interventions we have provided. This

Benefits of Problem-Solving Models

- Scientifically proven instructional methods
- Early identification and remediation of achievement difficulties
- More functional and frequent measurement of student progress
- A reduction in inappropriate and disproportionate special education placements of students from diverse cultural and linguistic backgrounds
- A reallocation of instructional and behavior support personnel to better meet the needs of all students. (Gresham, 2002)

model is designed to assist us in first solving our students' difficulties within the general education classroom (Tier 1). If students' difficulties are not met through this design, then the cycle of selecting intervention strategies and collecting data is repeated with the help of the building-level or grade-level intervention (Tier 2) or through the problem-solving team (Marston, 2002). This approach relies on the students' response to general education rather than test scores (e.g., math test or IQ test). The three-tiered problem-solving model relies on screening and assessment that is focused on student skills rather than classification; measuring response to instruction rather than relying on norm-referenced comparison; using evidence-based strategies within general education classrooms; and developing a collaborative partnership among general and special educators for consultation and team decision making (Marston, 2002). Problem solving provides a vehicle to facilitate communication across disciplines to resolve student difficulties in the classroom.

Within Tier 2, teams analyze data from universal screening and progress monitoring to identify groups of students who have similar mathematics instructional needs. As identified, we intervene and plan for these groups, often during supplemental instructional periods. Students are then matched with carefully selected interventions (standard protocols) that are research based (i.e., highly likely to produce student gains) and used with small groups in a highly scripted approach. This is done so interventionists can approximate the conditions that produce gains needed by our students (Fuchs & Fuchs, 2005).

RTI Problem-Solving Process

Plan

1. Identify the problem.
- Screen students (universal screenings and classroom data)
- Identify at-risk students
- Describe problems

2. Analyze the student data.
- Identify specific skill deficiencies
- Brainstorm possible areas of focus

Do

3. **Develop an action plan.**
   - Develop a student intervention plan
   - Match data to student needs
   - Identify who is responsible for implementing intervention
   - Decide the frequency, length, and group size of the intervention
   - Identify resources and materials needed for intervention
   - Identify the progress-monitoring tool
   - Determine goal for progress before intervention begins
   - Provide training if necessary

Check

4. **Implement the plan.**
   - Execute the intervention
   - Provide support through differentiation
   - Monitor progress of intervention
   - Maintain data and documentation

Act

5. **Evaluate effectiveness of the plan.**
   - Review data to determine the effectiveness of intervention
   - Revise or adjust the plan as needed

Source: Adapted in part from Florida Reading First Program

The purpose of the problem-solving process is to assist us in designing and selecting strategies for improving our students' academic and/or behavioral performance with a high probability of success by providing a structure for addressing the concerns we have identified. A problem-solving process requires full collaboration among a team of professionals along with parents to identify a specific, measurable outcome and to design research-based interventions to address the concerns. The process includes ensuring that interventions are implemented with fidelity according to their research base and that progress is monitored to determine the student's response. Our goal is to help you put into place a decision-making process that will lead to the development of instructional and intervention strategies with a high probability of success for your students. Any RTI system that is implemented must integrate the use of data to guide the development of effective interventions and to provide frequent monitoring of progress.

A TIME TO REFLECT

What curriculum decision rules are followed for Tier 2 (lesson checklists, mastery tests, etc.)? Does your school offer high pacing (high rate of student opportunities to respond) through Tier 2 instruction/intervention? Are students aware of expectations and are they explicitly taught for Tier 2? Explain how this is done.

Organizing for Instruction: Grouping and Scheduling

Developing a plan and organizing for instruction is critical to RTI's success because it is a blueprint for immediate, intensive intervention within the classroom. It is helpful to outline actions by answering the what, how, who, and when questions. We must take time to consider different protocols and instructional approaches through instructional organization and the grouping and scheduling of implementing those approaches. Collaboration with colleagues who have diverse expertise and knowledge enhances the specific action plan you have or will create. Creating an instructional or intervention plan begins with an implementation schedule. The implementation schedule lists the tasks to be completed, the beginning and ending dates for each task, and the necessary resources. (See Reproducibles #13 and #14 in Appendix A for blank Implementation Schedule and Observation Recording Table.)

As we organize our grouping and scheduling, there are several questions we must first ask ourselves.

- How much time do students spend practicing what is being taught?
- How much time is *needed* for skill practice?
- How much direct instruction is used in a class period?
- What grouping practices are currently in place?
- Is progress monitored continuously—weekly, biweekly, monthly, semiannually, annually?
- Is instruction for groups clear and focused? When/how is it defined?
- Do high expectations pertain to all groups of students? When should expectations be met?

Organizing for tiered instruction should be a collaborative effort with colleagues. Should tier time be scheduled in a block format for all students? Must we set aside time for Tier 2 in each school day? Do we need Tier 2 for three to five days per week? Scheduling considerations must be attended to early in the RTI process so other decisions will not be compromised. Remember that Tier 2 instruction is *in addition* to students' regular mathematics instructional time and should be scheduled outside that time frame.

We address this further in Chapter 6 as we discuss the collaboration and scheduling for all three tiers. However, let us describe how this can work as we illustrate a standard protocol model for grouping and scheduling tier time used by Crimson Elementary School. During tier time, all students were placed into an intervention group based on their data from universal screening. This included those students whose data indicated they were already at or above benchmark. All teaching staff for a grade, as well as assigned specialists, were devoted to delivering the specified instructional program for each group. For example, from 9:30 to 10:30 on Monday, first grade (consisting of 100 students) had its tier time. In this particular school, there were four general education first-grade classrooms. The school also had two mathematics coaches, two special education teachers, and two individuals hired as interventionists. Following universal screening, the grade had identified a total of fifty-five students who were at or above benchmark (Tier 1), a group of thirty students who were below benchmark but above the at-risk level (Tier 2), and fifteen students who were already high risk (Tier 3). During tier time on Monday, three benchmark groups of twenty students each were formed and assigned to three of the four general education teachers. During the thirty-minute tier time, these teachers delivered instructional enrichment to the students, providing instruction that was well aligned to the general education curriculum but with added opportunities to enhance the existing program. The thirty students assigned to Tier 2 were divided into five groups of six: one group (led by the general education teacher) focused on a standard protocol for teaching number families, two groups (led by the mathematics coaches) emphasized fluency in number facts, and two groups (led by the interventionists) reinforced number sense. The remaining fifteen students at Tier 3 (led by the special education teacher) were divided into four groups of three to five students and focused on basic development of mathematics number skills. Because all staff are deployed at the same time, there is a well-defined focus for the tier time, which shifts across the day to different grades and different standard protocols. This problem-solving model for block tier time scheduling requires personnel resource allocation. Because interventions are more individualized, there are generally more interventions needed with smaller groups; therefore, more seriously challenged schools will require more personnel.

The problem-solving model is common for emphasis of tiered instruction to be placed primarily on those students not at benchmark (Marston, 2002). When districts or buildings are getting started with RTI efforts, attention in the first year is often directed to the assessment systems, discussions about core and intervention approaches, and how personnel can and will be utilized. It is very important that scheduling to be at the top of the list of actions requiring early attention and careful construction. Usually this time is considered nonnegotiable because it is time scheduled for core instruction as well as tiered interventions. Time should be allocated for both core and supplemental instruction for students who demonstrate the need for mathematics intervention time beyond the core instruction. When scheduling is not attended to, the other decisions that will be made become compromised if full implementation is not a set goal.

Monitoring Student Progress for Instructional Decision Making

We set the stage for the decision making in our classrooms. We also set ambitious goals for students, perform assessments (biweekly, weekly, monthly, annually, etc.), graph student data, and use this data for our instructional decision making. How we do it, when we do it, and why we do it is the key to RTI success. The progress monitoring of our students moves us toward the decision-making process within the RTI in mathematics framework. As we work with the decision-making process we must consider several factors when applying the goals we have set forth. These include the age of our students, the frequency of our monitoring, the focus and frequency of the interventions we will provide, the gaps in our students' achievement, and the monitoring of trend data. As we regularly review the data based on our students' needs, we analyze the trends or trajectory we have set into place and make instructional decisions for them. To see this in action, we want to take you back to Ms. Holly's classroom to see the monitoring of student progress for the instructional decision-making process as it relates to Heather.

The mathematics instructional coach has now shared the CBM probe shown in Figure 5.9 with the RTI team. As indicated from the CBM, Heather's lack of knowledge remains with place value in multiplication. Although she does show mastery of multiplication of the easier facts, she does not exhibit evidence of adding with regrouping within the answer once she completes the multiplication process. Thus, her answers are incorrect on each of the problems presented. Further, she does not demonstrate knowledge of the place-value holder in the ones column as required when multiplying two-digit numbers by two-digit numbers. Students commonly misunderstand place value. Errors are evident in Heather's work, which seems to indicate that perhaps place value could have been learned in isolation from previous knowledge and with little meaning (Baroody, 1990). Heather does not seem to make the connection that zero will hold the place value because she has ignored zero as the placeholder in each of the problems.

Because the goal set for Heather (see Figure 5.5) was not obtained after intensive Tier 2 interventions and supports, we now expand the instructional decision-making process to determine what course of action to take in order for her to be mathematically successful. The RTI team continued the problem-solving questioning with Ms. Holly and the mathematics instructional coach to determine a new

FIGURE 5.9 Heather's CBM

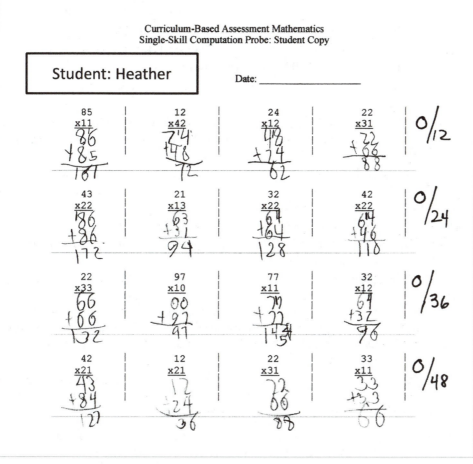

goal for Heather. It is through this discussion and decision-making process that the RTI team decided further intensive instruction and support was warranted and Tier 3 services were recommended.

Throughout this chapter and previous ones, we have described the RTI framework, Tiers 1 and 2, how to use data to select interventions for students to intensify and implement standard protocol and problem solving, and the monitoring of student progress for instructional decision making. We have provided examples of supports through lesson planning and collaboration with colleagues. Putting all of these pieces together in order to improve our students' mathematical outcomes requires a team effort. The goal for our students in RTI is to close the mathematics gap. If the gap is not being closed quickly enough, then more questions should follow as we consider more intensive interventions. It is important that we look at Tier 2 as an enhancement to our curricular goals. As we do so, we want to consider the following:

Tier 2 Considerations

1. What specific supplemental instruction will be implemented to improve the performance of at-risk students (more exposure, more practice, more focus, smaller group, type of delivery, program, etc.)?

2. How will the supplemental instruction/intervention be delivered?

   a. Academic engaged time: How much more time is needed?

   b. Curriculum: What will the students need?

    c. Personnel: Who, when, and where is it provided? How will support be provided to ensure fidelity of implementation?

    d. Parents: How will the student's parents be informed, involved, or engaged in supporting the instruction/interventions?

3. How effective is the supplemental instruction for groups of at-risk students?

    a. What assessments will be used for ongoing data collection?

    b. How frequently will assessments be conducted and analyzed by the teacher or team?

    c. How will the student's parents be informed, involved, or engaged in the progress monitoring and analysis of the student's level of performance and rate of progress?

    d. How will we determine whether the instruction/interventions are effective? What is our decision rule to determine that this student will require more intensive, individualized intervention?

4. Additional considerations: Has the student not made adequate progress after a reasonable period of time when provided appropriate instruction and intensive, individualized interventions?

    a. If not, obtain parental consent to conduct an evaluation of the evidence to determine whether the student has a disability and needs specially designed instruction and related services through IDEA and continue the problem-solving process in an ongoing effort to determine the student's instructional needs, thereby improving the student's rate of progress and level of performance.

    b. If the student has made adequate progress and can sustain that progress with decreasing levels of supports (Tier 2 or Tier 1), continue to monitor progress and adjust instruction/intervention levels as needed.

These considerations must be the center of our focus because they are used to better equip us in determining the scientifically based interventions we should use and which ones will be directly linked to the student's area of concern.

As you consider all the information from this book on RTI, we want to offer you an opportunity to put your new knowledge into practice. Included at the end of this chapter are four scenarios from different grade levels with samples of students' mathematics analyses with specific mathematics error patterns as identified by their teacher in Tier 1 instruction. They have been brought before the RTI team and are being considered for Tier 2 instruction. We have also included an RTI in algebra class case study. The case studies provided in this chapter have been included to help serve as a guide to help you with RTI implementation. We would like for you to develop a plan of action and select interventions based on the information and data given. (See Reproducibles #6 through #9 in Appendix A for OPTIONS Lesson Plan templates and Teacher Resources in Appendix A for interventions and ideas.)

As we enter the next chapter, we will focus on intensifying support within Tier 3. We will provide the specific classroom applications for Tier 3 implementation as it aligns with the curriculum focus, and as it works in conjunction with meeting our students' needs within the mathematics classroom.

Scenario 1

Student: Mae Montgomry

Age: 6

Grade: 1

Mae is a talker! She has difficulty staying on task and fails to listen to directions when presented by the teacher. Her work in most subjects is very neat and orderly, but not in math. She seems confused when trying to identify shapes. She does not have a good foundation with number sense, moving from the initial development of basic counting techniques to more sophisticated understandings of sizes of numbers, or number relationships, operations, place value, and patterns. She has difficulty recognizing "how many" in sets of objects. She does not connect number words to numerals or to the quantity they represent.

Universal screening indicates she scores in the thirtieth percentile in most mathematics skills and computations as compared to others within the classroom.

Tier 1 CBMs indicate many mathematical errors in scoring. Below is a sample of Mae's work.

$$\boxed{1} + \boxed{3} = \boxed{13} \qquad 6 + 7 + 2 = 9 \qquad 12 - 3 = 1 \qquad 2, \underline{4}, 6, \underline{7}, 10, 12, \underline{13}, 16$$

- Can you determine Mae's error patterns and mathematics misconceptions? (Record your analysis.)
- What is Mae doing correctly?
- What Tier 2 resources and supports should be implemented to help Mae?
- What interventions will you select for Mae based on the data and error pattern analysis?
- What concrete manipulatives and multiple representations can be included in the lesson?
- What probes will you use for key mathematical understanding?

Scenario 2

Student: Ronnie Frank

Age: 7

Grade: 2

Teacher observations show Ronnie has difficulty remembering and following instructions and staying on task. He is slow to complete mathematical tasks and needs prodding by the teacher. His class work is usually taken home for homework. Diagnostic assessment shows his scores average at 60 percent correct and indicates he experiences difficulty remembering his number facts, mixes up the meanings for the operations, has difficulty learning the algorithms for adding and subtracting, and does not estimate well. He struggles with most grade-level mathematics vocabulary words and has trouble moving from the concrete to the abstract.

Universal screening indicates he falls just below the forty-fifth percentile and is below average as compared to others within the classroom.

Tier 1 CBMs indicate many mathematical errors in scoring. Below is a sample of Ronnie's work.

$$
\begin{array}{cccc}
1. \quad 79 & 2. \quad 42 & 3. \quad 69 & 4. \quad 58 \\
\underline{-\ 4} & \underline{+\ 25} & \underline{-\ 14} & \underline{-\ 6} \\
35 & 04 & 25 & 12
\end{array}
$$

- Can you determine Ronnie's error patterns and mathematics misconceptions? (Record your analysis.)
- What is Ronnie doing correctly?
- What Tier 2 resources and supports should be implemented to help Ronnie?
- What interventions will you select for Ronnie based on the data and error pattern analysis?
- What concrete manipulatives and multiple representations can be included?
- What probes will you use for key mathematical understanding?

Scenario 3

Student: Kevin Courts

Age: 11

Grade: 5

Kevin is fluent with whole number computation, number sense, addition and subtraction, and multiplication and division. However, he is experiencing much difficulty remembering the algorithms associated with multiplication and division of fractions. His frustration prevents him from staying on task and he refuses to work. He looks for ways to exit math class as soon as it starts and his mathematics anxiety level seems to be increasing as the mathematics material becomes more difficult for him.

He likes to read books above his ability level and prefers to read instead of doing mathematics. Diagnostic assessment show his scores average at 90 percent correct on most skills, but fraction assessment results indicate scores of only 40 percent mastery. He expresses difficulty keeping the meanings of the two operations in mind along with their relationship to one another. His estimation skills appear low and his mathematics vocabulary is limited. (For example, he does not relate commutative property with multiplying fractions.)

Universal screening indicates he is at the seventy-fifth percentile, but is below average as compared to others within the classroom in regard to multiplication and division of fractions.

Tier 1 CBMs indicate many mathematical errors in scoring. Below is a sample of Kevin's work.

$$\frac{3}{4} \times 7 = \frac{12}{28} \qquad \frac{2}{3} \times \frac{4}{4} = \frac{12}{8}$$

- Can you determine Kevin's error patterns and mathematics misconceptions? (Record your analysis.)
- What is Kevin doing correctly?
- What Tier 2 resources and supports should be implemented to help Kevin?
- What interventions will you select for Kevin based on the data and error pattern analysis?
- What concrete manipulatives and multiple representations can be included in the lesson?
- What probes will you use for key mathematical understanding?

Scenario 4

Student: Tameka Bryan

Age: 12

Grade: 7

Teacher observations show Tameka has much success with most mathematics skills with the exception of geometry and measurement. She exhibits problems looking for patterns and over generalizes due to her limited experience and understanding in both areas. Tameka seems confused when trying to figure out area and perimeter, angles, altitude of angles, and ratios and proportions. She is fluent in completing most mathematical tasks, but is very slow to complete mathematical problems that involve the skills mentioned above. Her work is very neat and orderly, but she gets frustrated when she does not understand and seems to shut down when certain mathematical topics are discussed. She sometimes refuses to complete her assignments when her anxiety levels are high.

Universal screening indicates she scores in the eighty-fifth percentile in most mathematics skills and computations, but is well below average in geometry and measurement (thirtieth percentile) as compared to others in the classroom.

Tier 1 CBMs indicate many mathematical errors in scoring. Below is a sample of Tameka's work.

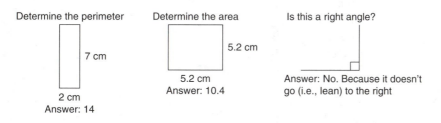

- Can you determine Tameka's error patterns and mathematics misconceptions? (Record your analysis.)
- What is Tameka doing correctly?
- What Tier 2 resources and supports should be implemented to help Tameka?
- What interventions will you select for Tameka based on the data and error pattern analysis?
- What concrete manipulatives and multiple representations can be included in the lesson?
- What probes will you use for key mathematical understanding?

RTI Algebra Case Study: Sixth Grade

Mr. Saban is in his third year of teaching sixth grade. He is part of a team of three other sixth-grade teachers at this school. The team also includes the school mathematics coach and curriculum resource teacher. They meet regularly to plan learning activities and are very knowledgeable regarding the RTI process. His class includes a mix of Hispanic (25 percent), African American (30 percent), and white (45 percent) students in a low socioeconomic section of the city. More than 30 percent of his students have performed below the fiftieth percentile according to universal screening in the area of algebra for the last three years. He also has two students identified as gifted within this class this year.

Mr. Saban's curriculum mapping tells him that the next learning objective he needs to address involves percent problems. He needs to identify the specific grade-level benchmark

MA.6.A.1.2 Solve percent problems, including problems involving discounts, simple interest, taxes, tips, and percent of increase or decrease. DOK: High. CRA levels: C, R, and A.

Once the benchmark has been identified, Mr. Saban plans for instruction. With keen awareness of his diverse population, he selects various strategies to implement instruction. He provides multiple opportunities for learning using various instructional methods. After two weeks of instruction, he reviews the assessment data from two formative assessments. Scores from the curriculum-based assessment are as follows:

Student	Week 1	Week 2	Mean
Ariel	4	8	
Cesar	9	12	
Cynthia	8	5	
Mary	1	1	
Emily	4	4	
Helan	6	7	
Ilene	2	3	
Jamarius	8	8	
Rhonda	2	0	
Leonel	5	6	
Martin	4	7	
Michelle	4	8	
Shelby	2	3	
Oscar	5	6	
Paul	1	3	
Raimi	9	12	
Sam	8	10	
Taylor	8	5	
Winter	12	16	

First, calculate the mean for each student. Next, identify the students who have a mean of 5 or less. These students will be monitored in primary prevention to determine their responsiveness to intervention.

Due to the scores on the formative assessments, Mr. Saban decided to complete an error analysis to determine the possible cause of student errors. Over 80 percent of the students made similar errors (see below). They correctly solved some percentage problems, but many answers are incorrect.

You need to help the RTI team analyze the error pattern students in Mr. Saban's sixth-grade class. You should also answer each of the discussion questions related to RTI and the error pattern presented for this case.

1. On a test with 30 items, Mary worked 24 items correctly. What percent did she have correct?

$$\frac{24}{30} = \frac{x}{100}$$ Answer: <u>80%</u>

2. Twelve students had perfect scores on a quiz. This is 40% of the class. How many students are in the class?

$$\frac{12}{40} = \frac{x}{100}$$ Answer: <u>30 students</u>

3. Jim correctly solved 88% of 50 test items. How many items did he have correct?

$$\frac{50}{88} = \frac{x}{100}$$ Answer: <u>57 items</u>

- When you think you have found the error pattern, use the error to solve the problems. Remember that you are looking for how the problem would be answered incorrectly using the students' procedures.
- Describe the error pattern (problem analysis). Why might these students be making this error?

Using the resources provided, use the problem-solving process to discuss this scenario. What would indicate that students (particularly Shelby) have needs beyond the core instruction?

- How do we know that this is not a classroom- or school-based issue?
- How does the teacher organize for instruction?
- What considerations does Mr. Saban need to address when planning for instruction?
- What resources may be involved?

Since more than 80 percent of the class is having similar problems with this type of exercise, the whole class should be involved in this intervention to remediate students' errors. Note that the intensity of the intervention would be different if only one or a few students made this error pattern, but the type of intervention might have been very similar. In this case, the students probably "successfully solved percent problems when the class first solved them, but as different types of problems were encountered, [the students] began to have difficulty" (Ashlock, 2010, p. 133). The students correctly solved the percent problems they wrote, but they are using a procedure that often does not accurately represent the ratios involved in the problem. They are using the following proportion for all of the problems presented (Ashlock, 2010):

$$\frac{\text{lesser number in the problem}}{\text{greater number in the problem}} = \frac{x}{100}$$

At this point, RTI Tier 1 is involved because the problem seems to be with the implementation of the curriculum and meeting the needs of more than 80 percent of the students in this class. This is an instructional issue, not a student issue.

- What would you do to help these students? Describe possible interventions.

You might have other ideas to be added to this intervention. You may want to gather or consider more information related to students' learning styles, attitudes, interests, mathematics anxiety levels, and backgrounds, among other variables. You should also consider the students' weaknesses and strengths. As indicated by Ashlock (2010), "when you assign percent problems, ask to see all of the work done on each problem. You need to see what ratios are derived from the problem, and whether the proportion itself is correctly developed" (p. 133). These students are correctly processing the proportion once it is determined. They do not need more instruction related to cross-multiplication procedures to solve the proportions once they are determined. These students seem to need more help with the concepts of percent, relating data in a problem to ratios (fractions), and equal ratios. You might want to use ten-by-ten squares of graph paper and redevelop the meaning of percent as "per 100," noting that $n\%$ is always $n/100$. For example, you may shade 40 out of 100 squares to show $40/100$ or 40 percent. You might also want to use base-10 blocks to redevelop the meaning of percent, using a flat base-10 block for 100, partially covering it with long base-10 blocks for 10, and unit base-10 blocks. Notice that the flat base-10 block is being used as a whole or unit divided into 100 parts (Ashlock, 2010).

After the intervention, most students were successful. However, Mr. Saban found that three students still needed help with percent problems. He provided intervention for the three students who were still having difficulties with percent problems.

This table displays the CBM scores for the nineteen students in Mr. Saban's class. Identify the students who have scores of 8 or less. These students will be monitored in primary prevention to determine their responsiveness to intervention.

Student	Week 3
Ariel	9
Cesar	9
Cynthia	10
Mary	6
Emily	10
Helan	10
Ilene	9
Jamarius	9
Rhonda	6
Leonel	9
Martin	10
Michelle	10
Shelby	7
Oscar	10
Paul	10
Raimi	9
Sam	10
Taylor	10
Winter	10

Using the resources provided, use the problem-solving process to discuss this scenario.

- What would indicate that Shelby (and others) has needs beyond the core instruction?
- How do we know that this is not a classroom- or school-based issue?
- How does the teacher organize for instruction?
- What considerations does Mr. Saban need to address when planning for instruction?
- What resources may be involved?

At this point, RTI Tier 2 is involved because the problem seems to be with a small percent of the students. The various methods of instruction are meeting the needs of more than 80 percent of the students in this class.

Mr. Saban knew he had to reteach the concepts involved with percents and provide small-group interventions for these students. He consulted with the math coach to design a new approach to learning the concept. Together they designed a lesson that included an activity in which students used themselves and moved around the room into different configurations to create percent situations, as well as an activity with the interactive whiteboard. He used practices of differentiated instruction to create small groups based on learning style preferences. Some used computers, others worked with a partner, and some worked independently. One group of students completed some exercises with Mr. Saban and he provided additional supports as they practiced.

Mr. Saban also provided more opportunities for learning using CRA methods, and more clarification of equivalent fractions and proportional reasoning related to percent ideas. At the concrete level, the students used base-10 blocks (using the flat block to represent a whole), centimeter cubes, tangrams, and geoboards (11-by-11 pin array). For example, 25 small cubes are equal to $\frac{25}{100}$ or 0.25 or 25 percent of the whole, and this is equal to ¼ of the whole. Similarly, at the representational level, the students used graph paper to represent percent values. For example, they took a closer look at converting ¾ to a fraction having a denominator of 100, and found of a number that multiplied by 4 is equal to 100. The number is 25 because $4 \times 25 = 100$. Then they multiplied the numerator and denominator by 25, as shown in Figure 5.10.

They multiply the numerator and denominator by 25 to convert ¾ to a fraction with a denominator of 100, which has the same effect of multiplying by 1 because $\frac{25}{25} = 1$. Notice that, in a similar manner, we can change $\frac{15}{20}$ to a fraction having a denominator equal to 100. We multiply by 4 this time. This is also equivalent to 0.75 or 75 percent.

After two days of instruction and practice during extra mathematics time and regular class instruction, Mr. Saban was more confident in his students' learning. While they were learning, he had implemented several probes as formative assessments. At the end of the second day, students were provided with five probes to complete independently to use as an assessment measure. This time the students were required to show their answers and explain their thinking using base-10 blocks and/or graph paper.

This measure reflected success in the students' learning. This time, twenty-one out of twenty-four students successfully completed at least four out of five probes correctly. Mr. Saban had been successful in the problem identification for the class.

Three students were still experiencing difficulties with the concept and skills of proportions. Although this is no longer a curriculum and instruction issue, Mr. Saban cannot ignore the needs of those three students. He creates time at the end of the class period to work with these three students each day for the following two weeks. During this time, Mr. Saban provides targeted interventions for these three students. On three of the days, the math coach comes to work with these students during that time. They implement a research-based program and collect data samples each day as part of the intervention. The data are recorded as a percent correct. The goal is 90 percent accuracy for all students.

The following table shows the percentages for these three students.

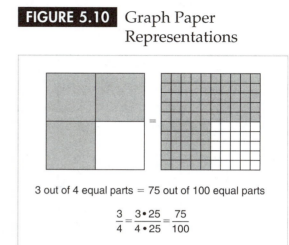

FIGURE 5.10 Graph Paper Representations

3 out of 4 equal parts = 75 out of 100 equal parts

$$\frac{3}{4} = \frac{3 \cdot 25}{4 \cdot 25} = \frac{75}{100}$$

	Day 1	Day 2	Day 3	Day 4	Day 5	Day 6	Day 7	Day 8	Day 9	Day 10
Rhonda	40%	40%	50%	40%	50%	80%	80%	100%	90%	100%
Mary	60%	70%	70%	80%	80%	80%	80%	90%	90%	90%
Shelby	60%	50%	60%	60%	50%	50%	40%	60%	50%	50%

Mr. Saban displayed the performance of the students in the form of a graph.

The graph is created so the data create a clearer picture. Gains or trends can be seen more easily and information can be communicated efficiently.

■ Was the intervention successful? Are there concerns with any of these students?

The intervention seems to be working for Rhonda and Mary, but not for Shelby. Both Rhonda and Mary are performing over the 90 percent proficiency level. Shelby is at or below the 50 percent level.

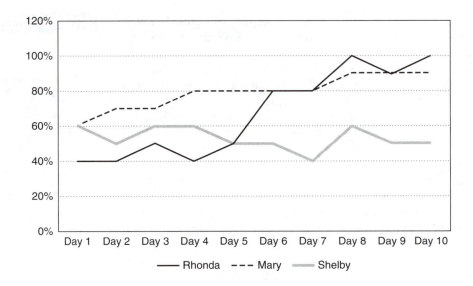

The data reflect the need for additional supports and services to help Shelby. Mr. Saban continues to provide supports to Rhonda and Mary three times a week with a mathematics specialist. Shelby will receive intervention activities with a high degree of curriculum fidelity. She will also be closely monitored weekly at Tier 3.

TEACHER'S CORNER

Keys to Getting You Started with RTI

- Review the Tier 2 Considerations on page 95. These are important questions to answer as you prepare for RTI and Tier 2 instruction.

- Using progress-monitoring data from Tier 1, engage in discussion with your RTI team regarding which students will need Tier 2 supports.

- Determine who, where, how and when Tier 2 supports will be delivered.

- Complete the Intervention Form (Reproducible #12 in Appendix A), the Classroom Implementation Schedule (Reproducible #13), and the Observation Recording Table (Reproducible #14).

- Determine the progress monitoring for Tier 2 students.

- Establish decision-making rules for instructional adjustments for students who will need additional supports (Tier 3) and how you will move students back into Tier 1 when progress goals have been met.

- Visit these websites for additional mathematics interventions and ideas regarding standard protocol:

  http://kc.vanderbilt.edu

  www.oci-sems.com

  www.voyagerlearning.com/vmath/index.jsp

  http://pearsonhighered.com/educator

  www.hmco.com/index.html

  www.proedinc.com

  www.harcourtachieve.com

  www.sraonline.com

- Complete Professional Learning Community Chapter 5 activities.

Intensifying Interventions within Tier 3

"Excellence in mathematics education requires equity—high expectations and strong support for all students. Assessment should support the learning of important mathematics and furnish useful information to both teachers and students."

—*National Council for Teachers of Mathematics (2000)*

What You Will Find in This Chapter

- Discussions about Tier 3, related to Tier 1 and 2, within a comprehensive RTI system
- Descriptions and examples of critical instructional variables to intensify instruction and interventions for individual students within Tier 3
- Characteristics, procedures, and examples of diagnostic teaching, error analyses, task analyses, and precision teaching in mathematics
- Examples of case studies and scenarios for consideration by mathematics teachers and other educators

Teacher's Voice

From the student results on the biweekly progress-monitoring assessments, I see the improvements in student learning for most of my students. It has been wonderful collaborating with my district's curriculum specialist and the instructional coach at my school to learn about and use some new manipulatives and teaching techniques with all of my students, but especially for the struggling students who were receiving Tier 2 interventions. They were so helpful as I was regrouping the students and finalizing my classroom schedule to provide the additional time for providing enrichment or intensive support for groups of my students based on their curriculum-based assessments. The students were so engaged in their learning, especially in the small groups, because the instruction and resources were scaffolded to meet their learning needs and included manipulatives to develop conceptual understanding. I didn't realize how important these strategies, manipulatives, and scaffolding techniques were to enhancing both student learning and engagement. Charting the students' progress from the curriculum-based assessments has been a visual reminder of their learning. The individual students and their parents appreciated seeing the charts of learning progress when I included them during routine parent conferences and as part of our school meetings. I was really excited to share the charts showing my students' results to the members of our school's RTI team last week. While my students continue to improve, most of the students that were receiving additional, intensive instruction as part of Tier 2 interventions were meeting the curriculum standards. I have learned so much already about differentiated instruction, evidence-based intervention programs, use of manipulatives to build conceptual understanding, and effective teaching techniques to scaffold instruction and engage my students in their learning. I feel so much more confident and knowledgeable to continue teaching other standards using these techniques, strategies, and resources. However, I am still not reaching all of my students. I am still concerned about Heather. Her results from the progress-monitoring data still show evidence that she has not yet mastered content in mathematics. I have this quote on my wall: "I cannot teach students well if I do not know them well" by Theodore Sizer. I do know my students, but I am not sure if I know enough about Heather to understand her thinking, skills, and misconceptions about math. The members of the RTI team tell me that this is an important part of providing instruction during Tier 3. Well, I am ready to continue learning to ensure that Heather will also be learning.

Ms. Holly, fourth-grade teacher

Our goal is to ensure that each and every student learns the curriculum. Every day we make instructional decisions in our classrooms using our knowledge and experience about evidence-based instructional practices and programs, strategies, and technology to meet the mathematical needs of our students. We collect assessment data from many sources: observations, curriculum-based assessments, interviews, and more formalized methods. We continuously adjust our lessons and resources to scaffold support during initial supplemental lessons as indicated by assessment data in a continuous process of teaching, assessing, and instructional problem solving. Most of the students master the curriculum as a result of effective, differentiated instruction in our classrooms during Tier 1. Some of our students may need additional, more intensive instruction, intervention resources, and/or additional scaffolding during Tier 2. There may be a very small group or an individual student who is not yet mastering the mathematical knowledge and skills of the curriculum. Critical instructional variables need to be considered when intensifying instruction and interventions during Tier 3. In order to make these decisions and maximize the instructional value of assessments, teachers need to move beyond a superficial "right or wrong" analysis of tasks and instead focus on how students are thinking about the tasks (NCTM, 2000). By analyzing error patterns from assignments and assessment probes, teachers engage in self-questioning and problem solving to design specific instructional alternatives for individual students during Tier 3 intervention.

Problem Solving for Individual Concerns during Tier 3

The problem-solving, self-questioning process is familiar to us as we proactively and continuously assess the progress of our students. Data from classroom progress-monitoring assessments are collected and used to enhance or revise instruction during Tiers 1 and 2. This instructional decision-making process (see Figure 6.1) also is used to decide how the instruction and interventions should be maintained and layered for individual students within Tier 3.

In Tier 3, efforts from several educators on your school's RTI team focus on the needs of individual students who continue to experience significant problems in mathematics despite effective initial instruction (Tier 1) and intensive supplemental interventions (Tier 2). In the sections that follow, we discuss previous student results from classroom instruction, interventions, and progress monitoring that are used by members of the RTI team. Instructional decision making and problem solving is a process used throughout Tier 3. During Tier 3, discussions center on diagnosing a solution from the data collected from Tier 1 instruction, Tier 2 intervention, and assessment results. RTI team members present for instructional decision-making and problem-solving discussions at Tier 3 may now include educators with additional expertise in mathematics, individuals with information

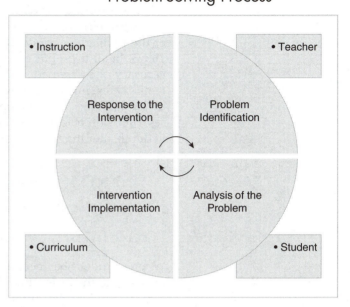

FIGURE 6.1 Instructional Decision-Making, Problem-Solving Process

about the identified students, and/or knowledge and access to evidence-based intervention programs in mathematics. Although Tier 3 is not considered special education in most schools and districts, special education personnel may contribute their expertise or provide services in alignment with district and state policies and procedures. In addition, students already identified as having disabilities may be receiving Tier 3 intensive interventions as part of their mathematics instruction. When the members of the RTI team are problem solving at Tier 3, the process is similar, but the considerations differ.

Step 1: Problem Identification — What Do I Know about the Problem or Concern?

The first step in the process is to define the problem by noting who is experiencing the problem and what has previously occurred (Tier 1 and Tier 2). When defining a problem, we must clearly describe what the problem "looks like" in objective, observable terms, so that all persons involved know they are talking about the same thing. It is helpful to describe the student's actual performance with the desired or expected performance for learning the mathematics content. We need to be aware of what the students need to know and what they should be able to do by a certain point in the school year. Annual curriculum maps and calendars for mathematics may assist with these targets for expected performance goals and trend lines.

Step 2: Analyze the Problem — Why Is This Occurring?

By Tier 3, we have already differentiated instruction, used various evidence-based resources, and engaged students with manipulatives to meet the curriculum outcomes and objectives in mathematics during Tier 1 instruction. Results of the curriculum-based assessments and ongoing progress-monitoring measures offer additional information to provide more intensive instruction and additional evidence-based interventions to smaller groups of students not yet reaching mastery within Tier 2. If students have not yet reached mastery, continued analysis of the problem is critical to provide appropriate, intensive interventions during Tier 3. In all tiers, but especially in Tier 3, we need to not only record student's accuracy of assessment results, but also identify valuable insights about our student's skills, misconceptions, and erroneous prior knowledge and/or conceptual understandings. This is done through in-depth diagnostic teaching, error analyses, precision teaching, and targeted diagnostic assessments. These are discussed in depth later in this chapter.

Step 3: Develop and Implement a Solution—What Are We Going to Do to Improve and Solve This Problem?

When a student has been identified as needing Tier 3 intervention supports, the next step in the instructional decision-making and problem-solving process is the selection and implementation of appropriate interventions. One option is to select an evidence-based intervention strategy that has a standard protocol for implementation. There are many intervention strategies (see the Teacher Resources section in Appendix A) that are evidence based. In addition, there are several websites that provide intervention resources.

A second option is to collect more information about the student's needs in mathematics. It may be important to conduct an analysis of the problem's context and specific error patterns. To do so, we must ask what factors are contributing to the problem (possibly identified in Tiers 1 and 2) and in what ways can we alter those factors to promote learning and reduce the severity of the problem. One goal of this stage in the process is to "diagnose the conditions under which students' learning is enabled" (Tilly, 2002, p. 29). This goal is accomplished by reviewing the gathered information (e.g., direct observation, interviews, rating scales, curriculum-based measures of academic skills, review of records) from a number of sources (e.g., the student, teacher, parent, peers, administrator) to answer questions that will be helpful in furthering our understanding of why or under what conditions the problem is occurring.

Although many questions can be asked at this stage, it is important to stay focused on identifying the factors that we can change (e.g., instructional strategies, curriculum materials). For example, when a student's classroom performance is below our expectations, we might ask whether the problem is with skill (something the student can't do) or performance (something the student won't do). Another important and related question to ask is whether the alignment between the student's skill level, the curriculum materials, and the instructional strategies is appropriate (Howell & Nolet, 2000). It is important to learn as much as possible about the individual student.

For examples of evidence-based intervention strategies, see the What Works Clearinghouse at www.whatworks.ed.gov, a resource developed by the Institute of Education Sciences, U.S. Department of Education.

When the problem involves performance that falls below what is expected, it is important to determine why the student has not yet been successful. Is it due to a lack of motivation, incorrect prior knowledge, lack of prerequisite skills, and/or incorrect conceptual understanding? Regardless of whether educators decide to move directly to intervention or to collect more information to analyze the problem, the focus of this step in the problem-solving process is on selecting a solution (intervention strategy) that successfully teaches the student and reduces the discrepancy between the student's current and expected performance. Interventions should be selected on the basis of their alignment and match to the problem.

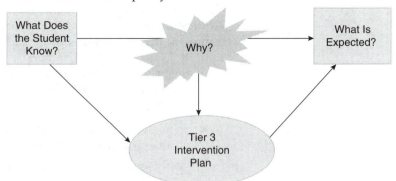

As a result, Tier 3 interventions require careful planning because they are designed to address significant problems for which students are in need of intensive interventions. Specifically, a Tier 3 intervention plan should describe the following:

1. What the intervention will look like (i.e., steps or procedures)

2. What materials and/or resources are needed and whether these are available within existing resources

3. Roles and responsibilities with respect to intervention implementation (i.e., Who will be responsible for running the intervention, preparing materials, etc.?)

4. The intervention schedule (how often, for how long, and at what times in the day?) and context (where and with whom?)

5. How the intervention and its outcomes will be monitored (i.e., what measures, by whom, and on what schedule?) and analyzed (i.e., compared to what criterion?)

In addition, an intervention plan should specify timelines for implementing objectives and for achieving desired goals. The end goal of this stage of the process is a clearly delineated intervention plan.

Step 4: Response to Instruction/ Intervention—Is the Plan Working? How Do We Know?

Student success can only be known following actual implementation of an intervention plan at Tier 3 and careful progress monitoring of learning over time. Classroom implementation of the invention plan and continuous progress monitoring are critical at Tier 3. Many members of the RTI team may become involved with solution finding and interventions during Tier 3. Remember, this is a team-based task.

Is the student now successfully learning mathematics?

The best way to determine whether a student is making progress toward the desired goals in mathematics is to continue collecting progress-monitoring data through curriculum-based assessments, similar to those used during Tiers 1 and 2. However, these are now specifically selected for students at Tier 3. The intervention process does not end until the problem is solved (i.e., the student has reached the expected goal) and the student is learning mathematics. Thus, continuous monitoring and evaluation are essential parts of an effective RTI process using curriculum-based assessments in Tier 3 (Lembke & Stecker, 2007).

When assessment data are reviewed and analyzed, a decision is made regarding whether the intervention plan should be revised or goals adjusted. The RTI team reviews assessment data from a student at Tier 3 who is still not making sufficient progress to reach benchmark goals for the end of the year and may recommend that the student be considered for evaluation for special education eligibility. Movement between tiers is an important decision that very much reflects the impact of the tiered instructional process.

To summarize, Tier 3 instruction/intervention differs from that provided in Tiers 1 or 2 in these ways:

- Increased emphasis: more problem diagnosis to determine the reasons the student is having the problem
- Increased intensity: more instructional time, smaller group size (individualized)
- Increased explicitness: more focus on teaching specific skills

A TIME TO REFLECT

Throughout the RTI process, communication with other educators is important. This is especially necessary if our students are still not learning the mathematics content and require Tier 3 interventions. Who are the members of your school's RTI team? Are there curriculum specialists, instructional coaches, other math teachers, and/or special education teachers who have the knowledge, skills, and expertise to assist with problem-solving solutions for your students at Tier 3? What resources are available (e.g., personnel, materials, time) when you codevelop the necessary intervention plans?

Variables to Intensify during Tier 3

Like Tier 2, Tier 3 instructional supports do not replace the classroom instruction—they are *in addition* to the mathematics instruction that each student receives. The same **instructional variables** apply here as they do in other tiers (see Figure 6.1), but in Tier 3 there is more purposeful intensity. At this tier, instruction is intensified by increasing the duration and frequency of instruction and intervention. Instruction and intervention should be explicit and systematic, based on diagnosed student learning needs, using verbalization of thought processes, guided practice, corrective feedback, and frequent cumulative review (Gersten, Jordan, & Flojo, 2005). Tier 3 services are usually provided one-on-one or in small groups and instruction is aligned with the core instructional program for an additional amount of time. Tier 3 interventions must be provided by highly effective and knowledgeable experts in the area of mathematics. To determine whether instruction and interventions have been successful, it is important to continue collecting sufficient assessment data. You will also find it very helpful to continue recording the methods used to intensify instruction for small groups of students (Tier 2) and/or individual students in Tier 3. This will help in determining the instructional practices you want to continue and ones you may need to change or discontinue. Some instructional practices to consider when intensifying instruction during Tier 3 include:

- Use a variety of classroom methods and resources, such as demonstrations, manipulative materials, charts, illustrations, diagrams, maps, and technology to provide multiple visual representations. Use visuals, demonstrations, and media to provide informational redundancy. Relate instructional topics, examples, and vocabulary to prior knowledge, interests, and backgrounds of the students. Encourage drawings and representations to translate and visualize word problems, (Gersten, Jordan, & Flojo, 2005)

- Develop multiple ways for students to demonstrate learning (e.g., role play, write a movie script, illustrate the concepts). Highlight key information. Provide highlighters, sticky notes, markers, and other resources (e.g., electronic dictionaries, calculators, instructional technologies) for student demonstration of learning and current understandings.

- Have students work in small groups of two to three to maximize opportunities for active student engagement and interactions.

- Encourage curriculum specialists, instructional coaches, other mathematics teachers, special education teachers, and other teachers with expertise in mathematics to provide additional assistance.

During Tier 3, students must have the most structured instructional time to provide additional opportunities for active learning. They also need scaffolded learning tasks and immediate, corrective feedback. This can be accomplished by increasing the intensity of the instructional delivery components throughout the tiers of instruction and intervention. Increasing the intensity of the instruction and interventions by varying the instructional delivery variables is very important during Tier 3. Making sure that students understand and demonstrate mastery of the stated outcomes is an important part of diagnosing misconceptions and error patterns in mathematics through more individual interactions and observations with knowledgeable and skillful teachers and curriculum specialists in mathematics. We will be more effective at providing valuable feedback to students through careful observations of student learning in smaller groups during Tier 3. It is important for teachers to document all of these intense interventions and/or modifications to the curriculum and the students' results. Documentation of OPTIONS at Tier 3 to meet more individual needs is equally important, as this will provide important background information if the student continues with minimal mathematical success. Please see the portion of the OPTIONS lesson plan where these notes can be quickly and accurately recorded in Figure 6.2.

If differentiation, scaffolding, accommodations, and increasing intensity across the various instructional components do *not* produce mastery, diagnostic

FIGURE 6.2 Recording Specific Instructional Components across Tiers

Instructional Component	Tier 1	Tier 2	Tier 3
Dosage: instructional time	Forty-five minutes	Thirty additional minutes	Fifteen to thirty additional minutes
Pacing appropriate for group size	Thirty students	Small groups of two to four students	One on one
Provide immediate, positive feedback	Teacher, peers: rubric	Resource teacher	Interventionist
Frequent student response opportunities Monitor/correct student responses	One to thirty response ratio	One to four response ratio	Each time 100 percent

assessments and teaching may be needed to provide further information about the needs of individual students. Although each of these instructional techniques and assessments can be used with students at any tier of services within RTI, their use is very important when diagnosing the continued learning challenges of students now in Tier 3 services.

A TIME TO REFLECT

How will your instruction be intensified for students needing Tier 3 interventions? Is there an evidence-based intervention program that you will be able to use as an initial solution for your students? Will you need to complete additional diagnostic teaching as an assessment to learn more about your students' knowledge of mathematics, including misconceptions and lack of prerequisite and prior knowledge?

We have provided information for Tier 3 instruction and its implementation. The next section of this chapter will provide examples about Tier 3 intervention within Ms. Holly's classroom.

Ms. Holly's Planning for RTI

As we think about these instructional variables within the tiers, we want to illustrate how the instructional focus has continued with Heather from Ms. Holly's classroom. Ms. Holly and the mathematics instructional coach were both working with Heather to improve her academic performance in mathematics (see Chapters 4 and 5) in both Tier 1 and Tier 2. According to the group's graphed results (Figure 5.4) and Heather's individual graphed results (Figure 5.7), minimal improvement occurred during Tier 2 interventions. As you remember, the RTI team recommended that Heather be placed in Tier 3 intervention based on discussion during their meeting and the assessments from the CBM administered (Figure 5.9). The mathematics specialist was chosen to work with Heather for Tier 3. She implemented the Intervention Grade Form (see Figure 6.3) to identify the Tier 3 interventions that Heather would be receiving and discussed these with the RTI team during the meeting.

The mathematics specialist also used the OPTIONS lesson plan for Tier 3 to implement instruction and interventions for Heather (see Figure 6.4). Analyzing student results from curriculum-based assessments and progress-monitoring probes from Tiers 1 and 2 becomes critical for the student at this point in Tier 3. We are trying to identify whether the problems are curriculum related, instruction related, teacher related, or student related. We offer more interventions to try and reach students academically, and we change the interventions to be individualized for each student's needs. We are now trying to determine if Heather's mathematical difficulties are a direct result of a learning disability and, if so, refer her for evaluation for special education services if further intensifying her instruction does not work. For Tier 3, the RTI team and Ms. Holly decided on intensifying several instructional variables.

The mathematics specialist worked daily with Heather and provided daily assessments and immediate feedback to her. She offered the strategies and interventions as identified in the OPTIONS lesson plan and continued collaboration with Ms. Holly and the RTI team. After nine weeks of intensive Tier 3 instruction, the mathematics specialist met with the RTI team again (including Ms. Holly) to discuss Heather's progress. As noted in Figure 6.5, Heather's academic progress began to greatly improve.

FIGURE 6.3 Heather's Intervention Form

Heather's Intervention Form A

Ms. Holly, Fourth-Grade Mathematics

Classroom Interventions and/or Standard Protocol Interventions

Tier 3

Primary Area of Concern	Strategic Intervention	Duration Start Date End Date	Intensity (Group Size/ Session Length)	Frequency (Number of Sessions per Week)	Student's Response to Intervention
■ Multiplication facts ■ Fails to record regrouped digit to tens column when multiplying numbers from ones column ■ Adds numbers presented instead of multiplying ■ Place-value concerns— using zero as place-value holder when multiplying	■ Concrete manipulatives ■ Individualized, one-on-one ■ More time on task ■ Games to build fluency ■ Guided practice ■ Independent practice ■ Word problem demonstrations ■ Review expectations ■ Intensive fluency with multiplying ■ Scaffolding approaches ■ Graphic organizers ■ Immediate feedback	Oct. 31–Dec. 20 (Daily assessments given each week for review)	One-on-one with student	Thirty minutes daily, five times per week (Ten minutes per session on multiplication facts to build quick retrieval of basic arithmetic facts using technology and flash cards)	■ Responds well with groups and teacher-led instruction ■ Is gaining recognition of using zero as place-value holder ■ Is showing mastery of multiplication facts ■ Is showing evidence of adding with regrouping within the answer in multiplication process ■ Responds well to verbal praise ■ Becomes engaged in the problem-solving process ■ Is rapidly progressing with mastery of concepts or procedures of multiplication

Note: Interventions at all elementary grade levels should devote about ten minutes in each session to building fluent retrieval of basic arithmetic facts (Gersten et al., 2009).

FIGURE 6.4 Intensifying Instruction and Interventions Using Targeted OPTIONS: Tiers 2 and 3

OUTCOME (Standard in mathematics):

PROGRESS-MONITORING DATA:

TIER 2/TIER 3 Objective:

TIER 2/TIER 3 EBP, Length of Time (in days):

INSTRUCTIONAL PERSONNEL (circle all that apply):

MT: Math teacher   IC: Instructional coach

SP: School psychologist   IRT: Instructional resource teacher

CT: Co-teacher

INTERVENTIONS	ONGOING PROGRESS MONITORING (OPM)
Record intervention, method to intensify, other professionals, and other classroom/student considerations used.	Record OPM assessment, results, and dates. Be sure to attach charts and graph results.

Tier 2: Mathematics

Students' Names:

| Tier 3: Mathematics

Students' Names:

Heather H. | <ul><li>Use clear, concise directions, questions, explanations, and instructions and walk her through the process.</li><li>Use as many concrete examples and experiences as possible and "chunk" the information (base-10 blocks, two-colored counters, ten frames, beans, abacus).</li><li>Present one or two problems at a time and review daily the skills she needs to memorize.</li><li>Provide immediate feedback, check for error patterns in computation, and have her explain her answers.</li><li>Use games, computer programs, word problem demonstrations, and representations to build fluency and understanding.</li><li>Use one-on-one (individualized) instruction.</li></ul> | <ul><li>Daily assessment and explicit feedback will be given to Heather.</li><li>CBM will occur weekly.</li><li>Student interviews will be conducted.</li><li>Student behavior will be observed and recorded.</li><li>Conceptual mapping and organizers will be used.</li><li>Analysis of error patterns will be ongoing.</li></ul> |

NEEDS OF INDIVIDUAL STUDENT

Remember to record all interventions, data from progress monitoring, and so forth for each individual student for possible referral as well.

INSTRUCTOR NOTES: _____

_____

SUMMARIZE

Date to review instruction/intervention and assessment data: _____

Team meeting members: _____

Location: _____

FIGURE 6.5 Heather's Instructional Graph

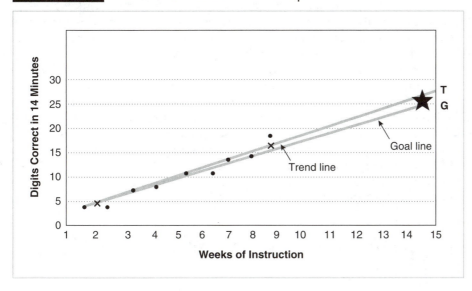

The mathematics specialist reviewed the intensity of supports through Tier 3 interventions that were effective with Heather. She indicated that Heather received individualized (one-on-one) instruction with more time to learn the mathematics content (thirty minutes, five days per week) *in addition* to other mathematics instruction. Heather was given more opportunities to work with concrete manipulatives to help her make the mathematical connections, and more time on task was provided to perform the mathematical operations. The mathematics specialist implemented both guided and independent practice; demonstrated word problems through modeling, visuals, and representations; and provided mathematical games (including those on the computer) to build fluency (Jittendra, Sczesniak, & Deatline-Bachman, 2005). She continually questioned Heather regarding mathematical understanding and provided immediate feedback to aid in correcting common errors and mathematics misconceptions with the material she was learning. In addition, preskills that were missed from prior learning were identified and addressed.

The examples of Heather's work (student portfolio samples, CBM assessments, diagnostic assessments, formative assessments, provisions and implementation of evidence-based instructional practices, fidelity of implementation, increased intensity of supports and interventions, and dosage) provided documentation that many academic problems that were evident in Tier 1 and Tier 2 instruction were vastly improving. The mathematics gap as compared to others in Ms. Holly's class was beginning to close. It was recommended that the mathematics specialist continue working with Heather for six to nine more weeks. If progress-monitoring and other assessment data continued to indicate Heather's mathematics gap was closing, then consideration would be given to placing her back into Tier 1 instruction and removing her from Tier 3 interventions. If continued improvement was not evident, then further analysis would be discussed to continue Tier 3 interventions and supports for longer durations.

As evidenced by the case study of Heather, a more individualized approach within Tier 3 assisted in helping her make the mathematics connections she needed in order to be mathematically successful. The results from Tier 1 and Tier 2 instruction still indicated a mathematical gap as per the progress-monitoring and other assessment data. However, when more intense instruction and supports were provided, progress for Heather steadily increased and the gap was narrowing.

This is how we want RTI in mathematics to work for our students. We want to assist them in whatever means are needed in order to help them link what they do know with what they are about to learn, to help correct the error patterns they may be making, and to void any mathematics misconceptions they may have that hinder them from learning the mathematical material.

We also need to realize that some students may not respond to Tier 3 instruction. RTI team decisions must be in place to determine whether additional supports may be needed for success (determined by progress monitoring in Tier 3) or if students may need referral for comprehensive evaluation and considered for eligibility for special education services. This is an instructional decision-making and problem-solving process that must be decided by your team and one that should be made *only* after you have exhausted all efforts within the RTI framework. It is important to determine the reason why the student has not yet been successful in mathematics during this tier of RTI.

Why?

Diagnostic Assessment and Teaching at Tier 3

Although we teach a group of students in our classrooms, learning is done by individuals. Our assessment tasks, especially during Tier 3, should help us teach individual students. We collect and analyze assessment data and prescribe additional assessments to further diagnose instructional concerns, to monitor student progress, and to summarize the outcomes for a specific period of time (e.g., length of intervention, grading period, annual progress). We use this information to identify a specific area of concern. Through interactions with our students, especially in Tier 3, we are clarifying, defining, and seeking to understand their specific knowledge, thinking, and conceptual understandings so we can intervene and remediate.

A TIME TO REFLECT

How do you check for student understanding during the lesson within Tier 3? How do you build in opportunities for students to discuss their solutions and rationale by using varied and complex thinking skills? How will you intensify instruction, considering instructional time, group size, positive feedback, and response opportunities, to learn more about individual students and their skills?

Diagnostic Teaching and Assessment

Assessing learning during Tier 3 instruction and interventions offers us invaluable insights on the learners' progress with the concepts and skills. By asking questions, observing behaviors, and providing feedback within the lesson, we not only provide guidance and explicit instruction during a teachable moment, but we also informally gather important assessment information to guide future instruction. Several specific diagnostic techniques include interviewing the student, observing student behavior, recording student behavior, using conceptual maps or organizers, and using commercially developed diagnostic assessments.

1. *Diagnostic mathematics interviews with the student.* Interviews are an effective way to collect information about a student's mathematical concepts, skills, and dispositions. The diagnostic interview provides information to determine what math skills to teach the student and how to teach them. This technique often is used in administering curriculum-based assessments in mathematics and is best completed individually with the student. The diagnostic interview enables the teacher and/or interventionist to identify specific problems, error patterns, or problem-solving strategies in math. As we pose questions to the student, we listen to his or her answers and explanations. Our diagnostic teaching can be focused on broad topics (e.g., measurement) or more narrow topics (e.g., linear metric measurement). The focus of diagnosis can also be specific concepts and principles (e.g., *equal* means *the same as*) or they can be specific procedures (e.g., renaming a fraction so it has greater terms). What we currently know about our student's learning determines the focus for diagnostic teaching. Assessment data from formative and progress-monitoring probes during Tier 1 instruction and Tier 2 intervention provide the focus for our interview when compared with the necessary preskills and prior knowledge necessary for the student to master identified grade-level mathematical skills and knowledge. By asking questions, collecting data, intervening, and continuously monitoring student progress, teachers prescribe instruction and interventions to meet the needs of their students in mathematics. These student academic results not only continuously inform the decisions made during the instructional process within the classroom, but also are valuable documentation of a student's responses to instructional variables and intervention programs when considering additional services to meet the student's needs. They are a way to gain insights into student learning and the student's feelings about the learning. Diagnostic interviews enable teachers to:

a. Gain insights into a student's understandings of concepts and procedures and identify any misconceptions or error patterns

b. Observe and hear how a student thinks about mathematics

c. Learn what the student thinks about mathematics.

Sam's answer: 87 + 49 = 1216

When interviewing Sam, the teacher needed to learn about his understanding of place value as demonstrated by his answer. Using base-10 blocks, the teacher asked Sam several questions about place value. After Sam counted out twelve tens blocks and sixteen unit blocks, the teacher asked Sam if he could show her another way to represent that same amount using fewer blocks. The teacher wanted not only to review and correct any conceptual misunderstandings using the concrete manipulatives, but also to discuss the revised procedures using multiple representations.

2. *Observing student behavior.* Informal observations take place whenever we have opportunities to observe students in our class. These can be a source of information as teachers listen to students' conversations, pose diagnostic questions, and observe the completion of mathematics assignments and tasks. At times, both interviews and observations will use a more diagnostic script.

Sample of a structured diagnostic interview:

- *Read the problem to me, please.*
- *What is the question asking you to do?*
- *How do you know that?*
- *How are you going to solve for the answer?*
- *Please solve this problem and talk to me as you work.*
- *Write down the answer to the question. Is it correct? Why or why not? Can you explain your answer?*

3. *Recording student behaviors.* At times, records of students' responses (e.g., written notes or audio or video recordings) will provide additional information. As we listen, we need to learn about an individual's understanding about specific ideas. This is done by asking and recording follow-up questions to probe the student for further understanding. We need to plan ahead to make records of all pertinent observations and interview information. An example

FIGURE 6.6 Tier 3 Observation Template

Tier 3 Observation Sheet

Name:_____ Date:_____

Date	Activity	Observed Behavior	Intervention Suggestions

of an observation sheet for an individual student during Tier 3 intervention is included in Figure 6.6.

4. *Conceptual maps or organizers.* Conceptual maps or graphic organizers that are used during instruction and/or intervention are especially useful during diagnostic teaching. Tasks incorporating graphic organizers often provide a visual format that focuses on relationships and understandings of mathematical concepts. While students are constructing or using the graphic organizers, teachers can observe and listen to students' understandings of important concepts.

A number line *can* be used for assessing numeration concepts.

10   20   ☐   40   50   60   ☐   80

5. *Commercial diagnostic tests.* Commercial diagnostic tests are available that are designed to help teachers identify and appropriately plan intervention for individual students. The diagnostic assessments are available for individual or group administration. The mathematical content will provide in-depth diagnostic information about subskills of student knowledge and mastery. There are examples of commercially available diagnostic tests in mathematics included in Table 6.1.

These techniques of diagnostic teaching are used to further determine the individual student's learning needs, misconceptions, and misunderstandings in relation to the curriculum in mathematics to be mastered. Often times, curriculum specialists, instructional coaches, and special education teachers may assist during this process. The entire diagnostic teaching and assessment process depends on the accurate identification of the underlying causes of the lack of understanding, progress, and demonstration of mastery by the individual student. When conducting diagnostic assessments and teaching, several considerations are important.

1. Allocate a time and location to properly plan and diagnose.
2. Begin with easier tasks, then gradually present more difficult material.
3. Use a nonjudgmental stance when providing feedback for student responses.
4. Ask probing questions.
5. Encourage the student to think out loud to solve the problems.

Another procedure to use as part of diagnostic teaching and assessment is error analysis of patterns of mathematical errors.

TABLE 6.1   Samples of Commercial Diagnostic Assessments

Test Name	Type	Age/Grade	Purpose	Publisher
Diagnostic Math Inventory	Individual, standardized	K–8	To diagnose math achievement and develop objectives	McGraw-Hill
KeyMath-Revised	Individual, standardized	K–6	To assess math concepts and skills	American Guidance
Stanford Diagnostic Mathematics Test	Group, standardized	K–12	To identify math achievement	Psychological Corporation
Enright Diagnostic Inventory of Basic	Individual/group, criterion-referenced	4–adult	To determine math levels, diagnose math errors	Curriculum Associates
Test of Early Mathematical Ability	Individual/group, criterion-referenced	3–9 years	To determine strengths and weaknesses, measure progress, guide instruction	Pro-Ed

Analysis of Error Patterns

As we illustrated in Chapter 5, error patterns are patterns observed within student work whenever an action is performed regularly that does not lead to correct results in every case. All of us make mistakes in mathematics. However, there is a difference between the careless mistakes made, and the misconceptions about mathematical concepts, ideas, and procedures that our students may have. Error patterns reveal misconceptions our students have learned. Because we connect new information with what we already know, it is important that we assess the preconceptions of our students. Prior knowledge may be incorrect or preskills may be missing. Error patterns are generally identifiable through several examples of similar errors. See the following examples of an error pattern in addition.

$$
\begin{array}{ccc}
75 & 67 & 84 \\
\underline{+8} & \underline{+4} & \underline{+9} \\
163 & 111 & 183
\end{array}
$$

Can you determine the error pattern? What concept is the student misunderstanding? How will you, as the mathematics teacher, intervene?

If we merely looked at the numbers correct on this assessment, the student would have received a zero. However, by reviewing samples of the student's assignments and assessments, we can determine the reasons why the student provided these answers by completing an error pattern analysis. (See Chapter 4 for Heather's error analysis samples in Figures 4.14 and 4.16 and Chapter 5 scenarios for practice in identifying students' mathematics error patterns.) As the example above demonstrates, the student appeared to know computation of whole numbers, but he has misinformation regarding place value and the procedures for addition.

Error patterns can be discovered in most concepts in mathematics (computation of numbers, fractions, and decimals) as well as in geometry, measurement, and algebra. We also use error pattern analysis during any of the tiers of instruction/intervention to correct misunderstandings in mathematics. However, this technique is especially important to use during Tier 3 intervention to discover and reteach misunderstood concepts, teach necessary prerequisite skills, and/or correct misunderstood or misapplied prior knowledge. Scope and sequence charts provide important task analyses of development skills needed as preskills for understanding a concept.

Often discovering and remediating error patterns is completed in conjunction with diagnostic teaching using several of the techniques previously described. These direct interventions are necessary to reteach important conceptual misunderstandings for Tier 3. The use of manipulatives while reteaching these important concepts is a visual representation for learning during these interventions. Overlearning the accurate algorithm or procedure may need to occur to ensure that the learning will be retained. We must be quick to offer Tier 3 students specific, immediate feedback and reinforcement during interventions.

Task Analysis

Task analysis is used to determine a hierarchical sequence of skills. Each mathematical operation or process can be broken down into discrete components or steps involved in arriving at a solution. Once the task is analyzed into these discrete steps, checklists can be developed that correspond to each step and students' progress toward mastery can be closely monitored. The sample in Figure 6.7 is a task analysis of some benchmarks and goals in fourth-grade curriculum. This grade-level scope and sequence chart, aligned with the state and district standards and outcomes, is a good source to use for determining the order of skills and identifying the individual student's strengths and needs.

A TIME TO REFLECT

Check with members of your grade-level team and your curriculum specialist for copies of your district's curriculum map and scope and sequence charts. Have the outcomes and goals been divided into specific tasks in a hierarchy of development for mastery of the outcomes? What are the prerequisite skills for the outcomes and benchmarks?

Precision Teaching

Precision teaching is a procedure to measure learning and proficiency of skills. It has three important components: direct measures, continuous measures, and learning rate and frequency (Lindsley, 1964). Let's look at all three of these components.

1. Direct measures are explicitly aligned with the skill or competency in mathematics to be taught and measured. Therefore, if accuracy and fluency of addition facts from $0 + 0$ to $9 + 9$ is the goal, we should count the number of addition problems the student does correctly in an assessment of that particular skill. The key here is to find the most direct measure of the skill of interest.

2. Continuous measures are frequent measures of the identified skill or competency.

3. Learning rate and frequency refers to collecting student performance assessment data that include both the number correct, as well as the amount of time to complete the assessment to measure and record both precision and fluency.

The use of precision teaching within Tier 3 interventions facilitates targeted teaching and assessment of very specific skills that can be determined from the instruction and assessment results from the previous tiers. Once specific skills to teach and/or remediate are identified, precision teaching has a set of procedures that are efficient for teachers and interventionists to complete. In addition, the collection of assessment data and charting the results by the teacher and the student is

FIGURE 6.7 Fourth-Grade Mathematics Concepts and Skills Checklist

Key: PR = Prerequisite, DOK = Depth of knowledge (low, moderate, or high as provided in the state standard)

Skill/Concept	Representation			Validation		Mastery		Retention	
	Concrete	Pictorial	Abstract	Say/write	Do	Yes	No	Yes	No
Big Idea 1: Develop quick recall of multiplication facts and related division facts and fluency with whole-numbers multiplication.									
General content limits related to big idea 1 ● Factors used may include up to two three-digit numbers, or, when a four-digit factor is used, the other factor may not exceed two digits. ● Divisors should not exceed one digit, unless it is a related division fact of 0 × 0 through 12 × 12. ● Dividends should not exceed three digits. ● Quotients may include remainders expressed only as whole numbers. ● Items will not require the use of long division.									
MA.4.A.1.1: Use and describe various models for multiplication in problem-solving situations, and demonstrate recall of basic multiplication and related division facts with ease.									
MA.4.A.1.1 is considered prior knowledge for MA.5.A.1.1, MA.5.A.1.4, and MA.5.A.6.2.									
1. Use and describe various models for multiplication in problem-solving situations (Part A of MA.4.A.1.1). DOK: moderate	X	X	X	X	X				
2. Demonstrate recall of basic multiplication facts with ease (Part B of MA.4.A.1.1). DOK: moderate			X	X					
3. Demonstrate recall of division facts related to multiplication facts with ease (Part C of MA.4.A.1.1). DOK: moderate			X	X					

(continued)

FIGURE 6.7 (continued)

Key: PR = Prerequisite, DOK = Depth of knowledge (low, moderate, or high as provided in the state standard)

Skill/Concept	Representation			Validation		Mastery		Retention	
	Concrete	Pictorial	Abstract	Say/write	Do	Yes	No	Yes	No
MA.4.A.1.2: Multiply multi-digit whole numbers through four digits fluently, demonstrating understanding of the standard algorithm and checking for reasonableness of results, including solving real-world problems. **Content limits for MA.4.A.1.2** • Items may include whole-number multiplication facts from 0 × 0 through 12 × 12 and the related division facts. • For items that require solving multi-digit multiplication problems, the two factors may not exceed three digits by three digits or four digits by two digits. • When both factors have three digits, at least one digit must be a zero. • Items may include finding partial products of a multi-digit multiplication problem or finding errors in multiplication problems. • Items may include checking for reasonableness of products. • Items may use properties (e.g., commutative, associative, inverse, identity, distributive, zero) to solve problems but will not include asking students to name the specific properties. • Also assesses MA.4.A.1.1. Prior knowledge for MA.4.A.1.2 includes MA.3.A.1.1–MA.3.A.1.3. MA.4.A.1.2 is considered prior knowledge for MA.5.A.1.1, MA.5.A.1.4, MA.5.A.6.2, MA.6.A.2.1, and MA.6.A.2.2.									
4. Multiply one- or two-digit whole numbers by two-digit whole numbers fluently, demonstrating understanding of the standard algorithm, and checking for reasonableness of results, including solving real-world problems (PR for MA.4.A.1.2).	X	X	X	X	X				
5. Multiply two- or three-digit whole numbers by two- or three-digit whole numbers fluently, demonstrating understanding of the standard algorithm, and checking for reasonableness of results, including solving real-world problems (PR for MA.4.A.1.2).	X	X	X	X	X				
6. Multiply two-digit whole numbers by four-digit whole numbers fluently, demonstrating understanding of the standard algorithm, and checking for reasonableness of results, including solving real-world problems (PR for MA.4.A.1.2).	X	X	X	X	X				
7. Multiply multi-digit whole numbers through four digits fluently, demonstrating understanding of the standard algorithm and checking for reasonableness of results, including solving real-world problems (MA.4.A.1.2). DOK: high	X	X	X	X	X				

Big Idea 2: Develop an understanding of decimals, including the connection between fractions and decimals.

General content limits related to big idea 2:
- Decimal place values could range from tenths through thousandths with no more than five total digits.
- Fraction items may have denominators of 1–10, 12, or 1000, or denominators that are derived from basic multiplication facts through 12 × 12 may also be used (e.g., 24 has the two factors 6 and 4; 72 has the factors 8 and 9).
- Items dealing with percents will not involve computation using the percent.

MA.4.A.2.1: Use decimals through the thousandths place to name numbers between whole numbers.

MA.4.A.2.1 is considered prior knowledge for MA.5.A.2.1, MA.5.A.2.2.

1. Use decimals through the thousandths place to name numbers between whole numbers (MA.4.A.2.1). DOK: low	X	X		X	X	

MA.4.A.2.2: Describe decimals as an extension of the base-10 number system.

MA.4.A.2.2 is considered prior knowledge for MA.5.A.2.1, and MA.5.A.2.2.

2. Describe decimals as an extension of the base-10 number system (MA.4.A.2.2). DOK: high	X	X	X	X		

quite reinforcing and motivating. Therefore, the five steps to follow when implementing precision teaching include:

1. Pinpoint the specific learning goal. From previous assessments and performance products, choose a goal to focus on. The learning goal in mathematics must be observable, repeatable, and have clear tasks to complete. For example, demonstrating mastery of basic addition facts would be an appropriate goal for precision teaching. Many teachers have found that some students in Tier 3 may need learning goals that are smaller subtasks of the overall goal. The student may need more instruction and practice with this skill before adding another component of the skill, similar to scaffolding.

2. After a learning goal has been pinpointed for an individual student, the next step is to determine materials needed and counting and recording methods to be used throughout the precision teaching. One-minute probes are the most frequently used counting period for goals in mathematics. They are quick and efficient measures of the student's knowledge and are a reliable demonstration of skills. Note that each digit of each answer is counted if correct. There are numerous precision teaching probes that can be uniquely created to pinpoint individual students' learning goals in mathematics by using the various resources included in the progress-monitoring assessments. When using electronic sources of assessments, remember to create and select probes that assess the individual student's learning goals.

3. Set individual goals for learning. It is important that we help students reach proficiency on each skill that is targeted for intensive intervention during Tier 3. Therefore, it is important to set individual goals for learning. Goals may need to be within a range of proficiency to allow for individual differences. Remember to consider student's individual needs and learning when setting goals. Also, students may be very motivated when engaged in establishing their own goals for learning.

4. Charting provides a visual picture of assessment results from the one-minute probes related to student learning. In addition, the charts provide the teacher (and others on the RTI team) with clearly displayed data of results to make further decisions for Tier 3 instruction.

5. After teaching intensive interventions, assessment with identified probes, and charting several scores for a couple of days or weeks (depending on the skill), the chart summarizes learning to date to aid in continued decision-making by the members of the RTI team. If the student's chart shows a positive change, it clearly shows that the student is progressing toward the learning goal. If not, the team may need to consider other interventions, increased intensity, and/or additional diagnostic teaching or assessment. When meeting with members of the RTI team, all assessment results may contain critical information to review and share with members of the team.

A TIME TO REFLECT

During each of the RTI tiers, but especially during Tier 3, our knowledge and use of various formative assessments are important to learning more about why the student is not mastering the curriculum standards. What assessments are readily available to use with individual students? Are the assessments aligned with your curriculum goals? Do they assess the necessary prerequisite skills defined through the task analysis?

In addition, it is important to record and keep track of your instructional techniques, interventions, and student assessment results. This is especially true for students that struggle with learning mathematics. Set up a file or folder for RTI instruction and interventions in your lesson plan book to keep track of the OPTIONS lesson plans you used to intensify instruction and interventions. Make additional copies of the OPTIONS lesson plan forms 6–9 in Appendix A so you can quickly and efficiently record your instruction and interventions and your students results in your RTI classroom.

In summary, when completing diagnostic assessment procedures, including error pattern analysis and precision teaching, we collect samples of student learning through multiple curriculum-based assessments, progress-monitoring probes, and observations or other informal assessments. There are numerous reasons to collect assessment data. The most important reason to collect data is to be assured that *all* students are mastering the critical learning objectives and standards for the curriculum. Assessments can be used at any grade level, in any content area, and in any instructional grouping arrangement. Therefore, during the lesson planning process, consider the methods to intensify intervention during Tier 3, especially for individual students.

Special Education Services within RTI

How special education fits into a tiered instructional model is always a question that arises when developing compressive school-wide RTI models. As we stated in the Author's Note in the Preface, different RTI models have placed special education in different ways within the process. We know there may be controversy regarding Tier 3 because some schools have students progress through each of the tiers, whereas some schools may have students jump from Tier 1 directly to Tier 3. Other schools may have students go through Tiers 1 and 2 and then refer students to Tier 3, during which time the RTI team (including a school psychologist, staffing specialist, and/or administrator in special education) may initiate the process to determine eligibility for special education. This level of intensity is typically for children who have not been responsive to the Tier 2 level of instruction and intervention; therefore, the students are considered in need of more individualized instructional delivery consistent with individualized education programs (IEPs). In our book, we refer to Tier 3 as intensive supports provided by a mathematics coach, mathematics specialist/interventionist, and/or possibly the special education teacher. If Tier 3 services are not working, then the student may need referral to special education services.

When considering the connections, then, between RTI and special education services, we need to consider students who have not been identified as eligible for special education and those with current IEPs. We intensify instruction, assessment, use multiple evidence-based practices and programs, and continuously collect student results through multiple formative assessments. All of this information is critical to share with the school-wide special education team, thus expanding collaboration and support for additional resources and services. When we make a referral for additional assessments to determine the existence of a disability that affects learning in mathematics, we contribute critical information regarding the student's previous learning and achievement in mathematics. The members of the special education team will guide mathematics teachers through the necessary procedures and assessments of the special education process. Today, there are about ten states that use the RTI processes we have described to determine eligibility for special education.

Consideration must be given to how to provide instruction to students with disabilities already receiving special education services within a comprehensive RTI model. Students with disabilities will need Tier 3 services in the content areas of their greatest need. However, a percentage of students with disabilities may be found to have skill deficits more consistent with those nonidentified students placed at Tier 2. The effectiveness of special education for these students would naturally result in some students having skills that are more consistent with those in the some-risk category than those at high risk. Of course, special education students will have skills in some content areas that are consistent with students placed into Tier 1 or the general classroom. The members of the IEP team for the student with a disability will make the decisions regarding the most appropriate placement based on the student's educational needs. RTI offers an organized continuum of support for all students, including students with disabilities, to receive increased scaffolding and resources in the mathematics classroom.

Some individuals may question the difference between a student at Tier 3 who is not identified and an identified special education student who is at Tier 3. The key differences lie in the development of an IEP for the identified students with disabilities that will bring multiple accommodations across many parts of the student's school life, beyond the instructional process taking place at any level of the tiered model. In addition, these students are afforded the legal protections and accountability that are required by law.

Collaboration and Scheduling: All Three Tiers

The key to providing tiered instruction lies in the establishment of a workable schedule that maximizes school personnel resources and a high degree of collaboration among all members of the entire instructional staff in a school. We have found that in many schools using RTI models, the assignment of specific blocks of time each day devoted to tiered instruction proves to be a workable mechanism for organization. Schools use various terms for the tiered instructional block, such as *tier time, power hour,* or *skill groups.* For instance, in the school schedule for implementing RTI for mathematics in an elementary school depicted in Figure 6.8 a block of thirty minutes identified as *tier time* is scheduled each day for each grade. Additional periods, called *X time* are used only for students at Tier 3.

The schedule assigns specific teachers to each block, with mathematics teachers assigned mostly to Tier 1, curriculum specialists and/or instructional coaches typically assigned to Tier 2, and Tier 3 and special education teachers assigned to Tier 3. Math teachers trained on the delivery of specific instructional and intervention programs are also periodically assigned to Tier 2.

A somewhat unique aspect of this particular model is the fact that during tier time, those students currently at benchmark are grouped together and teachers design instructional lessons that are viewed as enrichment to the curriculum. Teachers are encouraged to be creative and add new dimensions to instructional lessons that are aligned to the curriculum but may go beyond the existing required minutes of mathematics instruction delivered to all students. (Blocks of time for mathematics can be thirty to ninety minutes and vary from grade to grade and state to state). By dividing the entire grade into tiered instruction, the model provides opportunities for enrichment that go beyond the core instructional program to students who are already achieving at benchmark levels. Another aspect of the aforementioned school schedule is the inclusion of assigned times each week when progress-monitoring data would be collected for students in Tiers 2 and 3.

Some schools have established more streamlined approaches to scheduling by providing variation within grade-level teams within school-wide block. In the school schedule shown in Figure 6.9, the initial ninety minutes each day is the reading block to meet state legislative mandates. The next thirty-minute block is the school-wide "walk to intervention" time. During that period of time, each student is assigned to an intervention or enhancement group based on biweekly progress-monitoring data. Every certified educator, including librarians, special education teachers, and so forth, is assigned a group of students. Interventions, evidence-based resources, and standard protocols are decided by school and district curriculum specialists. Biweekly intervention groups may vary based on the most current progress-monitoring assessment data. Students needing Tier 3 interventions receive more individual interventions, diagnostic teaching, and so forth during "walk to intervention" time and/or other scheduled times during the rest of the school day.

FIGURE 6.8 Sample School Schedule Using a Daily Time Block for Tiered Instruction

	Monday	Tuesday	Wednesday	Thursday	Friday
9:00– 9:30	Tier time, grade 4	Tier 1 gen. ed. T1/ gen. ed.T2	Tier 2 math spec. 1/interv. 1	Tier 3 math spec. 2/sp. ed. 1	Tier 3 grade 5 X-time, sp. ed.
9:30– 10:00	Tier time grade 1	Tier 1 gen. ed. T3/ gen. ed. T4	Tier 2 math spec. 1/interv. 2	Tier 3 sp. ed. 1/ math spec. 2	Tier time grade 1
10:00–10:15	Tier time grade 3	Tier 1 gen. ed. T5/gen. ed. T6	Tier 2 gen. ed. T6/math spec. 1	Tier 3 sp. ed. 1 grade 3	Tier 3 grade 3
10:15–10:30	Tier time grade 2	Tier 1 gen. ed. T7/gen. ed. T8	Tier 2 math spec. 1/gen. ed. T9	Tier 3 sp. ed. 2/ math spec. 2	Tier time grade 2
10:30–11:00	Core team/ progress monitoring			Progress monitoring Tier 3	Tier 3 grade 6 X-time, math spec. 2
11:00–11:30	Core team/ progress monitoring			Progress monitoring Tier 3	Tier time grade 4
11:30–12:00	Core team/ progress monitoring			progress monitoring Tier 3	
12:00–12:30	Core team/ progress monitoring			Progress monitoring Tier 3	
12:30–1:00	Core team/ progress monitoring	Tier 3 grade 4 X-time, math spec. 1/math spec. 2	Tier 3 grade 4 X-time, math spec. 1/math spec. 2	Progress monitoring Tier 3	
1:00–1:30	Core team/ progress monitoring			Progress monitoring Tier 3	
1:30–2:00	Tier time grade 5 Tier time grade K	Tier 1 gen. ed. T10/ gen. ed. T11 Tier 1 gen. ed. T12/ gen. ed. T13	Tier 2 math spec. 1 Tier 2 math spec. 2	Tier 3 math spec. 2 Tier 3 math spec. 1	Tier time grade 5 Tier time grade K
2:00–2:30	Tier 3 grade 2 X-time, math spec. 2/sp. ed. 2		Tier 3 grade 2 X-time, math spec. 2/sp. ed. 2	Tier 3 grade 1 X-time, math spec. 2/sp. ed. 2	Tier 3 grade 1 X-time, math spec. 2/sp. ed. 2
2:30–2:45	Tier time grade 6	Tier 1 gen. ed. T14/ gen. ed. T15	Tier 2 math spec. 1	Tier 3 math spec. 2	Tier 3 grade 6
2:45–3:00	Tier 3 grade 3 X-time, math spec. 1	Tier 3 grade 3 X-time, math spec. 1	Tier 3 grade 3 X-time, math spec. 1	Tier 3 grade 3 X-time, math spec. 1	Tier 3 grade 6

FIGURE 6.9	Sample of School Schedule Using a Daily Time Block for Tiered Instruction

	Monday	Tuesday	Wednesday	Thursday	Friday
8:30–10:00	Tier 1 instruction: reading (school-wide)	Tier 1 instruction: reading (school-wide)	Tier 1 instruction: reading (school-wide)	Tier 1 instruction: reading (school-wide)	Tier 1 instruction: reading (school-wide)
10:00–10:30	Tier 2 time: walk to intervention (school-wide)	Tier 2 time: walk to intervention (school-wide)	Tier 2 time: walk to intervention (school-wide)	Tier 2 time: walk to intervention (school-wide)	Tier 2 time: walk to intervention (school-wide)
10:30–11:00	Core team/ progress monitoring	Tier 3 interventions (by grade-level teams)	Tier 3 interventions (by grade-level teams)	Progress monitoring Tier 3	Tier 3 interventions (by grade-level teams)
11:00–12:00	Content instruction/ lunch	Content instruction/ lunch	Content instruction/ lunch	Content instruction/ lunch	Content instruction/ lunch
12:00–1:00	Content instruction/ lunch	Content instruction/ lunch	Content instruction/ lunch	Content instruction/ lunch	Content instruction/ lunch
1:00–2:30	Tier 1 instruction: mathematics (school-wide)	Tier 1 instruction: mathematics (school-wide)	Tier 1 instruction: mathematics (school-wide)	Tier 1 instruction: mathematics (school-wide)	Tier 1 instruction: mathematics (school-wide)
2:30–3:00	Tier 2 time: walk to intervention (school-wide)	Tier 2 time: walk to intervention (school-wide)	Tier 2 time: walk to intervention (school-wide)	Tier 2 time: walk to intervention (school-wide)	Tier 2 time: walk to intervention (school-wide)
3:00–3:30	Core team/ progress monitoring	Tier 3 interventions (by grade-level teams)	Tier 3 interventions (by grade-level teams)	Progress monitoring Tier 3	Tier 3 interventions (by grade-level teams)
3:30–4:00	Content instruction and dismissal	Content instruction and dismissal	Content instruction and dismissal	Content instruction and dismissal	Content instruction and dismissal

After lunch, similar procedures are enacted in the content area of mathematics to ensure that Tier 1, 2, and 3 instruction and intervention times occur with students based on their assessed needs. Again, flexibility for scheduling is maintained within the grade-level teams during the content block of time. Grade levels may vary activities during the ninety-minute instructional block to ensure that other specialists within the school (e.g., mathematics curriculum teacher, math interventionist, etc.) are available at the given times.

We have described the three tiers of RTI discretely and explicitly in the last several chapters and the process of RTI has been illuminated. However, we want to offer a simple recap of the tiers here so you can refamiliarize yourself with each one. After reading through the tiers we will ask you to apply what you have learned.

Tier 1 Instruction

As shown in Table 6.2, all students receive high-quality mathematics instruction in their classroom for thirty to ninety minutes each day. This may be provided as whole-group instruction or through flexible grouping strategies (e.g., cooperative learning groups, paired instruction, and independent practice). Approximately 80 to 90 percent of all students are expected to learn during Tier 1 instruction. Universal screening assessments identify students who may be struggling with mathematics. After five to ten weeks of subsequent high-quality instruction and progress monitoring, students who continue to struggle—as indicated by progress-monitoring data—receive additional, more intensive instruction and intervention at Tier 2.

TABLE 6.2 Tier 1 Summary

Tier 1 Instruction	
Who receives instruction?	All students
Who provides instruction?	Mathematics or grade-level teacher
How is instruction delivered?	Whole group, cooperative learning groups, paired instruction, Independent practice
How long is the instruction provided?	Thirty to ninety minutes daily for entire school year

Tier 2 Instruction/Intervention

In addition to mathematics instruction in the classrooms, students not making adequate progress at Tier 1—approximately 10 to 15 percent of the class—receive different or additional support, as shown in Table 6.3. This instruction is provided by the classroom teacher or another educational professional in mathematics. Intervention should be provided in small groups of three to five students for fifteen to forty minutes two to five days per week. Educators should group students according to their area of difficulty (i.e., homogenous groups) and provide intensive, targeted instruction/intervention. For example, students struggling with addition problems that involve carrying should be grouped together, as should students having difficulty with fractions. Tier 2 instruction/intervention typically lasts ten to sixteen weeks, depending on the complexity of the skills to be taught and mastered. The length of the instructional period may depend on the instructional program being implemented.

Tier 3 Intervention

A small percentage of students who do not respond to Tier 2 intervention—1 to 5 percent of all students—will require even more intensive, individualized instruction, as summarized in Table 6.4. Students receive intensive instruction/interventions individually or in small groups of one to three students for at least twenty minutes each day. Often, instruction is typically provided by a specialist who designs individualized interventions. In addition, Tier 3 intervention may be provided through special education services. Statistically, 5 to 10 percent of all students have disabilities in mathematics (Little, 2009c). To qualify for special education services, a student must meet certain criteria: (1) he or she must have a disability, and (2) that disability must significantly affect his or her educational performance.

We have provided a template in Figure 6.10 to help you put your new knowledge into action. See what you can describe and do in each of the components. Place the following words in the RTI components section, then describe how you will implement RTI in your classroom for mathematics:

- Universal screening
- Progress monitoring
- Effective instruction
- Interventions
- Diagnostic teaching
- Curriculum-based assessments
- Scaffolding
- Intensifying instruction
- Manipulatives
- Differentiated instruction.

TABLE 6.3 Tier 2 Summary

Tier 2 Instruction/Intervention	
Who receives instruction?	Students not adequately responding to instruction in mathematics
Who provides instruction?	Math teacher or other knowledgeable professional (e.g., curriculum specialist)
How is instruction delivered?	In small groups of three and in homogenous groups determined by skill
How long is the instruction provided?	Fifteen to forty minutes, two to five days per week, for ten to sixteen weeks

TABLE 6.4 Tier 3 Summary

Tier 3 Intervention	
Who receives instruction?	Students not adequately responding to intensive instruction and interventions in Tier 2.
Who provides instruction?	Intervention specialist or special education teacher
How is instruction delivered?	Individually or in groups of no more than three students
How long is the instruction provided?	A minimum of twenty minutes daily, but the length of the instructional period is individualized

Please use words more than once and add other terms and components.

Placing the focus on our students involves many facets. We include ourselves in the instructional decision making, we involve our colleagues in the intervention process and in collaboration, we look for ways to help students approach mathematics in order to help them gauge understanding, and most important, we fulfill our obligation by not giving up on them. As we approach the next chapter, we want you to think about your school and the personnel involved. We want you to consider the following questions as they pertain to you and others: What do you have to offer other personnel? What do they have to offer you? How can you work together to meet the needs of all students in your school? How can you and your school-based team successfully embed RTI into the school's dynamic? If you are already implementing RTI, how can you enhance your current RTI framework to meet students' needs?

The next chapter will broaden your knowledge in both professional and collegial conversations and will center on enhancing lessons that serve as cornerstones for continuous improvement. We will discuss professional colearning to improve teaching, particularly for those who serve in the mathematics classroom.

FIGURE 6.10 RTI Template

	Tier 1	Tier 2	Tier 3
RTI components			
Classroom implementation: instruction and/or intervention			
Classroom implementation: assessments			

We will offer specific strategies for school reform and help you maximize your students' overall mathematics potential. Finally, we will encourage you to increase your role, opportunities, and rationale for collaboration within your school.

TEACHER'S CORNER

Keys to Getting You Started with RTI

- Review the considerations for a Tier 3 intervention plan on page 107. These are important questions to answer as you prepare for RTI and Tier 3 instruction.

- Using progress-monitoring data from Tiers 1 and 2, discuss with your RTI team which students will need Tier 3 supports.

- Determine for whom, where, how, and when Tier 3 supports will be delivered.

- Complete Intervention Form A (Reproducible #12 in Appendix A) and the Implementation Schedule (Reproducible #13).

- Determine the progress monitoring for Tier 3 students.

- Establish decision-making rules for instructional adjustments for students who will need additional supports (Tier 3) and how you will move students back into Tier 1 when progress goals have been met. You must also discuss what actions will take place when/if students do not respond to Tier 3 and need a possible referral for special education services.

- Complete Professional Learning Community Chapter 6 activities.

Supporting Students in Our School through Professional Learning about RTI

"Students benefit academically when their teachers share ideas, cooperate in activities, and assist one another's intellectual growth. Good instruction flourishes when teachers collaborate."

—*U.S. Department of Education, 2010*

What You Will Find in This Chapter

- Key features about changes needed in schools to support professional learning and implementation of RTI
- Professional learning structures (e.g., action research, professional learning communities, lesson study) and how they support teacher learning about RTI
- Action planning to enhance professional learning and collaboration in the school for success with RTI

Teacher's Voice

We had many meetings throughout the school year with my principal, my grade-level team, and the school district. On Wednesdays, there were grade-level planning meetings once per week where we would discuss the collected multiple types of student assessment data and completed multiple forms for the different purposes. At these meetings, we were also expected to discuss curricular needs and student concerns. On Thursdays after school, there were school improvement committee meetings. The RTI team meetings were held every other Monday right after dismissal. At the most recent faculty meeting (each Tuesday after dismissal), the principal shared that the school district will be mandating Lesson Study to improve student achievement, which will begin next month. Each grade-level team is to develop a set of procedures based on the school district guidance. We were lucky to already have an instructional coach in mathematics in the school. Where would the team find time to develop and implement one more thing in the current schedule?

When I attended the RTI grade-level meetings on Mondays, the suggestions shared by the instructional coach in mathematics were so helpful. While I was in the RTI meeting, I took notes about the resources and materials to use. I often felt, however, that I had nothing to share. I was not sure how to interact with the problem-solving process used in the meetings. How did this connect with the data I was already required to collect and share with other educators? Also, the discussions always made sense in the meetings. But when I tried the new materials, including the manipulatives to teach the lessons to some of my students, I felt that the lesson did not meet the students' needs. It was difficult to engage the students, as I was unsure of the lesson content and new materials. Although I am committed to improving my students' learning, I just feel so overwhelmed with all of these mandates. How could I learn and implement all of this new information to make a difference with my students? I want to learn, I want make a difference, and I want to learn how I can connect with other colleagues as part of an ongoing learning community to ensure my success and my students' success. At times, I felt this to be a little overwhelming, but soon discovered that team meetings provided much support and were beneficial as they helped each of us throughout the year. I have found this connection to be very important within the RTI in mathematics process.

Ms. Holly, fourth-grade teacher

At the beginning of this text, we described our goal not only as filling a pail, but also as lighting a fire. Through these previous chapters, we have described concepts and resources, provided examples, and encouraged action to implement RTI in mathematics within the classroom. Although we want to meet the learning needs of all students by implementing RTI in our classrooms and schools, sometimes there just seems to be too much to do every day. Most days, we already feel overwhelmed with all of the teaching responsibilities, as Ms. Holly described. Additional mandates usually mean more requirements, forms, and follow-ups. Most schools are already participating in school improvement processes that include many tasks for everyone in the school. So the questions remains, how can we work together to implement RTI in an already hectic schedule? Where do we find time to collaborate with other educators? How does RTI fit with the other professional learning and responsibilities already in place at your school? What is currently in place in your school to support professional learning and implementation of RTI in the mathematics classroom?

Education is a people-oriented business. Students are our business. We must remember that student improvement and achievement are linked to our learning as professionals. Schools do not improve unless the faculty improves. In high-achieving schools, teachers view their professional development and learning as a lifelong endeavor. Teachers in high-achieving schools feel they faced new challenges each year and could describe the various ways they had adapted, enhanced, and continued polishing their teaching repertoires. Teachers in "moving" schools tended to be collaborative and likely to seek out ideas from their colleagues (Rosenholtz, 1989). The goal is to be "movers" and make schools the high-achieving ones.

As we think of this, we know that Response to Instruction/Intervention (RTI) requires professionals who are highly knowledgeable in evidence-based instructional practices, as well as intervention materials, multiple types of assessments, and data collection methods. In addition to content expertise, we must also possess skills in differentiating and intensifying instruction, data interpretation, problem solving, and collaboration. A key component necessary for implementing RTI is continued professional learning and collaboration among multiple educators. As we continuously learn, our students continuously improve.

Building professional and collegial conversations centered on enhancing our multi-tiered lessons sets a cornerstone for continuous improvement. Specific strategies for school reform and renewal based on continuous learning serve as the catalysts for maximizing the potential for student improvement in mathematics within RTI. The focus of this chapter is professional co-learning to improve teaching by all educators in the mathematics classroom within a comprehensive system of school reforms. Various professional learning structures such as action research, lesson study, and professional portfolios will be discussed related to implementing RTI in your school.

Supporting Students through Collaboration within RTI

From your reading about RTI, it is clear that implementing RTI within districts, schools, and classrooms requires comprehensive support for students through our collaboration with colleagues. Successful implementation requires coordination and communication to ensure that a clear vision is articulated, sufficient resources are dedicated, necessary skills are supported, and incentives are identified within a clear action plan. No two schools are ever identical in staff, curriculum organization, teacher involvement, requirements, students, and so on. For example, some schools may have a mathematics instructional coach in each grade level; other schools may have no one designated as an instructional coach and additional personnel may be limited. It is very important to identify the staff and available resources in *your* school. School change is a complex process that requires the active involvement of everyone through explicit and thoughtful coordination of activities and procedures. This can be difficult to do, because we are often asked or required to do more with less. As Ms. Holly mentioned when describing her school, the meetings and responsibilities continue to be added. Many times, if we look at the purpose of the activity, we can align and meet the goal by enhancing something we are already doing within our school.

School change requires several important components, as you can see in Figure 7.1. Each of these components is critical to school reform efforts for implementing RTI within your classroom, school, and district. As we highlight the various components, reflect individually and discuss these with your colleagues.

FIGURE 7.1 Model for School Change

Managing Complex Change					
Vision	Skills	Incentives	Resources	Action Plan	→ Change
	Skills	Incentives	Resources	Action Plan	→ Confusion
Vision		Incentives	Resources	Action Plan	→ Anxiety
Vision	Skills		Resources	Action Plan	→ Gradual Change
Vision	Skills	Incentives		Action Plan	→ Frustration
Vision	Skills	Incentives	Resources		→ False Starts

We should not see RTI as "another new thing." Rather, we should think about how existing personnel, resources, and materials can be used in more coherent and interrelated ways to improve instruction for all students and to reduce the numbers of students struggling to learn mathematics within our classrooms. Alignment of available resources to the established curricular objectives and benchmarks is critical for students to be able to master the curriculum. Collaboration among various professionals is needed when planning, gathering resources, and delivering tiers of support across each of the grade levels in mathematics. Resource mapping will identify appropriate and available resources as you begin implementation of RTI within your school. We want you to think about what resources are available (e.g., personnel, materials, time, and funds). How can these resources be leveraged and maximized to ensure that we identify and use the necessary resources within our schools to meet our students' needs in mathematics?

Making RTI Work for Students

Getting started with RTI in schools can be difficult, especially if leadership for this initiative is not clear. One of the difficulties is that the responsibilities for RTI may be designated to different areas, such as curriculum, special education, school psychology, and building administration. The promise of RTI can be realized only if there is a genuine collaboration among the knowledgeable and expert professionals. Who are these experts in your school? How can you connect with them to effectively implement RTI in your classroom or school? Those who should be involved in planning and implementing RTI from the beginning include: (1) mathematics teachers (because this is where RTI begins), (2) mathematics coaches and interventionists (because of their broader knowledge of strategies and resources in mathematics), (3) special education teachers (because of their acquired knowledge of how to intensify and individualize instruction for struggling students, (4) school psychologists (because of their knowledge of various assessments and data), and (5) building administrators (because of their overall knowledge of school improvement). Once the members of the RTI team are identified, important decisions must be made while considering the other initiatives within the school and district to coordinate and build support. You should determine how and to what degree:

- RTI supports and coordinates with the state, district, and school visions, missions, guiding principles, and other initiatives and mandates
- RTI supports and enhances curriculum, instruction, and assessment
- RTI uses available data from multiple sources for instructional decision making
- RTI processes and procedures build on current school improvement procedures

A TIME TO REFLECT

Consider current implementation of RTI in mathematics in your school. Think about and write down the committees, meetings, and professional development resources that are available in your district and school that may be used for RTI implementation. What other resources, materials, and professional development resources are needed to fully implement RTI with quality? What if your school does not have anyone called the instructional coach or curriculum specialist? In this case, the question is who are the most knowledgeable mathematics teachers in your school and your district? How can they be involved with RTI? How can you connect with them to learn more?

On a daily basis, we strive to improve learning and outcomes for all students within our classrooms, schools, and districts. This goal is achieved through the *knowledge* and *skillful use* of evidence-based instruction and interventions by teachers and other school professionals. As we have identified, screening measures, diagnostic assessments, and continuous progress monitoring of students' learning in mathematics provide data and ongoing feedback to teachers, which we use to inform instruction. Beyond yielding targeted, differentiated instruction, data-driven decision making can be enhanced, implemented, and monitored as part of mandated accountability and considered before referrals for additional services, such as special education for identified students, are made.

Studies of effective elementary and middle school classroom teachers in mathematics provide us with powerful knowledge and skills for teaching. Skills such as the following are important in making RTI work for your students:

- *Positive expectations for all students.* All educators must believe that all students will learn mathematics, and our role is to enhance and guide learning to meet the expectations and standards for learning.

- *Classroom management.* A caring, organized, and efficient classroom is well-designed and well-managed to maximize teaching and learning opportunities in mathematics.

- *Lesson design for student mastery.* Each tier of instruction includes lessons that are well-designed, well-taught, and well-assessed to ensure student mastery of the curriculum in mathematics.

- *Multi-sourced curriculum.* Knowledge and use of multiple evidence-based instruction and intervention materials, resources, manipulatives, and technologies that meet the student levels of development, knowledge, and experiences are needed to scaffold learning and ensure cultural relevance.

- *Multi-level, diverse instructional methods.* Knowledge and use of multiple and explicit instructional pedagogical methods (e.g., small group, direct, cooperative learning) are necessary to support and guide learning within a continuum of teaching methods (large class to individual students).

- *Multi-level, diverse assessment methods.* Knowledge and use of multiple assessment methods (e.g., curriculum-based, observations) are needed to support and guide assessments within RTI (e.g., universal screening, progress monitoring, diagnostic, and outcome).

These are also the main components and resources for continued school improvement within classrooms and schools when implementing RTI. Your continued learning and expert use of these skills and competencies are the keys to continued student learning and improvement.

Professional Learning: Getting Connected with Colleagues

There are many collaborative professional development structures that enhance the knowledge and use of necessary skills and competencies of mathematics teachers to implement RTI in their classrooms and schools. First, we need to develop and use skills of **data-based instructional decision making** (e.g., action research, teacher inquiry) to implement RTI (as well as other continuous improvement processes within the school). Second, we need to continuously update knowledge of evidence-based resources and materials to improve our students' learning, especially if student progress-monitoring data show lack of learning to date. Professional learning communities (PLCs) have been instituted as a source of continued learning among educators within a school. Third, we need to continuously and collaboratively improve our use of the evidence-based instructional practices, resources, and interventions in our classrooms through **lesson study**. Last, we may need to collect and document student performance data and learning accomplishments related to student, grade-level, and/or school improvement plans (e.g., RTI plans, IEPs, SIPs) through professional portfolios. Through professional learning and collaboration with our colleagues, we will continue to improve, enhance, and polish our competencies and skills to implement RTI with quality and teach using evidence-based instructional practices and interventions with fidelity.

Connecting with colleagues can take many forms. **Action research** (also known as teacher inquiry or data-based instructional decision making) is a process of describing and testing theories through which we study student learning related to classroom instruction. This model of professional development and teacher learning requires us to know about data collection, evidence-based instructional practices and resources, and assessments used in classrooms. Through action research, we are provided opportunities to discuss with colleagues our findings for instructional practices. With that knowledge, we can systematically reflect on our practice and make changes to our instruction based on careful analysis of the current classroom performance of our students (Dana & Yendol-Silva, 2003; Little, 2003; Sagor, 2005). Conducting applied action research has been described as empowering for teachers, giving them opportunities to grow within their professional roles and responsibilities (Glanz, 2003; Little & Houston, 2003).

The cyclical problem-solving process to define, analyze, implement, and evaluate is central to the RTI process when determining instruction and intervention supports for students within the RTI tiers (see center of Figure 7.2). This problem-solving process is central to the action research process. Within this, classroom problems are identified, action plans are developed, data are analyzed and collected, and results are used and shared as teams of educators develop targeted instruction and/or intervention plans that address concerns in students' learning of mathematics.

Because learning is a cyclical process, both action research and the problem-solving process of RTI are continuous. An action researcher continuously observes, analyzes, hypothesizes, assesses, reflects, and adjusts. For example, you may be concerned about the current mathematics progress of students within the classroom as observed during small groups. By collecting the assessment information (data) from available classroom-, school-, district-, and state-administered tests, we analyze the current trends and hypothesize both possible causes and solutions to address the instructional needs of the identified students in our classroom. After implementing the instructional plan, assessment data are again collected to determine the student results after instruction. Reflection on the results and adjustment to instruction, including interventions as needed, continues until student improvement in mathematics is achieved. This cyclical nature of action research provides us with ongoing opportunities to reflect on and refine our own teaching practices (Little, 2009b). Therefore, we collect assessment data, analyze, hypothesize, and implement different instructional methods, programs, and procedures based on the initial mathematics classroom concerns. By collecting additional assessment data after instruction, analyzing the results, and reflecting on subsequent plans, we can determine whether additional adjustments to instruction, including possible interventions and resources from other sources (e.g., mathematics interventionists, special education teachers), may be needed to meet the instructional needs of identified students. This process may be repeated until student achievement is improved and the learning goals are achieved. The movement among the tiers, however, should be fluid as needed. If students (individuals or small groups) continue to experience difficulty mastering the instructional goals and the curricular standards for the grade level, increased and focused

FIGURE 7.2   Relationship between the Tiers of RTI and Cycle of Action Research

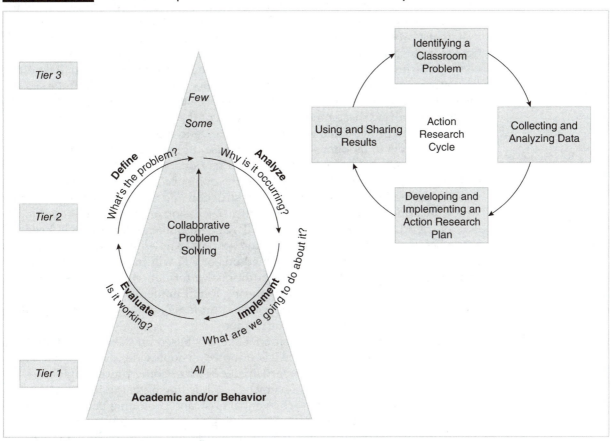

Source: Reprinted with permission from Little, 2009b.

strategies, accommodations, and/or various intervention programs are planned and implemented within the classroom.

Building Professional and Collegial Learning Communities for RTI Implementation

A **professional learning community (PLC)** is described as a model of professional development that focuses on student learning rather than teaching, collaborative work, and accountability for results for more than a decade (DuFour, DuFour, Eaker, & Karhanek, 2010). The professional learning community model flows from the assumption that the core mission of schools is not simply to ensure that students are taught, but to ensure that they learn. This simple shift (from a focus on teaching to a focus on learning) has profound implications within schools. With allocated time, resources, and collaboration, every professional in the school engages in the continuous exploration of three crucial questions that drive the work within a professional learning community.

1. What do we want each student to learn in mathematics?
2. How will we know when each student has learned it?
3. How will we respond when a student experiences difficulty in learning?

To address these crucial questions, educators within PLCs recognize that they must work together to achieve their collective purpose by promoting a collaborative school culture. The powerful collaboration that characterizes PLCs is a systematic process in which teachers work together to analyze and improve their classroom instructional practices. Teachers work in teams, engaging in a cycle of continuous improvement based on student learning (DuFour, 2004). These collaborative conversations and discussions enhance the learning of all professionals, including the teachers of mathematics, as goals, strategies, resources, and results are shared. During these times, the members of the PLC share related, additional resources from professional readings, websites, and other sources.

RTI works in tandem with PLCs because it gives us a way to structure our thinking about what instruction and interventions we should be providing. In collaboration, team members look at all the evidence-based practices and strategies in differentiating and intensifying instruction and interventions to determine which are appropriate for which students. Discussion among school-based members of the PLC about procedures, skills, and resources related to RTI needs to occur before RTI implementation in the schools. Knowledge and skills relating current mandates, procedures, and methods of RTI will improve the functioning and results of teams. The need for additional information may arise from multiple educators for different reasons during initial implementation. For example, we must receive the necessary support and professional development regarding evidence-based instruction and interventions.

Members of PLCs judge their effectiveness based on the results of students in their classrooms. When a PLC is adopted school-wide, every mathematics teacher within the teacher team participates in an ongoing process of identifying the current level of student achievement, establishing a goal to improve the current level, working together to achieve that goal, and providing periodic evidence of progress. Part of this process is developing a set of common formative assessments that are used to collect, analyze, and interpret results of student learning. Throughout the school year, each teacher can then identify how his or her students performed on each skill. Individual teachers have access to the ideas, materials, strategies, and talents of the entire team, including other mathematics teachers and curriculum specialists. In addition, teachers on PLCs have support from their colleagues as they try new ideas, materials, and strategies to meet needs of their students struggling in mathematics. PLCs are a model of sustained, job-embedded professional development for teachers to address the learning needs of their students and improve results. They require us to focus on our students' learning, to work collaboratively to enhance teaching techniques and implementation, and to be accountable for improved results for all students. Through continued conversations about new learning and approaches, PLCs offer an ongoing professional development structure to ensure continued learning for the teachers and other school educators to meet these goals.

Lesson study is a cycle of instructional improvements focused on planning, observing, and discussing lessons and drawing on their implications for teaching

A TIME TO REFLECT

Does your school currently use any of the following professional development structures: action research, professional learning communities, lesson study, and/or professional portfolios? How could these structures be used to support the implementation as an incentive for mathematics teachers and other members of the RTI team? Many school districts currently implement PLCs as part of their job-embedded professional development. Have you met and completed the PLC activities and/or the study questions provided in this text? If so, you have been collaborating and learning as members of a PLC on RTI. What a great way to learn!

and learning. Lesson studies are focused on classroom lessons that provide opportunities for us to implement new ideas, strategies, and/or evidence-based instructional resources and practices to address student learning needs in mathematics and carefully record student learning and behaviors during the lessons.

Within this process, we observe a designated lesson and collect and record teacher and student behaviors to share and discuss with other teachers after the lesson has concluded. In lesson study, we work together to

1. Form goals for student learning and long-term development.

2. Study existing curricula, standards, and resources and relate them to the student results and discuss possible adaptations and enhancements.

3. Collaboratively plan a lesson designed to meet both immediate and long-term goals for all students in the classroom.

4. Teach the lesson, with one team member teaching and others gathering evidence about student engagement and learning.

5. Discuss the observed information gathered during the lesson, using it to improve the lesson, the unit, and the overall instruction, including specific instructions for students who were struggling with the content of the lesson.

6. Teach a revised and enhanced lesson, incorporating suggestions for teaching the lesson to all of the students, from the entire classroom of students to individual students struggling with content. Additional resources and new materials may be suggested and added to the revised lesson. (Lewis, 2002)

Through this cycle, we deepen our knowledge of content, instruction, and student thinking through collaboration with other teachers. These opportunities deepen our own content knowledge in mathematics as we compare various curricula and standards, select and modify a lesson, try the problems ourselves, anticipate student thinking, and analyze student responses to the lesson (Lewis, 2008). Lesson study focuses on the heart of the educational process: what actually happens between us and our students in the classroom. Successful RTI implementation has the exact same focus—that being the improved learning by all students in our classrooms. The components of lesson study support and enhance critical elements of RTI implementation in all classrooms, including mathematics.

During lesson study, we collect data on the supports and barriers to students' learning during actual classroom lessons. This information is used by the teachers and teacher observers to improve their instruction. Similarly in RTI, progress-monitoring assessment data collected by teachers provides important information for intensifying instruction, deciding about evidence-based interventions, and making instructional decisions during problem solving. Teachers and instructional coaches, as members of the lesson study team, meet continuously as a lesson study group. During observations as determined by the visited teacher, observational data are collected and shared with the teacher to improve teaching practices within the classroom. The goal is to enhance current practices to ensure the most effective and skilled teaching. Within RTI, this goal is referred to as *fidelity of implementation*. In other words, we are using the teaching techniques and/or the instructional resources as they were designed. Through this process we continuously improve our teaching, using resources and evidence-based instructional methods and intervention practices with fidelity.

Through this continuous process to enhance, improve, and perfect effective teaching skills (pedagogy) and expert use of resources in mathematics, we collaborate with fellow teachers to plan, observe, and reflect on the results of a lesson. While continuously learning to teach through multiple tiers of instruction and intervention, the lesson study structure encourages us to improve our learning and teaching to meet our students' needs. Discussions of effective teaching practices, student engagement, evidence-based instructional practices and intervention programs, and formative assessment results are facilitated as we collect student assessment data, set instructional goals, and teach our students within a cycle of continuous improvement.

Professional portfolios showcase the learning and results of both teachers and students. A teacher's portfolio can serve many different purposes, depending on the professional goals of the teacher and the mandates of the school and district. As RTI is implemented in conjunction with other school improvement initiatives and ongoing professional development structures (described previously), contents of a teacher's professional portfolio document both the journey of change and learning, as well as the positive results from these changes. At any time, but especially when changes are implemented, it is very important to document and collect items that account for the impact of the actions, especially as related to student learning. Reflecting on student learning is one of the greatest incentives and motivators for us as teachers. The professional portfolio serves to document attainment of goals, both personal and professional, and to stimulate professional discussions and action planning.

Assembling items for a portfolio is a powerful vehicle for professional reflection and analyses. Various documents (e.g., videos from lessons, lesson study planning documents, assessment results for mathematics unit, individual student learning graphs) provide evidence of impact and effectiveness and also assessment data for professional growth and development. We may use similar artifacts to extend the scope of discussions to set new goals. Specifically, the portfolio contents serve as the "data" for the continued professional development of the mathematics teachers. Logs of implementation, lesson planning documents, and videotapes of lessons provide current and accurate information to extend and enhance professional discussions covering all aspects of teaching.

Professional portfolios not only are used formatively with colleagues, but also are used with continued professional learning for the development of teacher knowledge, skills, and competencies. Additionally, professional portfolios can be used as summative evaluations by building principals and for professional advancements, such as when applying for national board certification and/or another professional position. Indeed, the contents of professional portfolios can provide evidence of planning for instruction and interventions, interactions with students, feedback to students, student learning, and contributions to the school, district, and profession. Contents of the professional portfolio should be aligned with the professional standards and requirements of the school district, as available. Suggested contents for your portfolio include:

- Three-week unit plan
- Instruction plan for a single lesson
- Samples of assessment procedures
- Student work samples and other and resources
- Videotape of instruction
- Instructional artifacts of in-class assignments and homework
- Samples of student work
- Written reflections (Danielson, 1996)

Professional portfolios provide artifacts and data related to professional teaching and learning—the critical components of RTI and school improvement—as directly related to student learning. These artifacts provide both formative and summative information for multiple audiences. Most school reform efforts to date have focused on peripheral features of schooling (e.g., school schedules, different instructional materials, grouping patterns) rather than on core instructional features (Elmore, Peterson, & McCarthy, 1996) such as lesson design to intensify instruction. With implementation of RTI, school districts and mathematics teachers have a personal and professional responsibility to engage in professional development. Professional development and sustained support is a two-way street. Schools and districts need to offer supportive, collaborative, and sustained professional development structures to learn about, implement, refine, and polish the necessary skills to implement RTI in mathematics classrooms. We have the responsibility to take full advantage of the opportunities offered, as well as share the results of the professional development. A professional portfolio provides this important venue.

A TIME TO REFLECT

How do you receive feedback about your instruction? Is there another math teacher, an instructional coach, or a teacher in your grade level who can observe and provide feedback? To get started, you may want to make audio or video recordings of your lessons and review them yourself to see strengths or to set goals and targets for improvement.

As a mathematics teacher, do you know that all of your students are learning the established benchmarks? What assessment data do you have to show this? What have you learned and implemented that improved student learning this year? Do you have a lesson that addresses the tiers of RTI? As teachers, it is very important to keep these important artifacts in a portfolio of your successes to share with others (e.g., your principal, the intervention teacher) throughout the year as you continue to learn. If you do not have a professional portfolio, start one today.

RTI Embedded within Continuous School Improvement

Improving student achievement requires proactive problem-solving approaches in the teaching and learning process. Both teachers and students must be involved in the decisions that directly affect that process. As we become engaged in our own professional learning related to the RTI school-based framework, we become the agents of change. We are consciously planning for changes in our classroom and using data to plan and to monitor students' learning. Using problem-solving skills, evidence-based instructional methods, and progress-monitoring assessments is continued through the three tiers of the RTI framework, and intensity and interventions are increased as needed until student improvement is realized. As you consider implementing RTI in your mathematics classrooms, remember that professional development structures such as action research, lesson studies, and professional portfolios (among numerous other structures) have similar goals and necessary skills, as well as needed resources to accomplish them. Table 7.1 compares the components of these professional development structures to RTI. If your school or district has already engaged in significant curriculum design, professional development, and conversations about student data, then you will be able to move relatively quickly into creating a system of data management and progress monitoring needed to implement RTI. Decisions about organization, streamlined procedures, and collaboration are the most critical. Decisions will need to be made about the following:

- What are the sources of data? Are they accessible to teachers? Are they within a data management system that is available, accessible, and useful for instruction and intervention in mathematics as aligned with state and district benchmarks?

TABLE 7.1 Comparing Action Research, Professional Learning Communities, and Lesson Study with RTI

Characteristic	Action Research, Instructional Problem Solving	Professional Learning Communities	Lesson Study	Response to Intervention
Approach	Process, data-based approach to classroom instructional concerns	Continuous improvement approach based on student results	Framework for enhancing instruction through collaboration	Framework of data-based, school-wide instruction and interventions
Goal	To improve student achievement through teacher inquiry and problem solving of instructional concerns	To ensure that all students learn through continued learning of educators	To increase fidelity of instruction, student engagement, and student results	To improve student achievement through high-fidelity implementation of evidence-based instruction
Format	Cyclical	Continuous	Continuous, as determined by team	Cyclical through three described tiers
Members	Teachers (with assistance from other educators, as needed or requested)	Teams of educators, organized as per school-wide system	Teams of educators, organized as per grade-level team	Teams of teachers, school psychologists, math coaches, and other school personnel, as appropriate
Purpose and use	Student achievement, teacher professional development, endorsement, certification	Focus on improved student learning and results by working collaboratively	Improve effective teaching methods to improve student engagement and learning	Student achievement, student prereferral and eligibility for special education, if appropriate
Skills needed	Collaboration, trust, communication, problem solving, organization	Collaboration, trust, communication, organization	Collaboration, trust, effective teaching practices	Collaboration, trust, communication, problem solving, organization
Resources needed	Time for collaboration, knowledge of and access to evidenced-based instructional strategies and assessment, problem-solving processes, administrative support, and skilled colleagues	Time for collaboration, knowledge of and access to evidenced-based instructional strategies and assessment, problem-solving processes, administrative support, and skilled colleagues	Time for collaboration, knowledge of and access to evidenced-based instructional strategies and assessment, problem-solving processes, administrative support, and skilled colleagues	Time for collaboration, knowledge of and access to evidenced-based instructional strategies and assessment, problem-solving processes, administrative support, and skilled colleagues

- How will school-wide data teams work?
- How will existing schedules be adapted to maximize time and align with mandates and activities of school improvement planning, RTI implementation, professional development, and other program responsibilities?
- How will time be allocated for professional development, collaboration, teaming, and additional intervention needed for identified students in mathematics?
- What should/could be done to strengthen core instruction in mathematics across the district and school? How will these plans be completed and supported?

- What types of evidence-based programs for instruction and interventions in mathematics are available? What professional development has occurred for teachers to learn about and use these resources with expertise and fidelity?
- How will these important components be sustained?

Guidelines for successful RTI implementation within a school include the following (adapted from Lau, Sieler, Muyskens, Canter, VanKeuren, & Marston, 2006):

1. Establish a diverse RTI team that includes teachers as well as other educators with diverse expertise.

2. Comprehensively map current initiatives in place related to improving student achievement and supporting teachers and other educators in the areas of curriculum, instruction, and assessment.

3. Communicate with and encourage participation by key stakeholders (teachers, parents, administrators, and community members).

4. Complete a comprehensive needs assessment and action plan for RTI implementation including vision, skills, incentives, and resources (see Teacher's Corner for this chapter).

5. Provide time for planning, professional development, meetings, and ongoing monitoring and evaluation.

6. Complete comprehensive resource mapping and consider developing school-wide use of assessments, evidence-based instruction, and interventions that use current resources (e.g., school-wide after-school tutoring programs).

7. Develop and prepare an implementation manual detailing procedures, expectations, specific forms, and time frames for each tier and step of the process.

8. Provide in-depth professional development (awareness, coaching, and mentoring) to assist teachers and other educators in understanding and implementing action research, professional learning communities, teacher portfolios, and other sustained professional development within the RTI process.

A TIME TO REFLECT

As you review the guidelines for implementing RTI, what is your school doing well and what do you have in place? What would be some next steps to take?

Teaching mathematics to students is not easy. However, with the knowledge, skills, and commitment of classroom teachers and other educators, classroom instructional concerns will be solved through the continued discourse and collaborative professional learning in our classrooms and schools. It is up to *us* to deliver instructional practices that focus on students' strengths and decrease their mathematical weaknesses as we work to help them to be mathematically self-reliant. We have to create learning environments that offer students fresh, clear, and inviting structures that focus on the use of concrete manipulatives, strategies, activities, and opportunities that engage and excite them enough that they keep coming back for more mathematics! As we continue our professional learning, the mandated new procedures, policies, and practices of Response to Instruction/Intervention will be met. Remember, together we can make a difference, together we will make difference, together we *are* making a difference!

TEACHER'S CORNER
Keys to Getting You Started with RTI

- Complete Professional Learning Community Chapter 7 activities.
- Collaborate with colleagues through lesson study to improve your use of evidence-based instructional practices, resources, and interventions in your classroom. You may consider Reproducible #19, The Lesson Study Process (in Appendix A), for your discussion.
- Begin your professional portfolio by collecting any documents of student performance data and learning accomplishments (needs assessment) related to student, grade-level, and/or school improvement plans (RTI plan, IEPs, SIPs, etc.).
- Begin action research opportunities to study student learning as related to classroom instruction.
- Discuss your role within the RTI process. You may want to use Reproducible #18, Team Members and Roles in RTI (in Appendix A), for your discussion.
- Consider Reproducible #20, RTI in Mathematics Implementation Plan (in Appendix A). Discuss your thoughts about this plan with colleagues.

Best wishes for every success with RTI in Mathematics!

Appendix A

Reproducibles and Teacher Resources

Develop your personal action plan for RTI implementation based on the core components of RTI. Then, refer to your plans as opportunities to continuously learn anwd improve your current practices to meet your students' instructional needs in mathematics.

Core Concepts of RTI	How do I currently use this in my classroom?	How would I like to use this in my classroom?	What areas need improvement? How can the improvements be accomplished?
Universal screening and data collection for all students			
High-quality evidence-based instruction			
Differentiated instructional practices			
Continuous progress monitoring of student learning related to curricular standards			
High-quality evidence-based interventions			
Continuous progress monitoring of student learning resulting from instruction and interventions			
School-wide problem solving and classroom instructional supports			
Professional development practices			

Reflect on the following characteristics to assess your relative strengths and to set professional goals as an effective teacher in all three tiers of instruction/intervention.

	Strengths	Professional Goal/Actions
Positive Expectations and Attention		
Classroom procedures are clear and positive.		
High level of student involvement in learning.		
Relaxed and pleasant classroom climate focused on learning.		
Learning assignments emphasize students' interests, strengths, and talents.		
Interesting activities and experiences are matched to students' individual needs.		
Students are encouraged to join after-school groups/clubs/teams.		
Other teaching personnel are involved with students in the class to intensify instruction and interventions for students.		
Teachers and other educators model respect and collaboration.		
Student supports are available and used.		
Classroom Management		
Students are seated in the classroom in a way that best meets their needs (e.g., near the front of the classroom, near the teacher, near the door, near a window, near a supportive peer, away from unsupportive peers).		
The classroom is arranged for learning and to facilitate cooperative interactions and the sharing of materials and ideas between students and adults.		
Materials, centers, and resources are arranged according to curricular goals and tiers of instruction (learning centers, etc.).		
Teachers and students are aware of resources and materials and the procedures for their use and storage.		
Materials and resources are available and set up in advance.		
Lesson Design for Student Mastery		
Academic learning time continues to increase.		
Students are actively engaged in learning.		
Resources and materials are aligned with the curricular outcomes and standards.		
Students can articulate the goals and objectives for learning.		
Multiple opportunities for learning and demonstrating content and skills are provided.		
Students are actively engaged in assessing their learning.		
Students are demonstrating content and skills of the curriculum across the tiers of instruction and intervention.		

	Student Name/ID #		Parent Name	Contact Info.	State Assessment Data—Math	Math Level: _____	Language, Exceptionality, or Special Need	Other
1								
2								
3								
4								
5								
5								
6								
7								
8								
9								
10								
11								
12								
13								
14								
15								
16								
17								
18								
19								
20								
21								
22								
23								
24								
25								
26								
27								
28								
29								
30								
31								
32								

Other notes: _____

_____

Teacher:_____ Grade: _____ Content: _____

Team members: _____

Curricular goals to master as aligned with district/state/national standards:

Assessments necessary/available:	Criteria for mastery (progress monitoring):
District-/school-based:	District-/school-based:
Curriculum-based:	Curriculum-based:
Other:	Other:
Name:	
Source:	

	Aug.	Sept.	Oct.	Nov.	Dec.	Jan.	Feb.	March	April	May	June
Outcomes											
Criteria for performance											
Critical skills											
Prior knowledge											
Resources											
Supplemental materials											
Assessments											

Place names of students in boxes as your seating chart (feel free to use a copy of your seating chart, as well). During allotted time, record the information about class expectations and activities. For five minutes, record student behaviors for any identified students, using key below.

Class: _____ Time of day: _____ Learning activity: _____

Instructional arrangement: _____ Observer: _____

Key: Write letters to record students who *did not exhibit* the behavior in box above.

E: Engaged in math activity as described

Q: Quietly completed task

A: Answered questions correctly

R: Represented problem (visually)

U: Used manipulatives, calculators, etc.   Other: _____

M: Demonstrated mastery with skills   Other: _____

Needs/concerns: _____

O—Outcomes and objectives: (1) NCTM process standards this lesson will focus on (problem solving, reasoning and proof, communication, connections, representation); (2) attitude and mathematics anxiety; (3) math standards and expectations this lesson will address (numbers and operations, algebra, geometry, measurement, data analysis and probability); (4) state and local standards you must include.

Objectives of lesson and concept to teach: What is the purpose/learning goal of each lesson segment? What will students learn? How does this align with the standards? Does this lesson build on previous content or different content?

P—Prior knowledge, prerequisite skills, and/or necessary concepts: What prior knowledge/scaffolding is necessary for this lesson?

Indicate the cognitive levels you will use and explain how and why you chose each.

concrete	concrete-representational	concrete-abstract
representational	representational-concrete	representational-abstract
abstract	abstract-concrete	abstract-representational

Materials/resources: What materials will you need as the teacher? What materials will students need? Complete this for each of the tiers.

Personnel: Which instructional personnel have the knowledge and skills to assist with teaching: coteacher, instructional coach, instructional resource teacher, special education teacher, others? Complete this for each of the tiers.

T—Teaching within the tiers: Teaching/learning strategies: Which strategy (s) and student interests are you going to focus on in this lesson? Include all that apply in EACH of the Tiers.

whole group	small group	cooperative grouping
peer tutoring	choice boards	compacting
differentiation	visuals	teacher-led discussions
student-led discussions	whole-group discussions	small-group discussions
learning contracts	learning centers	task choice
flexible grouping	tiered assignments	interest centers or groups
design a mural	put on a demonstration	set up an experiment
build a model	write a report	develop a computer presentation
write a song	make a movie	vocabulary development
compare/contrast	classify/categorize	create a diagram/drawing
experiments	role playing	use models
reflective thinking	jigsaw	debate
freewriting	thematic approach	think and wait time transitions
K-W-L	dialogue journal	brainstorming
predicting	observing	explaining
interviews	graphic organizer	concept mapping
storytelling	games	questioning techniques
exploration	problem solving	manipulatives (which ones?)
technology		

Others:

Teaching with motivation: How will you get your students excited about what you are teaching them? What invitations will you provide to get them to learn? How will you keep their attention and interest?

Teaching tied to previous learning: How will you tie to what you are about to teach with what they already know, their readiness, and so forth? What scaffolding is necessary?

(continued)

Teaching sequence: (1) How will you introduce the lesson? After posing an initial setting, ask students to begin brainstorming about possible problem-solving strategies (modeling, acting, drawing, diagrams, simplifying, looking for patterns, etc.).

(2) What is your instructional outline? Direct students to analyze the problem for knowns/unknowns. Introduce strategies to help students arrive at possible solutions, use models, draw pictures, diagrams, patterns, and so forth.

(3) What higher order questions will you ask?

(4) How will you model or offer instructional input?

(5) What will you provide as guided practice to check for understanding of an activity?

(6) What will you offer for independent practice?

(7) Wrap-up, closure, or closing remarks: How will you encourage your students to reflect on or discuss what they have just learned? Some examples include journal writing, discussions, exit cards.

I—Instruction/intervention to intensify through the tiers: How will you enhance this lesson to meet individual learning needs of your students who may need additional support? Review the decisions and questions included in the teaching area to add enhancements/revisions to personnel, materials, and instruction/intervention through Tier 2 (targeted for smaller groups) and/or Tier 3 (intensive interventions for a very small group of students or an individual). Also, consider the following instructional components to intensify instruction: dosage; instructional time; pacing appropriate for group size; provide immediate, positive feedback; frequent student response opportunities; and monitor/correct student responses.

O—Ongoing progress monitoring of assessment procedures and results: How will you know the students have mastered/acquired the knowledge, skills, content, and behavior taught? How will you know the objective was met? Summarize, synthesize, and analyze, and include results for each of the following:

Universal screening

Progress monitoring (including curriculum-based assessments)

Diagnostic assessments

Precision teaching

Observations

Interviews with students

Other forms of data collection relevant to instruction and interventions

N—Needs of the small groups/individual students: What accommodations and backgrounds will be considered during the lesson? Include all that apply for Tiers 1, 2, and/or 3.

Adapt the number of items

Adapt time allotted

Adapt skill/ability level (allow calculators, simplify tasks)

Adapt problem type and how the learner may approach the problem/task

Adapt goals/expectations while using same materials

Use technology/computers

Adapt/increase the amount of personal assistance to student to address:

Poor motor skills	Poor memory	Difficulty following directions
Poor written expression	Reading below grade level	Difficulty with concepts/skills
Poor vision	Poor number alignment	

S—Summarize: Write the results of all curriculum-based assessments, informal observations/assessments, and your observations and interviews with your students. These data and assessments will be important as decisions are made regarding necessary enhancements to instruction and interventions within the tiers of instruction in mathematics. These assessment results for instruction and interventions will also be important as individual students may need more intensive interventions and/or specialized programs and services, such as special education, if appropriate.

Planning Considerations for Lesson Planning—Overview

Mathematics concept/standard:.	Unit:	Grade:
Lesson objective:	Student interests/needs:	

District/state/national standards:

Prior knowledge/prerequisite skills:

Resources/materials:

Textbook:

Other:

Lesson motivation/rationale for learning:

Instruction (introduction and concept development)	*Cognitive level and materials*:	*Teaching/ learning strategies:*	*Student active engagement strategies:*	*Informal assessment/ progress monitoring:*
Small Groups (individuals if needed):	*Cognitive level and materials*:	*Teaching/learning Strategies:*	*Student active engagement strategies:*	*Informal assessment/ progress monitoring:*
Independent Practice and Application	*Cognitive level and materials*:	*Teaching/learning Strategies:*	*Student active engagement strategies:*	*Informal assessment/ progress monitoring:*

Comments on and description of progress monitoring used:

Results:

Next steps:

Teacher comments after reflection:

_____

_____

_____

Teacher name: _____ Grade: _____ Dates: _____

Outcomes and objectives:				
Prior knowledge and preskills:				

	Teaching with Tiers Instruction/Intervention			**Ongoing Progress Monitoring**
	Instruction/ Intervention to Intensify	Personnel (circle)	Materials/Resources	Classroom Assessments and Results
Tier 1: Core	Core instruction:	MT: Math teacher IC: Instructional coach IRT: Instructional resource teacher CT: Coteacher ESE: Special education		Assessment: Results:
Tier 2: Targeted	Small group(s)	MT IC IRT CT ESE		Assessment: Results:
Tier 3: Intensive	Individual	MT IC IRT CT ESE		Assessment: Results: Results:

Needs of Students to Intensify Instruction/Interventions (Sprenger, 2005)

Instructional Component	Tier 1	Tier 2	Tier 3
Dosage: Instructional time	forty-five minutes	thirty additional minutes	fifteen to thirty additional minutes
Pacing appropriate for group size	thirty students	small groups of six	one on one
Provide immediate, positive feedback	teacher, peers—rubric	resource teacher	interventionist
Frequent student response opportunities Monitor/correct student responses	one to thirty response ratio	one to six response ratio	each time 100%

Summarize and share: Reflect on students' results
SUMMARIZE Date to review instruction/intervention and assessment data: _____ Team meeting members: _____ Location: _____

FOR GROUPS/GUIDED MATH/SCAFFOLDING

OUTCOME (Standard in mathematics):

PROGRESS-MONITORING DATA:

TIER 1 Objectives:

Essential Questions:

Length of Time (days):

INSTRUCTIONAL PERSONNEL (circle all that apply):

MT: Math teacher

IC: Instructional coach

SP: School psychologist

IRT: Instructional resource teacher

CT: Coteacher

Interventions Record intervention, method to intensify, other professionals, and other classroom/student considerations used.	**Ongoing Progress Monitoring (OPM):** Record OPM assessment, results, and dates. Be sure to attach charts and graph results.

Group 1	Group 2		Group 3	Group 4
Day 1	Day 2	Day 3	Day 4	Day 5
Math rap (10/12) Whole-group lesson Guided practice Diagnostic assessment Introduce independent learning stations (see below)	Homework check Mini-lesson Homework check Independent learning station groups	Homework check Mini-lesson Independent learning station groups	Homework check Mini-lesson Independent learning station groups	Summative assessment

(continued)

Concepts for Knowing	Concepts for Learning	Websites:

Needs of Individual Students

Independent learning stations:

Computer stations:

Questions to ask:

SUMMARIZE

Date to review instruction/intervention and assessment data: _____

Team meeting members: _____

Location: _____

Intensifying Instruction and Interventions using targeted OPTIONS in Tier 2 and Tier 3

OUTCOME (Standard in mathematics):

PROGRESS-MONITORING DATA:

TIER 2/TIER 3 Objectives:

TIER 2/ TIER 3 EBP, Length of Time (days):

INSTRUCTIONAL PERSONNEL (circle all that apply):

MT: Math teacher

IC: Instructional coach

SP: School psychologist

IRT: Instructional resource teacher

CT: Coteacher

	INTERVENTIONS Record intervention, method to intensify, other professionals, and other class-room/student considerations used.	**ONGOING PROGRESS MONITORING (OPM)** Record OPM assessment, results, and dates. Be sure to attach charts and graph results.
Tier 2: Mathematics Students' Names:		
Tier 3: Mathematics Students' Names:		

NEEDS OF INDIVIDUAL STUDENTS
Remember to record all interventions, data from progress monitoring, and so forth for each individual student for possible referral as well.

SUMMARIZE

Date to review instruction/intervention and assessment data: _____

Team meeting members: _____

Location: _____

Reflect on and complete the following open-ended probes to assist you in investigating your initial concerns and identifying a classroom problem or area of concern.

In my classroom I am currently concerned about:

In order to investigate my concern, I need to collect information on:

I will gather this information by collecting the following sources of data:

After analyzing my data, I found that my students are having difficulty with:

To meet my students' instructional/behavioral needs, I need to focus my instruction on:

Florida Department of Education. (2004). *Improving student learning through classroom action research.* Tallahassee, FL: Author. Reprinted with permission.

Instructional Characteristic	Evaluation Question	Well Met	Somewhat Met	Not Met
Clear instructional targets	Are the purpose and outcomes of instruction clearly evident in the lesson plans?	☐	☐	☐
Clear purpose for learning	Do the students understand the purpose for learning the skills and strategies taught?	☐	☐	☐
Clear and understandable directions and explanations	Are directions clear, straightforward, unequivocal and without vagueness, need for implication, or ambiguity?	☐	☐	☐
Adequate modeling	Are the skills and strategies included in instruction clearly demonstrated for the student?	☐	☐	☐
Guided practice and corrective feedback	Do students have sufficient opportunities to practice new skills and strategies with corrective instruction offered as necessary?	☐	☐	☐
Instructionally embedded assessments	Are instructionally embedded assessments used to monitor students' mastery of skills and strategies and to pace students' learning?	☐	☐	☐
Summative assessments	Are summative assessments used to monitor students' retention and reinforcement of skills and strategies following instruction?	☐	☐	☐

Curriculum Characteristic	Evaluation Question	Well Met	Somewhat Met	Not Met
Instructional scope	Does the curriculum include all key instructional content necessary to achieve the goals of instruction?	☐	☐	☐
Instructional sequence	Is the curriculum sequenced in a logical order that builds skills from prior skills and extends skills in order to move students to independent mastery?	☐	☐	☐
Consistent instructional format	Are the instructional strategies consistent from lesson to lesson?	☐	☐	☐
Addresses multimodality instruction	Are a variety of instructional methods used to provide the students with auditory, visual, and hands-on learning activities?	☐	☐	☐

Source: www.pattan.k12.pa.us/files/SpEd/conf05/Marchand.ppt

Classroom Interventions and/or Standard Protocol Interventions

Tier 1

Primary Area of Concern	Classroom Intervention	Duration		Intensity (Group Size/ Session Length)	Frequency (Number of Sessions per Week)	Student's Response to Intervention
		Start Date	End Date			

Tier 2

Primary Area of Concern	Strategic Intervention	Duration		Intensity (Group Size/ Session Length)	Frequency (Number of Sessions per Week)	Student's Response to Intervention
		Start Date	End Date			

Tier 3

Primary Area of Concern	Strategic Intervention	Duration		Intensity (Group Size/ Session Length)	Frequency (Number of Sessions per Week)	Student's Response to Intervention
		Start Date	End Date			

Tasks	Timeline (Beginning/Ending)	Resources

Small group or class:

Date:

Objective:

Name:	Name:	Name:	Name:	Name:
Name:	Name:	Name:	Name:	Name:
Name:	Name:	Name:	Name:	Name:
Name:	Name:	Name:	Name:	Name:

As you identify resources to provide intensive Tier 3 services for identified students, complete this overview of evidence-based resources. Please consult websites listed at end of this form. Share your resources with your colleagues.

Part 1. Why Your School/District/State Should Implement Progress Monitoring

1. What efforts have you already made toward implementation of progress monitoring?	
2. What are your implementation goals for next year?	
3. What are you implementation goals for the next three years?	

Part 2. Considerations for Selecting a Progress-Monitoring System

1. What type of information do you hope to collect about student progress in reading?	
2. What approach will you use?	
3. What is the scope of implementation at your school?	
4. What resources do you have/need? a. time b. money c. personnel d. technology	

Part 3. Print-Based Curriculum Measures in Mathematics

1. With which measures are you most familiar?	
2. Which measures would you like to examine that are aligned with your standards?	
3. What resources do you have/need? a. time b. money c. technology d. training	

Part 4. Considerations for Data-Based Decision Making

1. How will you determine what goals to use? Universal goals? Use of slope data? Goals from a particular system?	
2. How often will you collect data and with whom? School-wide? With individual students?	
3. How will you prompt yourself to apply decision-making rules and how often? Or how will you prompt others?	
4. How will instructional interventions be determined, and how will their implementation be monitored?	

(continued)

Part 5. Considerations When Selecting a Web-Based System of Progress Monitoring

1. What measures are needed?	
2. What types of information are provided?	
3. What is the cost?	
4. Other academic areas covered?	

Part 6. Effective Mathematics Intervention Programs

1. When will you implement interventions?	
2. How will you determine what intervention to implement?	
3. How often will you make decisions about which interventions to implement and whether interventions are working?	
4. What evidence-based programs are available to intensify instruction/intervention?	
5. What evidence-based intervention programs are aligned with your curriculum from the What Works Clearinghouse?	

Websites: Evidence-Based Resources for Implementing RTI in Mathematics

National Council of Teachers of Mathematics

http://standards.nctm.org/document/eexamples/index.htm

National Library of Virtual Manipulatives

http://nlvm.usu.edu/en/nav/vlibrary.html

Intervention Central

www.interventioncentral.org

Access Center: Improving Outcomes for All Students K–8

www.kbaccesscenter.org

National Center on Student Progress Monitoring

http://studentprogress.org

The National Center on Response to Intervention (RTI)

www.rti4success.org

Doing What Works

http://dww.ed.gov

Center on Instruction

www.centeroninstruction.org

IRIS Center for Faculty Enhancement

http://iris.peabody.vanderbilt.edu

Notes:

As you meet with the RTI team, discuss the following questions as you problem solve solutions for the students who may need Tier 1 interventions.

Name of student: _____ Grade: _____ Date: _____

Attendees at meeting: _____ Next meeting date: _____

1. Is the core instruction well-delivered, using evidence-based practices? How was this verified?
2. What assessment tools or processes were used to identify instructional needs and the students' response to instruction/intervention?
3. Is the core instruction effective?
    a. What percent of students are achieving standards/benchmarks (approximately 80% or more)?
    b. What percent of students in subgroups are achieving standards/benchmarks (approximately 80% or more)?
    c. If core instruction is not effective,
        *   Is the curriculum appropriately matched to the needs of the students?
        *   Is support provided for implementation fidelity?
        *   How effectively has the school-based leadership team engaged in Tier 1 level problem solving in order to increase the effectiveness of core instruction?
4. How are parents and students informed, involved, or engaged in supporting and monitoring effective core instruction? Provide documentation.

Action steps:

Person responsible:

Tier 2 Considerations for RTI Team

As you met with the RTI team, discuss the following questions as you problem solve solutions for the students who may need Tier 2 interventions.

Name of student:_____ Grade:_____ Date:_____

Attendees at meeting:_____ Next meeting date:_____

1. What specific supplemental instruction was implemented to improve the performance of at-risk students (more exposure, more practice, more focus, smaller group, type of delivery, program, in addition to and aligned with core instruction, etc.)?
2. How was the supplemental instruction/intervention delivered?
    a. Academic engaged time: How much more time was needed?
    b. Curriculum: What did the students need?
    c. Personnel: Who, when, and where was it provided? How was support provided to ensure fidelity of implementation?
    d. Parents: How were the students' parents informed, involved, or engaged in supporting the instruction/interventions?
3. How effective was the supplemental instruction for groups of at-risk students?
    a. What assessments were used for ongoing data collection?
    b. How frequently were assessments conducted? Analyzed by the teacher or team?
    c. How were the students' parents informed, involved, or engaged in the progress monitoring and analysis of the students' level of performance and rate of progress?
    d. How did you determine whether the instruction/intervention was effective? What was your decision rule to determine that this student would require more intensive, individualized intervention?

Action steps:

Person responsible:

(continued)

Tier 3 Considerations for the RTI Team

As you met with the RTI team, discuss the following questions as you problem solve solutions for the students who may need Tier 3 interventions.

Name of student: _____ Grade:_____ Date:_____

Attendees at meeting:_____ Next meeting date:_____

1. What specific, individualized, intensive instruction/intervention was implemented to improve the performance of the student (more exposure, more practice, more focus, smaller group, type of delivery, program, in addition to and aligned with core instruction, etc.)? At least four pieces of information must be included: amount of additional time, focus of the instruction/intervention, specific instructional strategies, and evidence of fidelity and sufficiency of instruction.
2. How was the intensive, individualized instruction/intervention delivered?
   a. Academic engaged time: How much more time was needed?
   b. Curriculum: What did the student need?
   c. Personnel: Who, when, and where was it provided? How was support provided to ensure fidelity of implementation?
   d. Parents: How were the student's parents informed, involved, or engaged in supporting the instruction/interventions?
3. How effective was the intensive, individualized instruction/intervention for the student?
   a. What assessments were used for ongoing data collection?
   b. How frequently were assessments conducted? Analyzed by the team?
   c. How were the student's parents informed, involved, or engaged in the progress monitoring and analysis of the student's level of performance and rate of progress?
   d. How did you determine whether the instruction/intervention was effective? What was your decision rule to determine any necessary adjustments to the instruction/interventions?

Action steps:
Person responsible:

Grade level: _____ Members: _____ Date: _____

Name of Resource	Skills	Use	Location
Curriculum Materials			
Personnel			
e.g., parent volunteers			
e.g., instructional coach			

Times for meetings/problem-solving sessions:

_____

_____

Sources of additional resources/funds:

_____

_____

Available resources on websites/through school district:

_____

_____

What are the Responsibilities of Each Team Member?

Role	Tier 1—Classroom Instruction	Tier 2—Small-Group Targeted Interventions	Tier 3—Intensive Interventions
Classroom Teachers			
District Leaders			
Special Program Teachers			
School Psychologists/Diagnosticians			
Counselors			
Campus Leaders			
Parents			

Name of teacher to be observed: _____

Lesson study team members: _____

Grade level: _____ Date of observations:_____

Scheduled meeting dates and times:_____

Characteristics and Actions of Your Lesson Study Team	
Defining the Problem	
What instructional focus in content of mathematics and/or student engagement concern will be defined and studied?	
Planning the Lesson	
What research, methods, and resources in mathematics and teaching in the RTI classroom will provide important knowledge and skills to consider?	
Teaching the Lesson	
What observational data about teacher actions and student engagement will be collected during the agreed-on lesson?	
Feedback and Reflection of the Lesson	
What was the teacher's reflection on the effectiveness of the lesson? What observational data did the members of the lesson study team collect and share?	
Lesson Revision and Enhancement	
What revisions and enhancements to the observed lesson could be suggested to increase fidelity of instruction and student engagement in learning?	
Teaching the Revised Lesson	
Using similar observation rubrics, how did the lesson enhancements impact fidelity and student engagement?	
Feedback and Reflection of Enhanced Lesson	
What was the teacher's reflection on the effectiveness of the second lesson? What observational data did the members of the lesson study team collect and share?	
Sharing Results	
What learning was observed by the teacher? What observational and assessment data were collected and shared regarding student impact?	

As you consider continued and sustained implementation of Response to Intervention in your district, school, and classroom within a comprehensive system of continuous improvement within mathematics, consider the following questions and complete the action plan.

Component of Complex Change	Action Plan
Vision • Who are the members of the RTI team? • What is the vision for RTI? • Has a comprehensive, coordinated plan of action been developed/shared for RTI? • What specific outcomes are expected? • Have resources, materials, personnel, and so forth been dedicated to RTI related to other school and district initiatives?	What is needed? Who will complete? When?
Skills • What are sources of needs assessment data to determine specific skills for RTI? • What are the current skills of educators in collaboration; problem solving; effectively planning, teaching, and differentiating instruction and interventions; using assessment data; organizing for multi-tiered instruction? • What sustained professional development will be provided in the above-listed skills?	What is needed? Who will complete? When?
Incentives • How has planning for implementation of RTI involved all educators? • What continued support for the learning of educators will be provided? • How will student results be collected and shared with multiple teams?	What is needed? Who will complete? When?
Resources • Have resources, professional development, materials, assessment tools, evidence-based instructional and intervention materials, technology, and time been identified and allocated for RTI implementation? • Has resource identification and mapping occurred, including available personnel? • Have school improvement resources and other finds been dedicated to RTI implementation?	What is needed? Who will complete? When?

Teacher Resources for RTI and Differentiated Instruction

1. Examples of Math Intervention

2. Intervention Strategies to Help Struggling Learners in Mathematics

3. Problem-Solving Strategies for Elementary and Middle School Students

4. Manupulatives to Concepts—Concepts to Manipulatives

5. Guided Math Group Templates

6. Guided Math Planning Sheet (example and blank template)

7. Extension Menu (example and blank template)

8. Choice Board Activity (example and blank template)

9. Think-Tac-Toe

10. Mathematics Anxiety Survey for Elementary Students

11. Student Interest Inventory

12. Learning Contract (2)

13. My Math Mind-ers (templates for daily and weekly record keeping for students)

14. My Personal Math Journal (template)

15. My Learning Journal (template)

16. Journal Writing Template

17. Literature Template

18. Exit Card Questions

19. Group Work Templates (5)

20. Progress Report (template)

Examples of Math Interventions

General

- All directions, questions, explanations, and instructions need to be delivered in the most clear and concise manner and at the appropriate pace for the student.
- Check to ensure understanding of the concept of numbers and the relationship of symbols to number of objects.
- Allow student to perform alternative assignments. Gradually introduce more components of the regular assignments when he or she is ready.
- Make sure the student understands the reason behind learning. Give concrete examples and opportunities to apply the concepts they are learning.

Students who cannot remember facts

- Separate + and – facts by sets to be memorized individually.
- Use as many concrete examples and experiences as possible (e.g., paper clips, pencils, buttons, milk caps).
- Do not have competitive activities while students are memorizing facts. It may cause them to hurry and reinforce incorrect answers.
- Present a few facts at a time and track the student's success in a visible way.
- Put a number line on the desk to use for adding and subtracting.
- Have the student solve half the problems on their own and use a calculator for the other half.
- Review daily the skills that you want memorized.
- Let students use calculators to correct and check math facts.
- Use Peg-boards, abacuses, and base-10 blocks to teach facts while providing a visual cue.
- Only add one fact at a time as the student shows mastery.
- Use computer games that provide immediate feedback as reinforcement.

Students who have trouble moving from the concrete to the abstract

- Have the student use "sets" of objects from the room to practice the facts.
- Use concrete examples associated with each problem. For example, 4–2 becomes 4 boys went out to recess, 2 boys come in, how many boys are still outside?
- Demonstrate to students how to associate concrete with abstract. For example, 2 pencils + 2 pencils=. Walk students through the process.
- Use a peer tutor, then allow the student to be the peer tutor (learn and teach)
- Review abstract terms daily.
- Limit the amount of information to be learned at any one time.
- Make concepts as real-life as possible.

Students who mix up operations when solving problems

- Have flash cards of the operational signs.
- Have the student use a reminder next to the problems to help them understand the symbols' meanings. Gradually remove the reminders.
- Color code the operation on each problem. Use a different color for each operation.
- Have the student go through daily work first and highlight the operation to be used before doing the problems.
- Enlarge the symbols to cue the student. Use separate pages for the different operations. Gradually combine them.
- Put the operation symbols randomly around the room and have students identify and label them periodically.

Students who have trouble skip counting

- Have the student count concrete items: nickel, dimes, pairs, and so forth.
- Use a number line to help the student see the increments. Keep it on their desk.
- Have the students count and write the number as they count.
- The student should use tangible items to see the numbers increase by the increment used in the counting.
- Help the student understand the why of this concept. Use real-life situations in which skip counting (multiplication) would be used.

Students who have trouble solving addition or subtraction problems

- Have students demonstrate the way they solved the problem, stating the process used and manipulating objects.
- Find opportunities for the student to solve addition problems in real life (lunch money, calendar activities, etc.).
- Be consistent with math terms used.
- Use graph paper to make sure that the numbers line up correctly.

Students who have trouble solving multiplication or division problems

- Have the student use a manipulative to solve the problem.
- Use calculators to reinforce the facts and/or for drill activities. Provide students with shorter tasks but more of them throughout the day (e.g., four assignments of five problems each versus one assignment of twenty problems).
- Explain to the student the real-life applications of learning the concept. Give concrete examples and opportunities to apply these concepts throughout the day.
- Provide the student with self-checking materials, requiring correction before turning in assignments.
- Teach zero elements.

Intervention Strategies to Help Struggling Learners in Mathematics

✓ Identify students using both formal and informal assessments.

✓ Use questioning that focuses on student thinking and reasoning.

✓ Use small groups and pairs.

✓ Have students illustrate understanding of content through graphs, drawings, charts, tables, and models.

✓ Differentiate instruction through learning styles, models, manipulatives, and technology.

✓ Seat struggling learners in the best location in the classroom.

✓ Consider "chunking" the information presented to students so they can manage what they need to learn.

✓ Build and scaffold learning on prior knowledge.

✓ Self-correct mistakes.

✓ Increase task structure (e.g., directions, rationale, checks for understanding, feedback).

✓ Increase task-relevant practice.

✓ Increase opportunities to engage in active academic responding.

✓ Provide a mini-lesson on skill deficits.

✓ Decrease group size.

✓ Increase the amount and type of cues and prompts.

✓ Teach additional learning strategies: organizational, metacognitive, work habits.

✓ Change curriculum.

✓ Change scope and sequence of tasks.

✓ Increase guided and independent practice.

✓ Change types and method of corrective feedback.

✓ Use both teacher and student think-alouds to help understand and solve problems.

✓ Foster student interaction.

✓ Have students solve math problems in group settings and communicate their problem-solving strategies with their peers.

✓ Ensure that instructional materials include a cumulative review in each learning session.

✓ Ensure that intervention materials are systematic and explicit and include numerous models of easy and difficult problems.

Problem-Solving Strategies for Elementary and Middle School Students

- Describe any stumbling blocks along the way.
- What is the unknown, challenge, or question?
- Can the problem be simplified or paraphrased?
- Is there any information that is unnecessary, contradictory, or redundant?
- Describe what you were thinking as you were solving the problem.
- Are there any words to define?
- Have you taken into account all the information?
- Where can I get more information?
- Is there a strategy I can use?
- Has all the information been considered?
- Where did frustrating moments occur?
- Where did the "Aha!" moments occur?
- Were there any times you wanted to give up?

Trial and error

Guess and check

Make a model

Generalize

Make a diagram or draw a figure

Look for a pattern

Work backward

Solve a similar (analogous) but simpler problem

Use a computer

Seek a resource

Make an organized list, write an equation, or use a formula

Looking Back
- Was the problem too easy, too hard, or just right? Why?
- Have you done a problem like this before?
- What if conditions were different? How would your answer change?
- Can the solution be proven?
- Is there more than one solution?
- Does the solution make sense?
- Are the steps correct?
- Can the solution be used to solve other problems?

Manipulatives to Concepts — Concepts to Manipulatives

Manipulative	Concept
Algebra tiles	Integers, equations, inequalities, polynomials, similar terms, factoring, estimation
Attribute blocks	Sorting, classifying, investigation of size, shape, color, logical reasoning, sequencing, patterns, symmetry, similarity, congruence, thinking skills, geometry, organization of date.
Balance scale	Weight, mass, equality, inequality, equations, operations on whole numbers, estimation, measurement
Base-10 blocks	Place value, operations on whole numbers, decimals, decimal-fractions-percent equivalences, comparing, ordering, classification, sorting, number concepts, square and cubic numbers, area perimeter, metric measurement, polynomials
Calculators	Problems with large numbers, problem solving, interdisciplinary problems, real-life problems, patterns, counting, number concepts, estimation, equality, inequality, fact strategies, operations on whole numbers, decimals, fractions
Capacity containers	Measurement, capacity, volume, estimation
Clocks	Measurement, capacity, volume, estimation
Color tiles	Color, shape, patterns, estimation, counting, number concepts, equality, inequality, operations on whole numbers & fractions, probability, measurement, area, perimeter, surface area, even & odd numbers, prime & composite numbers, ratio, proportion, percent, integers, square & cubic numbers, numbers, spatial visualization
Compasses	Constructions, angle measurement
Cubes	Number concepts, counting, place value, fact strategies, classification, sorting, colors, patterns, square and cubic numbers, equality, inequalities, averages, ratio, proportion, percent, symmetry, spatial visualization, area, perimeter, volume, surface area, transformation geometry, operation on whole numbers & fractions, even & odd numbers, prime & composite numbers, probability
Cuisenaire rods	Classification, sorting, ordering, counting, number concepts, comparisons, fractions, ratios, proportions, place value, patterns, even & odd numbers, prime & composite numbers, logical reasoning, estimation, operations on whole numbers
Decimal squares	Decimals, place value, comparing, ordering, operations, classification, sorting, number concepts
Dominoes	Counting, number concepts, facts, classification, sorting, patterns, logical reasoning, equality, inequality, percent, perimeter area
Factor blocks	Primes, composites, factors, multiples, least common multiple greatest common
Fractional models	Fractions-meaning, recognition, classification, sorting, comparing, ordering, number concepts, equivalence, operations, perimeter, area, percent, probability
Geoboards	Size, shape, counting, area, perimeter, circumference, symmetry, fractions, coordinate geometry, slopes, angles, Pythagorean theorem, estimation, percent, similarity, congruence, rotations, reflections, translations, classification, sorting, square numbers, polygons, spatial visualization, logical reasoning
Geometrical solids	Shape, size, relationships between area & volume, volume, classification, sorting, measurement, spatial visualization
Math balance	Equality, inequality, operations on whole numbers, open sentences, equations, place value, fact strategies, measurement, logical reasoning
Money	Money, change, comparisons, counting, classifications, sorting equality, inequality, operations on whole numbers, decimals, fractions, probability, fact strategies, number concepts
Number cubes (dice)	Counting, number concepts, fact strategies, mental math, operations on whole numbers, fractions, decimals, probability, generation of problems, logical reasoning

Number cards	Counting, classification, sorting, comparisons, equality, inequality, order, fact strategies, number concepts, operations on whole numbers, fractions, decimals, logical reasoning, patterns, odd & even numbers, prime & composite numbers
Pattern blocks	Patterns, one to one correspondence, sorting, classification, size, shape, color, geometric relationships, symmetry, similarity, congruence, area, perimeter, reflections, rotations, translations, problem solving, logical reasoning, fractions, spatial visualization, tessellations, angles, ratios, proportions
Polyhedra models	Shape, size, classification, sorting, polyhedra, spatial visualization
Protractors	Constructions, angle measurement
Rulers and tape measures	Measurement, area, perimeter, constructions, estimation, operations on whole numbers, volume
Spinners	Counting, number concepts, operations on whole numbers, decimals, fractions, fact strategies, mental math, logical reasoning, probability, generations of problems
Tangrams	Geometric concepts, spatial visualization, logical reasoning, fractions, similarity, congruence, area, perimeter, ration, proportion, angles, classification, sorting, patterns, symmetry, reflections, translations, rotations
Two-color counters	Counting, comparing, sorting, classification, number concepts, fact strategies, even & odd numbers, equality, inequality, operations, ratios, proportions, probability, integers

Concept	Manipulative
Angles	Protractors, compasses, geoboards, rulers, tangrams, pattern blocks
Area	Geoboards, color tiles, base-10 blocks, decimal squares, cubes, tangrams, pattern blocks, rulers, fractional models
Classification	Attribute blocks, cubes, pattern blocks, tangrams, two-color counters, Cuisenaire rods, dominoes, geometric solids
Constructions	Compasses, protractors, rulers
Coordinate geometry	Geoboards
Counting	Cubes, two-color counters, color tiles, Cuisenaire rods, dominoes, numeral cares, spinners, 10-frames, number cubes, money, calculators
Decimals	Decimal squares, base-10 blocks, money, calculators, number cubes, numeral cards, spinners
Equation Inequalities Equivalence	Algebra tiles, math balance, calculators, 10-frames, balance scale, color tiles, dominoes, money, numeral cards, two-color counters, cubes, Cuisenaire rods, decimal squares, fraction models
Estimation	Color tiles, geoboards, balance scale, capacity containers, rulers, Cuisenaire rods, calculators
Fact strategies	10-frames, two-color counters, dominoes, cubes, numeral cards, spinners, number cubes, money, math balance, calculators
Factoring	Algebra tiles
Fractions	Fractional models, pattern blocks, base-10 materials, geoboards, clocks, color tiles, cubes, Cuisenaire rods, money, tangrams, calculators, number cubes, spinners, two-color counters, decimal squares, numerical cards
Integers	Two-color counters, algebra tiles, thermometers, color tiles
Logical reasoning	Attribute blocks, Cuisenaire rods, dominoes, pattern blocks, tangrams, number cubes, spinners, geoboards
Measurement	Balance scale, math balance, rulers, tape measures, capacity containers, thermometers, clocks, geometric solids, base-10 materials, color tiles
Mental math	10-frames, dominoes, number cubes, spinners
Number concepts	Cubes, two-color counters, spinners, number cubes, calculators, dominoes, numeral cards, base-10 materials, Cuisenaire rods, fractional models, decimal squares
Odd, even, prime, composite	Color tiles, cubes, Cuisenaire rods, numeral cards, two-color counters, factor blocks
Patterns	Pattern blocks, attribute blocks, tangrams, calculators, cubes, color tiles, Cuisenaire rods, dominoes, numeral cards, 10-frames

Concept	Manipulative
Percent	Base-10 materials, decimal squares, color tiles, geoboards, fractional models
Perimeter & circumference	Geoboards, color tiles, tangrams, pattern blocks, rulers, base-10 materials, cubes, fractional circles, decimal squares
Place value	Base-10 materials, decimal squares, 10-frames, Cuisenaire rods, math balance, cubes, two-color counters
Polynomials	Algebra tiles, base 10-materials
Probability	Spinners, number cubes, fractional models, money, color tiles, cubes, two-color counters
Pythagorean theorem	Geoboards
Ratio & proportion	Color tiles, cubes, Cuisenaire rods, tangrams, pattern blocks, two-color counters
Similarity, congruence	Geoboards, attribute blocks, pattern blocks, tangrams
Size, shape, color	Attribute blocks, cubes, color tiles, geoboards, geometric solids, pattern blocks, tangrams, polyhedra models
Spatial visualization	Tangrams, pattern blocks, geoboards, geometric solids, polyhedra models, cubes, color tiles
Square, cubic numbers	Color titles, cubes, base-10 materials, geoboards
Surface area	Color tiles, cubes
Symmetry	Geoboards, pattern blocks, tangrams, cubes, attribute blocks
Tessellations	Pattern blocks, attribute blocks
Transformational geometric translations, rotations, reflections	Geoboards, cubes, pattern blocks, tangrams
Volume	Capacity containers, cubes, geometric solids, rulers
Whole numbers	Base-10 materials, balance scale, number cubes, spinners, color tiles, cubes, math balance, money, numeral cards, dominoes, rulers, calculators, 10-frames, Cuisenaire rods, clocks, two-color counters

Guided Math Group Template

Week of: _____ Concept to learn: _____

Whole-Group Plan					
	Day 1	Day 2	Day 3	Day 4	Day 5
Group 1					
Group 2					
Group 3					
Group 4					

Group 1 Members:

Group 2 Members:

Group 3 Members:

Group 4 Members:

Whole-Group Plan
Whole-Group Lesson

	Day 1	Day 2		Day 3		Day 4		Day 5
Group 1	Whole Group							Whole Group
Group 2								
Group 3								
Group 4								

	Day 2	Day 3`	Day 4	
First Meeting				
Second Meeting				

Small-Group Lessons
GUIDED MATH PLANNING SHEET Example

Group 1 Members:	Group 2 Members:	Group 3 Members:	Group 4 Members:
Jennifer	Meredith	Heather	Mary
Brian	Ronnie	Tameka	Alecean
Mae	Kirby	Tawana	Gigi
Corey	Roderick	Kevin	Amelio

Standard(s):

Center/Station **A**:
Materials Needed:

Measuring distance traveled

Center/Station **B**:
Materials Needed:

Addition/subtracting distance traveled

Center/Station **C**:
Materials Needed:

Graphing distance results of paper airplanes flown

Center/Station **D**:
Materials Needed:

Mean, median, mode of results

Center/Station **E**:
Materials Needed:

Area and perimeter of wings on each plane

Center/Station **F**:
Materials Needed:

Width of tail on each plane flown

Guided Math Planning Sheet

Group 1 Members:	Group 2 Members:	Group 3 Members:	Group 4 Members:

Standard(s):

Center/Station A:	Center/Station B:
Materials Needed:	Materials Needed:
Center/Station C:	Center/Station D:
Materials Needed:	Materials Needed:
Center/Station E:	Center/Station F:
Materials Needed:	Materials Needed:

Extension Menu for Middle School Example

Source: Used with permission from Tricia Parks, Cherokee High School.

Circle A and Circle B are externally tangent. Suppose you know the equation of Circle A, the coordinates of the single point of intersection of Circle A and Circle B, and the radius of Circle B. Do you know enough information to find the equation of Circle B? Explain and show your answer with a drawing. 50 points	Given points A and B, describe the locus of points P such that Triangle APB is a right triangle. 30 points	A zoo has a large circular aviary, a habitat for birds. You are standing about 40 feet from the aviary. The distance from you to a point of tangency on the aviary is about 60 feet. Describe how to estimate the radius of the aviary. 20 points
A cellular phone network uses towers to transmit calls. Each tower transmits to a circular area. On a grid of a city, the coordinates of the location and the radius each tower covers are as follows (integers represent miles): Tower A is at (0,0) and covers a 3 mile radius, Tower B is at (5,3) and covers a 2.5 mile radius, and Tower C is at (2,5) and covers a 2 mile radius. Tell which towers, if any, transmit to a phone located at J(1,1), K(4,2), L(3.5,4.5), M(2,2.8), or N(1,6). 20 points	A dog's leash is tied to a stake at the corner of its doghouse, as shown. The leash is 9 feet long. Make a scale drawing of the doghouse and sketch the locus of points that the dog can reach. 3 ft 4 ft 9 ft 50 points	The Greek mathematician Apollonius (c. 200 B.C.) proved that for any three circles with no common points or common interiors, there are eight ways to draw a circle that is tangent to the given three circles. The red, blue, and green circle are given. Two ways to draw a circle that is tangent to the given three circles are shown below. Sketch the other six ways. 30 points
Suppose you are operating the camera located at point B. If you want a 20 degree angle of the stage, should you move closer to the stage or further away? Explain. Stage 80° $X°$ 1 70° Q 2 30° A 50° 3 B 30 points	Why do you think people historically thought that Earth was flat? Explain, using drawings if needed. Use as many mathematics vocabulary words as you can. You get 2 bonus points for each one used. 20 points	Make a conjecture about tangents to intersecting circles. Then test your conjecture by looking for a counterexample. 50 points

Extension Menu Activities

Name: _____

Unit/Theme: _____

Choice Board Activity Example

Geometry and Measurement

Fourth-Grade Mathematics

Computer Whiz Complete an online game with 100 percent accuracy. You may visit any of these three sites: www.aaamath.com http://aplusmath.com www.ezgeometry.com Print the results and show your teacher.	**"Rapping" It Up** Choose at least six polygons and create a song or rap of polygons. Be sure to include the definitions.	**Don't Be a Square** Draw a square in the middle of a piece of construction paper with an area of 16 square inches. Use each side to create four equilateral triangles. (The side of the square will be the base of the triangle.) Cut out your design and create your new 3D shape. Identify the figure and the number of faces, vertices, and edges.
Name That Street Sign Think of five road signs you may see in the real world. Draw and color each one. The signs should be classified as specific polygons.	**Define Design** Answer the following: Can a rhombus be a square, or can a square be a rhombus? Use a geoboard to explain your answer.	**Garden Center** You are asked to plant a garden with an area of 30 square feet. Using the seed packs provided, decide how you will plant your crops to allow enough growing space.
Angle Dangle! Design a poster that could be used by others to learn how to find a missing angle of a quadrilateral and a triangle.	**It's My Devine Design!** Create a picture using only geometric shapes in your design. You may use construction paper to cut and glue your shapes to form your picture.	**Space Transformation** You have a rectangular-shaped room with an area of 180 square feet. You must paint the walls, carpet the floors, and add any other details that may fit the space. Create a guide sheet for the items and amount of space/materials needed for each.

Choice Board Activity

Name: _____

Unit/Theme: _____

Think-Tac-Toe Menu

1.	2.	3.
4.	5.	6.
7.	8.	9.

Directions: Choose activities in the think-tac-toe design. When you have completed the activities in a row (horizontally, vertically, or diagonally) you may decide to be finished. Or you may decide to keep going and complete more activities on your board.

I choose activities # _____, # _____, # _____, # _____

Do you have ideas for alternate activities you'd like to do instead? Talk them over with your teacher.

I prefer to do the following alternate activities: _____

_____

Name: _____ Date: _____

Mathematics Anxiety Survey for Elementary Students

Do You Have Math Anxiety?

Choose from the scale of 1 to 5 to the right of each question, where 5 corresponds to strong agreement with the statement and 1 corresponds to little or no agreement with the statement.

1. I become physically agitated when I
   have to go to math class.   1 2 3 4 5

2. I am fearful about being asked go to the
   board in a math class.   1 2 3 4 5

3. I am afraid to ask questions in math class.   1 2 3 4 5

4. I am always worried about being called on
   in math class.   1 2 3 4 5

5. I understand math now, but I worry that
   it's going to get really difficult soon.   1 2 3 4 5

6. I tend to lose my concentration in math class.   1 2 3 4 5

7. I fear math tests more than any other kind.   1 2 3 4 5

8. I'm afraid I won't be able to keep up with
   the rest of the class.   1 2 3 4 5

9. I don't know how to study for mathtests.   1 2 3 4 5

10. It's clear to me in math class, but when I go
    home it's like I was never there.   1 2 3 4 5

If you score in the 40–50 range it is likely that you have math anxiety to some extent. You should use the results of this survey to help you to understand your current attitude toward math. Do not consider a high total to mean that you are hopeless and will always feel this way. Mathematics anxiety can be reduced and/or prevented.

Student Interest Inventory

Name:_____

Today's Date: _____ Birth Date: _____

Brothers and Sisters:

Name: _____ Age: _____

Name: _____ Age: _____

Name: _____ Age: _____

Name: _____ Age: _____

Name: _____ Age: _____

My special friends are:

_____

What I like to do most at home:

_____

These are my favorite hobbies:

_____

These are my favorites:

Book: _____ TV show: _____

Movie: _____ Food: _____

Singer: _____ Song: _____

If I had one wish, it would be:

_____

School would be better if:

_____

If I had a million dollars, I would:

_____

This is what my teacher did last year that I liked the most:

_____

This is what my teacher did last year that I liked the least:

_____

Learning Contract

Name

_____

My question or topic is:

To find out about my question or topic…

I will read:

I will look at and listen to:

I will write:

I will draw:

I will need:

Here's how I will share what I know:

I will finish by this date:

Learning Contract

To demonstrate what I have learned about _____,
I want to

_ Write a report
_ Put on a demonstration
_ Set up an experiment
_ Develop a computer
    presentation
_ Build a model

_ Design a mural
_ Write a song
_ Make a movie
_ Create a graphic organizer or
    diagram
_ Other _____

This will be a good way to demonstrate understanding of this concept because

_____

To do this project, I will need help with

_____

My Action Plan is

_____

The criteria/rubric which will be used to assess my final product is

_____

My project will be completed by this date_____

Student signature: _____
Date ___/___/___

Teacher signature: _____
Date ___/___/___

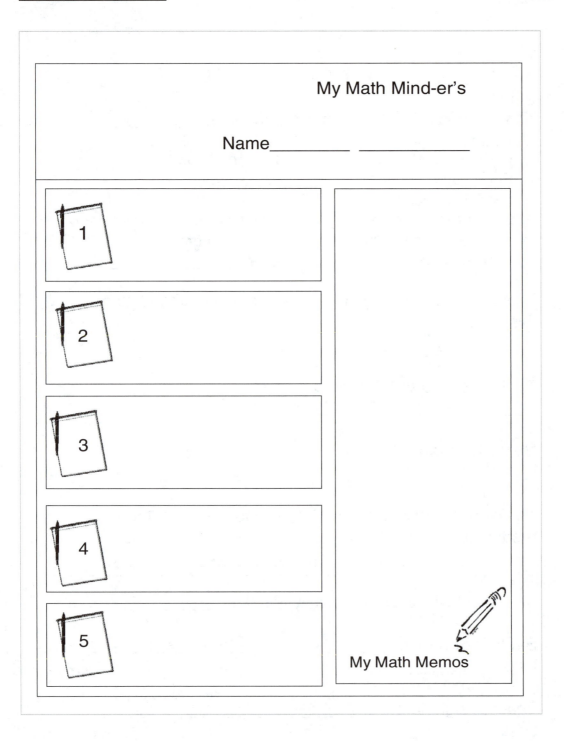

My Math Mind-er's

Name_____ _____

1

2

3

4

5

My Math Memos

My Math Minder's

Name _____ Week of _____

Monday	Tuesday	Wednesday	Thursday	Friday
1	1	1	1	1
2	2	2	2	2
3	3	3	3	3
4	4	4	4	4
5	5	5	5	5
Math Challenge	Math Challenge	Math Challenge	Math Challeng	Math Challenge

I learned from this activity because

_____

_____

I chose this activity because

_____

_____

My Personal Math Journal

Week of _____

Monday

Tuesday

Wednesday

Thursday

Friday

What I learned that was most important to me was . . .

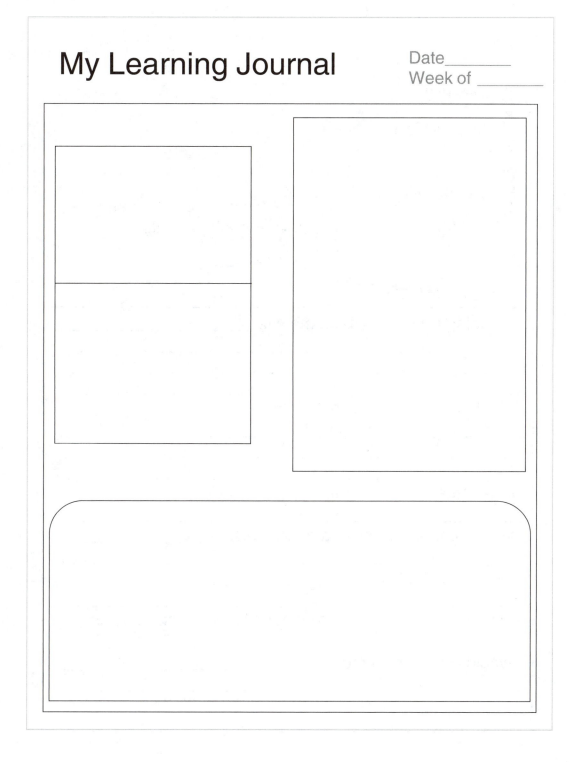

My Learning Journal

Date_____
Week of _____

NAME_____DATE_____

Math + Me =

Journal Writing

Use this page as the first entry in your math journal...

One thing I like best about math is_____
_____
_____
_____

One thing I don't like about math is_____
_____
_____
_____

My favorite math materials are_____
_____

When it comes to math I am strongest at_____
_____

And weakest at_____
_____

A math idea I've heard of but don't know much about is____
_____

I would like to know more about_____
_____
_____

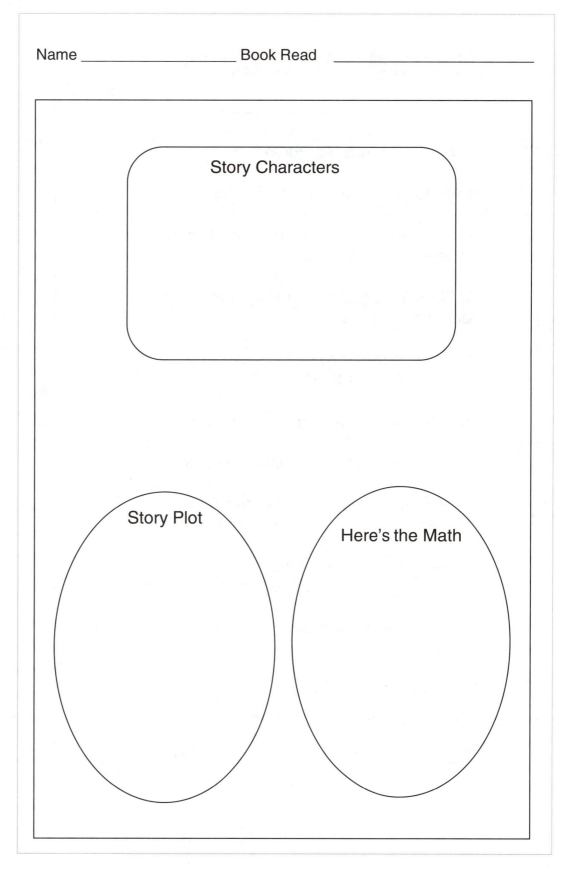

Name _____ Book Read _____

Story Characters

Story Plot

Here's the Math

Exit Card Questions

A. General open-ended questions

1. Write one thing you learned today.

2. What area gave you the most difficulty today?

3. Something that really helped me in my learning today was . . .

4. What connection did you make today that made you say, "AHA! I get it!"

5. Describe how you solved a problem today.

6. Something I still don't understand is . . .

7. Write a question you'd like to ask or something you'd like to know more about.

8. What mathematical terms do you clearly understand or have difficulty understanding?

9. Did working with a partner make your work easier or harder. Please explain.

10. In what ways do you see today's mathematics connected to your everyday life?

NAME_____DATE_____

Group Experiment Outline

Group Members or Group Name: _____

_____

Roles of Team Members: _____

_____

Problem to Solve: _____

_____

Materials Needed: _____

_____

Procedure:	What We Did	What We Observed
_____	_____	_____
_____	_____	_____
_____	_____	_____

What We Found:

_____

_____

What Is the Outcome?

_____

_____

Evaluation of Group, Experiment, and What We Could Have Done Differently or Better:

_____

_____

_____

Group Goals

Group:_____

Date:_____

Goal	Plan of Action	Completed

What we accomplished today:_____

_____

Tomorrow we would like to accomplish:_____

_____

Teacher response:_____

_____

Group Project Study Plan

Group Members or Group Name_____

_____

Roles of Members:	Topic:_____
_____	Type of Project:_____
_____	Beginning Date:_____
_____	Completion Date:_____
_____	

What Do We Want to Discover:_____
_____

What We Will Need for the Study:_____
_____

What We Will Do:_____
_____

How We Will Evaluate:_____
_____

How We Will Share Our Project with Others:_____
_____

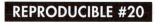

Group Evaluation

Activity:_____

Group Cooperation:_____

Individual Member Cooperation:_____

Use of
Materials:_____

Use of Time:_____

Major Problems within Group:_____
_____

Major Group Strengths:_____
_____

Summary:_____
_____
_____
_____

Next Time We Would Like to:_____
_____

Signatures:_____   _____
                  _____
                  _____   Date:_____

Group Update

Group Members or Group Name:_____

_____ Date: _____

We Are Learning:_____

_____

Questions We Would Like Answered:
1._____
2._____
3._____
4._____

Projects and Activities	Given to Group	Finished On
1._____	_____	_____
2._____	_____	_____
3._____	_____	_____
4._____	_____	_____
5._____	_____	_____
6._____	_____	_____

Problems We Had: Solutions We Used:

_____   _____

_____   _____

Overall Progress of Our Group as of Today:_____

_____

Progress Report

Student:_____ Date:_____

Dear Parents:

This progress report will tell you how your child is doing academically and socially in my classroom. It will reflect your child's growth and development over the past _____ weeks. After you have read this report, please fill out the form below and return to me with your signature by _____. Thank you so much!

Areas of growth:_____

_____

_____

Suggested areas to work on:_____

_____

_____
Teacher Signature

Parent Comments:_____

_____

_____
Parent Signature

Appendix B

Book Study Questions

Chapter 1: Response to Instruction and Intervention in Mathematics

1. How would you define Response to Instruction/Intervention? What are the critical core components when implementing RTI that you see in your classroom and in your school? Explain your answer.

2. Discuss some of the typical challenges for students learning mathematics. What have been your experiences and observations with your students this year? What strategies, programs, and resources have you already used to improve student learning?

3. What are the major goals of your mathematics program? Explain.

4. What are the principles that ground your current mathematics program? Explain.

5. What does your mathematics classroom look like? What does high-quality instruction look like in your classroom/school? Explain.

6. Has your state adopted the Common Core Standards in mathematics? Discuss your knowledge about these standards.

7. How do you know that your students are learning? How do you measure the rate of student learning over time?

8. How do you currently differentiate to meet your students' abilities, knowledge, and skills in mathematics?

9. Are professional development opportunities provided for collaboration among colleagues to discuss mathematical programs and student progress? Are these held daily, weekly, monthly? Are they within the school, unit, or grade level?

10. Do you currently implement RTI in your mathematics program? If not, how might you apply what you have learned about RTI from reading this chapter? How might you enhance what you are currently doing with RTI in your mathematics program within your school/classroom?

Chapter 2: Setting the Stage for RTI in the Classroom by Understanding the Fundamentals

1. How do you define the tiers within Response to Instruction/Intervention?

2. Discuss the major characteristics of instruction within each of the three tiers.

3. What are several effective teaching practices necessary to teach with fidelity? Explain.

4. Name and describe the four steps and questions within instructional, data-based decision-making processes that we use as educators in mathematics.

5. Discuss the necessary teacher characteristics to implement RTI: expert, effective, analytic, and reflective (Allington, 2009).

6. Discuss several ways to differentiate instruction in mathematics during lessons. Name several techniques that Ms. Holly used in her fourth-grade classroom.

7. Reflect on your current knowledge and skills to differentiate instruction based on your students' instructional needs.

Chapter 3: Knowing the Students are Learning: Use of Assessment Data

1. What are the benefits of assessment for you as the teacher? What benefits will the assessment have for your students? Explain.

2. What sources of assessment data are continuously collected, aggregated, and available for school staff, especially faculty?

3. Is your assessment system comprehensive and multi-sourced? What do you do with the different assessments currently in place?

4. How can you determine if your students are learning and what processes can be used to determine the rate of students' mathematical learning over time?

5. What do you do when scores from one instrument are vastly different than scores from another instrument? What tools do you use?

6. What important details can you gain from the assessments?

7. How will assessment assist in the instructional planning for your particular students?

8. How do you promote students' active engagement in the process of tracking their own data?

9. Consider who else is available and knowledgeable to assist with the interpretation of scores and the processing of data in order to understand assessments.

10. How can technology be used to manage data and record it in a way that will help other teachers?

11. Where is there time to discuss student data within the school schedule? How do you find time to collect data about students when they are participating in remediation or small-group instruction?

Chapter 4: Teaching All Students in My Classroom: Tier 1

1. Describe your core curriculum. Verify and list the evidence-based practices as matched to students needs. Discuss your findings with your colleagues.

2. How can you help students focus on instruction and do so effectively?

3. How could this benefit you and others within your school as you "gauge the pulse of your own teaching"?

4. What resources, manipulatives, and programs are available to students with differing abilities within Tier 1 instruction?

5. As you consider formative assessment in the classroom, describe the how you will share learning goals with students. Will you involve them in

self- or peer assessment? Will you use teacher–student conferencing, provide feedback, and so on?

6. As we prepare for Tier 1 instruction, we want to consider as many opportunities, strategies, and ideas as possible to reach all students. Describe the new discoveries you have made after reading information on Tier 1 instruction. How will you use these discoveries to reach your particular students?

7. What is meant by guided instruction? How do cues, prompts, and questions differ, and how can each be used during guided instruction?

Chapter 5: Interventions within Tier 2

1. Describe the fidelity of your curriculum, particularly within Tier 2 instruction.

2. Why is it important to set academic goals for students in Tier 2?

3. Are all lesson parts taught within Tier 2 following outlined procedures? Why or why not?

4. What assessment data are available to the members of your RTI team when developing an intervention plan for Tier 2 services?

5. Are the interventions in Tier 2 matched to student needs? Explain your answer.

6. What decisions and/or rules are in place for your students who no longer need Tier 2 supports?

7. How are those decisions and/or rules made and implemented?

8. Is participation and effort in Tier 2 consistently reinforced in your school? Why or why not?

Chapter 6: Intensifying Interventions within Tier 3

1. What assessment data are available to the members of the RTI team when developing an intervention plan for Tier 3 services?

2. How will you use various methods of diagnostic teaching (error analysis, interviews, observations, etc.) to understand more about your students' needs in mathematics?

3. Are there currently curricular materials that include prerequisite skills and/or preskills? Why would these skills be important in planning for interventions?

4. As you review the sample schedule in this chapter, think about how you will organize your classroom to provide time and resources for multi-tiered mathematics lessons (and other academic areas) as needed.

5. How do you comprehensively describe your responsibilities to provide multi-tiered instruction and interventions in mathematics?

6. Intensive interventions should be delivered individually to students. How can this recommendation be realized?

Chapter 7: Supporting Students in Our School through Professional Learning about RTI

1. As you consider the important elements of the change process in the Figure 7.1, discuss implementation of RTI in your school. Is there a clear, shared vision for RTI? Do faculty and staff have the necessary knowledge and skills? Are there supports available to learn these skills? What incentives are provided (e.g., planning time, classroom resources)?

2. What do you currently do to learn about and use new instructional techniques, strategies, and resources? Who can assist with this learning within the grade level, school, and district?

3. What professional learning opportunities are currently in your school? Are these opportunities related to RTI? What common components do you see? (Feel free to review and discuss the chart at the end of this chapter.)

4. As you complete the RTI in Mathematics Implementation Plan (see Reproducible #20 in Appendix A), what are needs that you identified for teachers in your grade level and within your school? How can you meet these needs to sustain RTI implementation in your school?

Appendix C

Professional Learning Community (PLC) Resource

Book Summary

This book provides specific, evidence-based instructional strategies and resources for use by classroom teachers, instructional coaches, curriculum specialists, and administrators in both elementary and middle school classrooms when implementing Response to Instruction/Intervention (RTI) in mathematics. The strategies presented address RTI mandates for the classroom. The purpose is to connect these strategies and ideas to classroom practices to improve student learning in mathematics, specifically for students that may struggle and/or have other specific difficulties in mathematics. Strategies, resources, and activities within this book range from checklists and teaching tips that can be used with little to no teacher preparation, to more involved instructional decision making and lesson planning for use in the mathematics classroom. After each chapter, activities for continued learning and discussions are provided to enhance learning and classroom use.

Goal of This PLC

The first goal of this particular PLC resource is to foster an understanding of the "big ideas" and issues related to RTI. The second and primary goal, however, is to provide educators with clear extension activities that can be immediately implemented within their mathematics classrooms at a particular elementary or middle school site.

Expectations and Procedures for Completing This Study

Establish the following expectations of the group:

- PLC time, date, length (if necessary).
- Establish PLC norms for conversations and activities.
  - Revisit norms/post norm for each session
- Establish goals for each session.
  - Everyone reads material before each session
  - Everyone is able to identify their own insights, personal ties, implications
- Establish a frame for the PLC. Possible frames could include:
  - Insights from reading
  - Discussions based on book study guide

- Implications from reading
- So what? Now what?

■ Consider how everyone will participate in the professional learning community.

- Consider identifying a facilitator for each session

Chapter-by-Chapter Activity Guide

Chapter 1: Response to Instruction and Intervention in Mathematics

> "In 2007, the National Council of Teachers of Mathematics (NCTM) stated that all students' instructional needs can be met by knowledgeable teachers who use evidence-based instructional practices and strategies designed to increase student achievement."

Consider the above quote from NCTM as included by the authors in Chapter 1. Discuss their purpose for including this statement. Identify and record specific goals of your PLC for choosing this particular topic (RTI) to study.

■ To help your PLC in identifying these goals, review data related to reading from your school site and identify strengths and areas of need. Also, peruse the chapter titles and headings and have each member consider his or her personal knowledge level on the chapter topics and ask themselves what areas are most critical for them and their students and/or their school site.

■ The authors included the seven core components necessary to implement RTI (Figure 1.1). Discuss RTI implementation in your school and district related to each of these core components.

- Review your school's current RTI implementation plan and school improvement plan, if available. Discuss evidence-based practices, assessments, and professional development currently available that will be useful with RTI implementation. (Throughout the chapters, this question will be important to consider.)
- If participants completed their RTI Personal Action Plan (Reproducible #1 in Appendix A), discuss goals and needs of PLC members to implement RTI in mathematics.

■ Lastly, discuss new learning from several of the websites included in this chapter that focus on RTI and curriculum standards in mathematics.

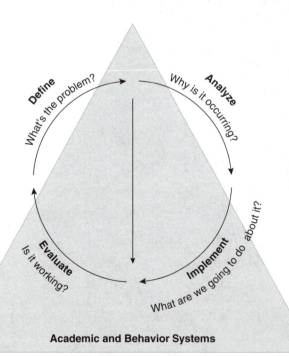

Chapter 2: Setting the Stage for RTI in the Classroom by Understanding the Fundamentals

> "The goal of RTI is to meet the learning needs of the students by considering, analyzing, and differentiating the learning environment, the mathematics curriculum and skills being taught, and the delivery of that instruction within a comprehensive system of school improvement."

■ Consider the above quote by the authors in Chapter 2. Discuss their purpose for including this statement. Identify and discuss issues related to your specific goals, current learning, and new knowledge about implementing RTI in your classroom.

- As you look at Figure 2.1, discuss RTI and the tiers of instruction related to the language of RTI, which is also included in the Glossary.
  - Review the characteristics of each of the tiers.
  - Discuss your roles with instruction, intervention, and assessment within each of the tiers.
  - Discuss what you currently know and do in your classroom related to these characteristics and skills.

- As you complete the Considerations for Effective Teachers self-assessment (Reproducible #2 in Appendix A), explain what you learned about your teaching. How could you use this self-assessment to continuously improve your teaching practices?

- Instructional decision making includes many variables. As you review Figure 2.4, discuss these variables and your resources and learning within your classroom and school.
  - What assessment data and other sources of information do you have to learn about your students at the beginning of the year and as you plan for a new unit to teach? (See Reproducible #3, Student Demographics within RTI Universal Screening, in Appendix A.)
  - Do you have clear, aligned, and sequenced curriculum maps that frame the curriculum content standards that you are required to teach? (See Reproducible #4, Curriculum Mapping and Pacing Chart to Use with RTI, in Appendix A.)
  - Are there others in your school who may have additional assessment data that could help you learn more about your students?
  - Do you have dedicated planning time for data discussions, team planning, and curriculum discussions?
  - Other thoughts?

- Lastly, discuss new learning from several of the websites included in this chapter that focus on RTI and curriculum standards in mathematics.

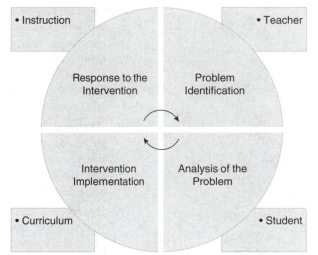

Chapter 3: Knowing the Students Are Learning: Use of Assessment Data

"We use assessment data every day to learn about our students . . . . Gathering formative assessment data from many sources builds a complete picture of our students' abilities, skills, dispositions, and learning."

Consider the above quote by the authors in Chapter 3. Discuss their purpose for including this statement. Identify and discuss your current assessment practices and the assessment data resources available to you within your school to learn about your students and plan for instruction.

- Observations of students tell you so much about your students' knowledge, skills, and thinking. Use the Student Observation Form (Reproducible #5 in Appendix A) for a five-minute block of time two or three times during your instruction in mathematics. (Hint: Feel free to make a copy of your seating chart and add a key, if that is easier.) Discuss new learning about your students after these observations. What changes are you considering as a result? Explain.

- Discuss the new learning you gained from viewing several of the websites included in this chapter that focused on RTI and multiple assessments mathematics.

- Make a list of appropriate universal screening tools you can use to identify at-risk students at the beginning of the school year.
- Lastly, identify appropriate progress-monitoring tools you can use to check student progress. Create a calendar for the administration of these tools.

Chapter 4: Teaching All Students in My Classroom: Tier 1

"'An effective and coherent mathematics program should be guided by a clear set of content standards, but is must be grounded in a clear and shared vision of teaching and learning—the two critical reciprocal actions that link teachers and students and largely determine education impact' (Leinwand, 2009, p. 90)."

- Consider the above quote by the authors in Chapter 4. Discuss their purpose for including this statement and its importance in Tier 1 instruction.
- Considerations for Tier 1 (p. 78) were produced to facilitate your conversations and decision making for students who may require the most intensive interventions at Tier 1. We have provided a template for you in Reproducible #16, Tier 1 Considerations for the RTI team (in Appendix A). After you use the format within your RTI and/or data team meetings, discuss how these questions guided the instructional decision making for your particular students. You may consider using your responses to the Student Observation Form (Reproducible #5) and the Classroom Problem Identification Plan (Reproducible #10) for additional discussion.
- As you think of your own curriculum and planning for instruction, teaching practices, and lesson delivery, we want you to think of the considerations when teaching within Tier 1 of RTI. Use the Worksheet for Evaluating Explicit Instruction and Systematic Curriculum (Reproducible #11 in Appendix A) as a guide. Discuss the questions posed per page.
- It is very important for us to reflect on our current teaching techniques and instructional approaches in the mathematics classroom. As you investigate your students concerns as per the Classroom Problem Identification Plan (Reproducible #10) think about what other information can be gathered to address students' needs. Consider the following questions to help facilitate this collection of information:
  - Who is affected by the problem?
  - Why is there an issue that needs to be addressed and/or changed?
  - Why is student learning breaking down?
  - What is causing the problem?
  - What may be missing within the instructional learning environment that my students need in order to be mathematically successful?
  - What is the goal for improvement?
  - What will be done about the problem to help my students gain the needed mathematical knowledge?
- Discuss with colleagues what you believe are some of the most important components of effective teaching, especially since classroom instruction is the primary focus of Tier 1. Discuss how you successfully and effectively teach the mathematics skills and concepts so all students can focus, understand, and remember the content. List some ideas and strategies you currently use and share them with colleagues.
- Identify key concepts, skills, and principles to be learned within Tier 1. How may you become proficient at implementing the different strategies and managing differentiation/scaffolding within your lessons?

- Several scenarios were presented in this chapter. Discuss your thoughts, ideas, and responses as they pertain to each one. Explain what you gained to better equip your knowledge base of Tier 1 instruction.

Chapter 5: Interventions within Tier 2

"If a student is not performing as expected, we will change what we are doing and continue problem solving until we find what works."

Consider the above quote by the authors in Chapter 5. Discuss their purpose for including this statement and its importance in Tier 2 instruction. Identify and discuss your current strategies (standard protocols) in Tier 2. Is more supplementary instruction needed? Are the standard protocols effective? Why or why not? How are you determining their effectiveness and what is the criteria for establishing those protocols?

- As you consider Tier 2 instruction, identify the specific supplemental instruction that is being delivered to students. Is improvement in mathematical performance of struggling learners occurring for *most* students? Why or why not? If the answer is no, what can be changed so more students are successful? More exposure, practice, focus, smaller groups, delivery of instruction, better alignment with core instruction? Explain and/or justify your answers.

- The instructional decision-making process allows us to set forth the goals our students need to be mathematically successful. Review this process and set goals for your students. If you are just beginning RTI, the identification of these should be a top priority as you set the stage for its implementation. If you are already involved in RTI implementation you should be reviewing them periodically with your school-based RTI team for continued mathematical success and overall effectiveness.

- Several scenarios were presented in this chapter. Discuss your thoughts, ideas, and responses as they pertain to each one. Explain what you gained from each one to better equip your knowledge base of Tier 2 instruction.

- Considerations for Tier 2 (p. 95) were produced to facilitate your conversations and decision making for students who may require intensive interventions at Tier 2. After you use the format within your RTI and/or data team meetings, discuss how these questions guided your instructional decision making. We have provided a template for you in Reproducible #16, Tier 2 Considerations for the RTI Team (in Appendix A).

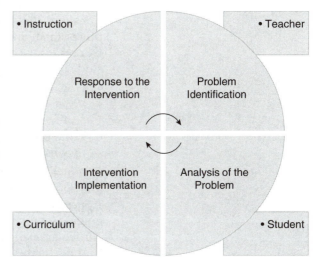

Chapter 6: Intensifying Interventions within Tier 3

"Although we teach a group of students in our classrooms, learning is done by individuals. Our assessment tasks, especially during Tier 3, should help us teach individual students. We collect and analyze assessment data and prescribe additional assessments to further diagnose instructional concerns, to monitor student progress, and to summarize the outcomes for a specific period of time (e.g., length of intervention, grading period, annual progress). We use this information to identify a specific area of concern."

Consider the statement by the authors about Tier 3 and diagnostic teaching and assessment. How do you see your role in diagnosing and assessing, especially during Tier 3 in RTI? What instruments do you have to diagnose and prescribe?

- As you consider your resources to learn more about the individual students, what knowledge, skills, and resources do you need? What is the availability of these resources? Please use Reproducible #15, Evidenced-Based Resources and Planning for Tier 3 (in Appendix A). What other professionals are available to assist you on your RTI team?

- Reproducible #16, Tier 3 Considerations for the RTI Team (in Appendix A) was produced to facilitate your conversations and decision making for students who may require the most intensive interventions at Tier 3. After you use the format within your RTI and/or data team meetings, discuss how these questions guided your instructional decision making.

- Planning, teaching, and assessing within a differentiated classroom may include students at multiple tiers of instruction and intervention. There may also be multiple professionals (math coaches, curriculum specialists, etc.) who are part of your instructional considerations. Talk about Reproducible #9, Intensifying Instruction/Interventions Using Targeted OPTIONS in Tier 2 and Tier 3 and discuss how this format will assist and organize your planning for instruction and intervention in Tier 3.

- Lastly, discuss new learning you gained from viewing several of the websites included in this text that focus on evidence-based intensive interventions in mathematics.

Chapter 7: Supporting Students in Our School through Professional Learning about RTI

"Building professional and collegial conversations centered on enhancing our multi-tiered lessons sets a cornerstone for continuous improvement."

- Consider the quote above from Chapter 7 regarding the building of professional and collegial conversations for enhancing multi-tiered lessons. During your conversations about RTI in mathematics, PLC activities, and study questions, consider your professional learning regarding the following:
  - How have your goals as members of this PLC been met?
  - What have been some areas of professional learning, both individually and within various teams?
  - What other questions and actions do you, as a PLC in mathematics, need to consider to continuously improve and maintain the momentum?

- Complete a scavenger hunt of available resources in mathematics. Take a look at Reproducible #17, Resource Mapping for RTI in Mathematics (in Appendix A). Check your storeroom, teachers' textbook guides, CDs, resource guides, samples of textbooks, and so forth for resources that align with your curricular standards in mathematics. These resources could be used for learning centers, peer tutors, instructional coaches, and so forth to intensify instruction within RTI. Remember to also identify personnel reosources. Who can assist you when intensifying instruction for students in mathematics? Once your available resources are identified, what additional resources are needed? How can available resources be shared with your colleagues?

- Identify the current school-based teams at your school. How will they interface with an RTI team? When an RTI team is identified, discuss roles and responsibilities, logistics (scheduling, resources, support, etc.) data sources, and communication methods with others within your school. Reproducible #18, Team Members and Roles in RTI (in Appendix A) may help guide you in this process.

- Lesson study is a complex process, supported by collaborative goal setting, careful data collection on student learning, and procedures that enable productive disucssions. Are there two or three of your colleagues in mathematics who might agree to visit each other's classrooms, provide feedback, and collaboratively discuss teaching and learning in mathematics? Do you have thirty to forty-five minutes once or twice a week to begin these discussions? See Reproducible #19, The Lesson Study Process (in Appendix A), for an outline of the lesson study process and some additional resources.

- How do you begin or continue implementing RTI in your school and district? First, remember that change is a process that takes continued dedication, collaboration, and time. Second, consider the components of complex change described in this chapter as related to *your* school. Then, look at your RTI in Mathematics Implementation Plan (see Reproducible #20), ask the difficult questions, and continue building an action plan of next steps.

- Lastly, discuss how you will continue to increase and sustain collaborative work with colleagues.

Glossary

Accommodations Refers to the teaching supports and services made available to students with special needs for accessing or demonstrating competency in the defined curriculum.

Accuracy Used to identify whether a student has acquired a skill; this is generally the area that is stressed in evaluation.

Action research A process of describing and testing theories through which we study student learning related to classroom instruction.

Affective readiness Considers the students' mathematical dispositions or motivations, and attitudes toward mathematics.

Assessment The process of determining a student's understanding of mathematics and measuring his or her ability to perform procedures.

Baseline data Basic information gathered before a program begins. It is used later to provide a comparison for assessing program impact.

Classroom instructional decision-making process Continued analysis of student progress-monitoring data to guide day-to-day instruction and interventions through systematic analyses of variables in instruction, curriculum, and environment to meet learner needs.

Conceptual understanding The comprehension of mathematical concepts, operations, and relations.

Content readiness Involves students' ability to work with ease on a specific mathematics area.

Contextual readiness Students' awareness of the ways mathematics are used or applied in real-life problem solving, and realization of the importance of mathematics.

Continuous improvement cycle Ongoing process of data collection (assessment) through screening, diagnostic, and outcome measures to inform instruction.

Curriculum-based measurement (CBM) A reliable and valid assessment system that is used to screen students or to monitor student progress and mastery in mathematics.

Curriculum mapping A procedure for reviewing the operational curriculum.

Data-based instructional decision making See Action research.

Diagnostic assessment Assessment administered with special knowledge and skills in the specific assessment area to provide more in-depth information about students' skills and instructional needs to plan for interventions.

Differentiated instruction Tailors the learning environment and teaching practices to create appropriately different learning experiences for students in order to meet their individual needs. Teachers recognize students' varying interests, readiness levels, and levels of responsiveness to the standard core curriculum and plan responsively to address these individual differences through content, process, products, and learning environment.

Dosage Amount of time teaching and learning specific to a curriculum goal.

Evidence-based practices Instructional practices and educational programs that have been researched to show positive learning outcomes.

Explicit instruction A clear and overt purpose and process that provides models for solving a problem type using an array of examples.

Fidelity The delivery of instruction and interventions in the ways they were designed to be delivered.

Flexible grouping Prescriptive, focused, research-based interventions provided to students by any trained or skilled staff member, regardless of the student's education categorization or the educator's special or general education job description.

Fluency How quickly students are able to perform or recall a math fact, process, or procedure.

Formative assessment Formal or informal assessments used to plan instruction in a recursive way through systematic and continuous feedback to both the student and the teacher concerning successes and failures.

Gap analysis A tool for measuring the difference between the student's current level of performance and benchmark expectations (i.e., determining a student's response to an intervention as well as the appropriate intensity level of an intervention).

Goal (or trend) lines Depict the anticipated growth and offer a comparison for the trend line and are typically shown as the expected rate of progress toward either the district goal or a goal developed by the problem-solving team.

Guided practice Modeling of skills to be learned while providing a high level of direction (questioning, additional modeling, student demonstration of skills performance, and immediate teacher feedback) to help obtain mastery of mathematical content.

Instructional variables The instructional factors that teachers should consider in meeting individual needs that are much the same for various groups of students.

Intensity increasing levels of instructional intensity.

Intervention Specific services, activities, or products developed and implemented to change or improve student knowledge, attitudes, behavior, or awareness.

Lesson study A cycle of instructional improvements focused on planning, observing, and discussing lessons and drawing on their implications for teaching and learning.

Mathematical readiness The level of total development that enables a student to learn a behavior, comprehend a concept, or perform in a given way with ease.

Math probes Brief, timed exercises to complete using the mathematical skills and materials that are drawn directly from students' school curriculum.

Maturational readiness Students' natural developmental and cognitive stages and mental abilities.

Outcome assessment Provides data related to a student's comprehensive learning at an established period of final assessment at the end of a unit of study, the end of the school year, and/or after state and/or district assessments.

Pedagogical readiness Considers students' understanding and appropriate use of materials, including objects, pictures, representations of objects, symbols, models, manipulatives, technology, and other instructional materials used to facilitate mathematics learning.

Problem-solving model A collaborative approach that involves a team (which includes parents and general and special educators) that meets to evaluate student data and to plan and monitor prescribed interventions.

Professional learning community (PLC) A model of professional development that focuses on student learning rather than teaching, collaborative work, and accountability for results. The model flows from the assumption that the core mission of schools is to ensure that students learn.

Professional portfolios A showcase of the learning results of both teachers and students; documents both the journey of change and learning (e.g., videos from lessons, lesson study planning documents, assessment results from a mathematics unit, individual student learning graph) through impact and effectiveness.

Progress-monitoring data Data compiled from the continuous use of various assessments and probes to measure student academic performance on a regular basis (weekly or monthly) to adjust and/or intensify instruction/interventions, as needed.

Review of previous records Information gathered through recording of student skills and competencies through trends or inconsistencies in student learning.

RTI team A group of professionals (e.g., teachers, mathematics coaches, school-based personnel) working together to improve educational outcomes for all students by collaborating on decisions. The team uses data analysis, curriculum planning, sharing of best practices, and discussion of intervention strategies to plan for student success.

Scaffolding A carefully designed learning progression that provides assistance to students learning new material through explicit instruction, modeling, questioning, and feedback by breaking learning into small steps, allowing students to grow gradually in independence as learners.

Standard implementation protocol A structured schedule/framework for providing the use of extended learning time blocks for each grade level or for each grade level during the school day.

Standardized assessments Any empirically developed examination with established reliability and validity as determined by repeated evaluation of the method and results.

Summative assessment Assessment that typically takes place at the conclusion of an instructional cycle and informs stakeholders of student achievement in mathematics (e.g., chapter and quarter tests). The assessment provides an evaluation of the effectiveness of instruction and compares students' achievements to core grade-level and course performance standards.

Systematic instruction An approach in which teachers guide students through a defined instructional sequence and may be either teacher- or student-directed, inquiry based, or explicit.

Targeted instruction Instruction focused on the specific skill deficits among particular struggling learners.

Task analysis Analysis used to determine a hierarchical sequence of skills. These skills can be broken down into discrete components or steps in arriving at a solution.

Teacher inquiry *See* Action research.

Think-Pair-Share A strategy designed to provide students with "food for thought" on a given topic, enabling them to formulate individual ideas and share these ideas with another student.

Tiers Three (or more) levels of instruction and intervention services that increase in intensity to meet needs of students within the RTI framework.

Trend lines Graphed data that provide visual representations of student achievement (learning) related to the expectations (trend line), especially when collecting progress-monitoring data for students receiving Tier 2 and Tier 3 interventions.

Universal screening assessments Assessment used for initial determination of students' current performance levels and identifying students in need of additional interventions.

Work-sample analyses A critical aspect of comprehensive assessment in mathematics that can include performance tasks from in-class assignments, board work, and problem-based learning assignments.

Zone of proximal development A systematic sequence of prompted content, materials, tasks, and teacher and peer support to optimize learning until students can apply those learned skills and strategies independently. It is the distance between what students can do by themselves and the next level learning that they can achieve with competent assistance.

References

Allington, R. (2009). *What really matters in response to intervention: Research-based designs.* Boston: Pearson.

Allsopp, D., Kyger, M., & Lovin, L. (2008). *Teaching mathematics meaningfully.* Baltimore: Paul H. Brookes.

Ashlock, R. (2010). *Error patterns in computation: Using error patterns to help each student learn.* Boston: Allyn & Bacon.

Baroody, A., (1990). How and when should place-value concepts and skills be taught? *Journal for Research in Mathematics Education, 21,* 281–286.

Bender, W., & Shores, C. (2007). *Response to intervention: A practical guide for every teacher.* Thousand Oaks, CA: Corwin Press.

Bennett, A., Maer, E., & Nelson, T. (1998). *Math and the minds eye.* Portland, OR: The Math Learning Center.

Berch, D., & Mazzocco, M. (2007). *Why is math so hard for some children? The nature and origins of mathematical learning difficulties and disabilities.* Baltimore: Paul H. Brookes.

Berh, M., Lesh, R., Post, T., & Silver, E. (1983). Rational number concepts. In R. Lesh & M. Landau (Eds.), *Acquisition of mathematical concepts and processes.* New York: Academy Press.

Bransford, J., Brown, A., & Cocking, R. (2000). *How people learn: Brain, mind, experience, and school.* Washington, DC: National Academy Press.

Brumbaugh, D., Ortiz, E., & Gresham, R. (2006). *Teaching middle school mathematics.* Mahwah, NJ: Lawrence Erlbaum.

Chappuis, S. (2005). The best value of formative assessment. *Educational Leadership, (65)*4, 14–19.

Clements, D. H., & Sarama, J. (2007). Effects of a preschool mathematics curriculum: Summative research on the Building Blocks project. *Journal for Research in Mathematics Education, 38,* 136–163.

Dana, N., & Yendol-Silva, D. (2003). *The reflective educator's guide to classroom research: Learning to teach and teaching to learn through practitioner inquiry.* Thousand Oaks, CA: Corwin Press.

Danielson, C. (1996). *Enhancing professional practice: A framework for teaching.* Alexandria, VA: Association for Supervision and Curriculum Development.

DeGeorge, B. (2004). Manipulatives: A hands-on approach to math. *Principal, 84*(2), 28–32.

Dickson, S. V., Chard, D. J., & Simmons, D. C. (1993). An integrated reading/writing curriculum: A focus on scaffolding. *LD Forum, 18*(4), 12–16.

DuFour, R. (2004). Schools as learning communities. *Educational Leadership, 61*(8), 6–11.

DuFour, R., DuFour, R., Eaker, R., & Karhanek, G. (2010). *Raising the bar and closing the gap: Whatever it takes.* Bloomington, IN: Solution Tree Press.

Ellis, E. S., & Larkin, M. J. (1998). Strategic instruction for adolescents with learning disabilities. In B. Y. L. Wong (Ed.), *Learning about learning disabilities* (2nd ed., pp. 585–656). San Diego, CA: Academic Press.

Elmore, R., Peterson, P., & McCarthy, S. (1996). *Restructuring in the classroom: Teaching, learning, and school organization.* San Francisco: Jossey-Bass.

Florida Department of Education. (2011). *Guiding tools for RTI implementation.* Tallahassee, FL: Author.

Fuchs, D., & Fuchs, L. S. (2001). Responsiveness-to-intervention: A blueprint for practitioners, policymakers, and parents. *Teaching Exceptional Children, 38,* 57–61.

Fuchs, D., & Fuchs, L. S. (2005). Introduction to response to intervention: What, why, and how valid is it? *Reading Research Quarterly, 41*(1), 93–99.

Fuchs, D., & Fuchs, L. S. (2008). Introduction to response to intervention: What, why, and how valid is it? *Reading Research Quarterly, 41*(1), 93–99.

Fuchs, L. & Fuchs, D. (2002). Principles for the prevention and intervention of mathematics difficulties. *Learning Disabilities and Practice, (16)*2, 85–95.

Gersten, R., Beckmann, S., Clarke, B., Foegen. A., Marsh, L., Star, J. R., & Witzel, B. (2009). *Assisting students struggling with mathematics: Response to intervention for elementary and middle schools* (NCEE 2009–4060). Washington, DC: National Center for Educational Evaluation and Regional Assistance, Institute of Educational Sciences, U.S. Department of Education. Retrieved from https://ies.ed.gov/ncee/wwc/publications/practiceguides

Gersten, R., Jordan, N. C., & Flojo, J. R. (2005). Early identification and interventions for students with mathematics difficulties. *Journal of Learning Disabilities, 38*(4), 293–304.

Glanz, J. (2003). *Action research: An educational leader's guide to school improvement.* Norwood, MA: Christopher-Gordon.

Gresham, G. (2004). Mathematics anxiety in elementary school students. *ComMuniCator, 28*(1), 28–29.

Gresham, G. (2005). Math anxiety: How you can help your children overcome it. *Home School Journal, 19,* 50–51.

Gresham, G. (2007). A study to reduce mathematics anxiety in elementary pre-service teachers. *Early Childhood Education Journal, 35*(2), 181–188.

Gresham, G. (2009). *Response to intervention: Practical strategies for intervening with students before they fall too far behind in mathematics (Grades K–6).* Bellevue, WA: Bureau of Education and Research.

Griffin, S., & Case, R. (1997). Re-thinking the primary school math curriculum: An approach based on cognitive science. *Issues in Education, 3,* 1–65.

Hall, T. (2002). *Explicit instruction: Effective classroom practices report.* Wakefield, MA: National Center on Accessing the General Curriculum. Retrieved from http://aim.cast.org/learn/historyarchive/backgroundpapers/explicit_instruction

Hall, T., Strangman, N., & Meyer, A. (2003). *Differentiated instruction and implications for UDL implementation.* Wakefield, MA: National

Center on Accessing the General Curriculum. Retrieved from http://www.k8accesscenter.org/training_resources/udl/diffinstruction.asp

Hembree, R. (1990). The nature, effects, and relief of mathematics anxiety. *Journal of Research in Mathematics Education, 21,* 33–46.

Hiebert, J., & Carpenter, T. P. (1992). Learning and teaching with understanding. In D. Grouws (Ed.), *Handbook for research on mathematics teaching and learning* (pp. 65–97). New York: Macmillan.

Hoover, J., & Love, E. (2011). Supporting school-based response to intervention: A practitioner's model. *Teaching Exceptional Children, 43*(3), 40–48.

Howard, M. (2009). *RTI from all sides: What every teacher needs to know.* Portsmouth, NH: Heinemann.

Howell, K. W., & Nolet, V. (2000). *Curriculum-based evaluation: Teaching and decision making* (3rd ed.). Belmont, CA: Wadsworth.

Jankowski, E. (2003). Heartland area education agency's problem solving model: An outcomes driven special education paradigm. *Rural Special Education Quarterly, 22*(2), 15–24. Retrieved from http://www.findarticles.com/p/articles

Jimerson, S., Burns, M., & VanDerheyden, A. (2007). *Handbook of response to intervention: The science and practice of assessment and intervention.* New York: Springer.

Jittendra, A. K., Sczesniak, E., & Deatline-Bachman, A. (2005). An exploratory validation of curriculum-based mathematical word-problem-solving tasks as indicators of mathematics proficiency for third graders. *School Psychology Review, 34*(3), 358–371.

Lau, M., Sieler, R., Muyskens, P., Canter, A., VanKeuren, T., & Marston, D. (2006). Perspectives on the use of the problem-solving model from the viewpoint of school psychologist, administrator, and teacher. *Psychology in the Schools, 43*(1), 117–127.

Leinwand, S. (2009). *Accessible mathematics: Ten instructional shifts that raise student achievement.* Portsmouth, NH: Heinemann.

Lembke, E., & Stecker, P. (2007). *Curriculum-based measurement in mathematics: An evidence-based formative assessment procedure.* Portsmouth, NH: RMC Research Corporation, Center on Instruction.

Lewis, C. (2002). Does lesson study have a future in the United States? *Nagoya Journal of Education and Human Development, 1*(1), 1–23.

Lewis, C. (2008). Lesson study. In L. Brown (Ed.), *Powerful designs for professional learning.* Oxford, OH: National Staff Development Council.

Lindsley, O. (1964). *Precision teaching.* Lawrence: University of Kansas Press.

Little, M. (2003). Professional development to improve student learning: A systems approach. In E. M. Guyton & J. Dangle (Eds.), *Teacher education yearbook XII: Research linking teacher preparation and student performance* (pp. 57–82). Dubuque, IA: Kendall/Hunt.

Little, M. (2009a). Teaching mathematics: Issues and solutions. *Teaching Exceptional Children Plus, 6*(1), Article 1. Retrieved from http://scholarship.bc.edu/education/tecplus/vol6/iss1/art1

Little, M. (2009b). Action research and response to intervention: Bridging the discourse divide. *Educational Forum, 23*(2), 23–31.

Little, M. (2009c). *Response to intervention (RtI) for teachers: Classroom instructional problem solving.* Denver, CO: Love.

Little, M. & Houston, D. (2003). Research into practice through professional development. *Remedial and Special Education, 24*(2), 75–88.

Little, M., & Witzel, B. (2009). Mathematics. In R. Evers (Ed.), *Learning disabilities: Research to practice.* Boston: Allyn & Bacon.

Maccini, P., & Gagnon, J. (2002). Perceptions and application of NCTM standards by special and general education teachers. *Exceptional Children, 68,* 325–344.

Marston, D. (2002). A functional and intervention-based assessment approach to establishing discrepancy for students with learning disabilities. In R. Bradley, L. Donaldson, & D. Hallahan (Eds.), *Identification of learning disabilities* (pp. 437–447). Mahwah, NJ: Lawrence Erlbaum.

Mellard, D., McKnight, M., & Woods, K. (2009). Response to intervention screening and progress-monitoring practices in 41 local schools. *Learning Disabilities Research and Practice, 24*(4), 186–195.

National Association of State Directors of Special Education (2005). *Response to intervention: Policy considerations and implementation.* Reston, VA: Author.

National Council of Teachers of Mathematics. (2000). *Principles and standards for school mathematics.* Reston, VA: Author.

National Council of Teachers of Mathematics. (2007). *Principles and standards for school mathematics.* Reston, VA: Author.

National Council of Teachers of Mathematics. (2008). *Principles and standards for school mathematics.* Reston, VA: Author.

National Governors Association. (2009). *Common core competencies.* Washington, DC: Author.

National Mathematics Advisory Panel. (2008). *Foundations for success: The final report of the U.S. national mathematics advisory panel.* Washington, DC: U.S. Department of Education.

National Research Council. (1993). *How students learn: History, mathematics, and science in the classroom. Committee on how people learn, A targeted report for teachers.* Washington, DC: The National Academies Press.

National Research Council. (2001). *How students learn: History, mathematics, and science in the classroom. Committee on how people learn, A targeted report for teachers.* Washington, DC: The National Academies Press.

Rosenholtz, S. (1989). *Teachers' workplace: The social organization of schools.* New York: Longman.

Sagor, R. (2005). *How to conduct collaborative action research.* Alexandria, VA: Association for Supervision and Curriculum Development.

Spectrum, Inc. (2010). *RtI adoption survey.* Retrieved from http://www.spectrumK12.com

Sprenger, M. (2005). *How to teach so students remember.* Alexandria, VA: Association for Supervision and Curriculum Development.

Tilly, D. (2002). Best practices in school psychology as a problem-solving enterprise. In A. Thomas & J. Grimes (Eds.), *Best practices in school psychology* (4th ed., Vol. 1, pp. 21–36), Bethesda, MD: National Association of School Psychologists.

Tobias, S. (1998). Anxiety and mathematics. *Harvard Education Review, 50,* 63–70.

Tomlinson, C.A. (1999). *How to differentiate instruction in mixed ability classrooms.* Alexandria, VA: Association for Supervision and Curriculum Development.

Tomlinson, C. (2003). *Fulfilling the promise of differentiated classroom: Strategies and tools for responsive teaching.* Alexandria, VA: Association for Supervision and Curriculum Development.

Troutman, A., & Lichtenberg, B. (2003). *Mathematics: A good beginning.* Stanford, CT: Wadsworth/Thomson Learning.

U.S. Department of Education. (2010). *ESEA blueprint for reform.* Retrieved from http://www2.ed.gov/policy/elsec/leg/blueprint/index.html

Vygotsky, L. S. (1978). *Mind in society.* Cambridge, MA: Harvard University Press.

Wong, H. K., & Wong, R. T. (1998). *How to be an effective teacher the first days of school.* Mountain View, CA: Harry K. Wong Publications.

Index